W9-BRS-503

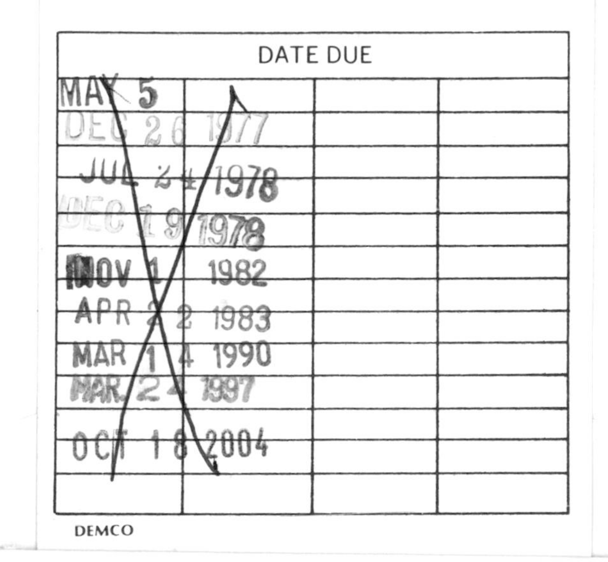
16386
301.41
HAH
HAHN, EMILY
Once upon a pedestal
DATE DUE
MAY 5
DEC 26 1977
JUL 24 1978
DEC 19 1978
NOV 1 1982
APR 22 1983
MAR 14 1990
MAR 24 1997
OCT 18 2004
DEMCO

ONCE UPON A PEDESTAL

Books by Emily Hahn

Hongkong Holiday
Raffles of Singapore
Miss Jill
England to Me
Purple Passage
Love Conquers Nothing
Chiang Kai-shek
Diamond
The Tiger House Party
China Only Yesterday
China to Me
Africa to Me: Person to Person
With Naked Foot
Romantic Rebels
Animal Gardens
Times and Places
On the Side of the Apes
Once upon a Pedestal

EMILY HAHN

THOMAS Y. CROWELL COMPANY
Established 1834 New York

I wish to thank Professor Gordon S. Haight and Professor Edmund S. Morgan, who lent me books and gave me advice, and David H. Springer, for advice on Anne Hutchinson.

 Published simultaneously in Canada by Fitzhenry & Whiteside Limited, Toronto.

Designed by Ingrid Beckman

Manufactured in the United States of America

Library of Congress Cataloging in Publication Data

Hahn, Emily, 1905–
Once upon a pedestal.

Bibliography: p.
1. Women's liberation movement—United States.
2. Woman—Legal status, laws, etc.—United States.
3. Woman—Suffrage—United States. I. Title.
HQ1426.H25 301.41'2'0973 74-5354
ISBN 0-690-00507-5

2 3 4 5 6 7 8 9 10

CONTENTS

ONCE UPON A PEDESTAL

CHAPTER 1

"Whistling Girls . . ."

THERE WAS A TIME not so long ago when she was talked of as the most pampered female in the world, with the possible exception of some prize-winning Persian cat. She was drawn by Gibson, painted by Sargent, written about by Henry James, costumed by Worth, gently but lovingly mocked by *Punch,* and described—though, admittedly, with a certain distaste—by Kipling. A rose was named for her. Noblemen courted her. She was the American Girl.

It goes without saying that she didn't burst on the world full-fledged. There were many American women ahead of her, as there have been thousands since, but somehow that period, about 1890 to 1914, seems to stand out as the Girl's epitome, her finest hour. Since then, slowly at first, and then with mounting speed, something has happened to her successors, and as the long-stemmed American Beauty fades from the scene we might wonder why. After all, American women have lost none of the Gibson Girl's advantages and have gained some of their own in recent years. She is still the envy of the other women of the world .... or is she? What has happened to bring forth this latter-day women's protest?

It may be that one can't sum up the processes. Perhaps feminism just happens from time to time, lurking in womankind like the flu virus, for if we look at history we can see that there is nothing new about feminine protest. It even crops up in mythology and literature. Twenty-three hundred years ago the citizens of Athens—men, of course; women didn't have citizenship in Greece, and were not permitted to visit the theater anyway—rocked with laughter at Aristophanes' comedy *Lysistrata*. In that play, you will recall, the women grew so tired of a long-drawn-out war between Athens and Sparta that they staged a revolt against the men, denying them sexual intercourse until peace should be declared. Then there was the myth about the Amazons: female warriors who fought like men, governed a nation of women only, and took mates temporarily, sending away all male infants at birth to be raised by their fathers somewhere outside the country.

But Lysistrata and the Amazons were figments of the imagination. Real-life Greek women lived much like women everywhere in all ages, mothering children and taking care of men. In ancient civilizations very few women became rulers and fewer were warriors or hunters, because fighting and hunting were men's work. Down through the centuries humans have continued to behave in much the same way—though in extraordinary circumstances, such as those in which Joan of Arc found herself, a few people must have given fresh thought to the subject. It is hard to believe that some women now and then, even when the Catholic faith was observed throughout the West, did not question the justice of St. Paul's philosophy.

Surely little girls of ancient Greece and Rome and Egypt, before they were brainwashed, must have rebelled when they were checked in their attempts to play the games boys played, and stormed in futile protest when they had to give way to their brothers in family disputes. Almost inevitably, life tamed them, but now and then a girl made history, and I cannot believe that such girls were confined to the class of queens like Nefertiti and Hatshepsut. The queens' records were engraved and so lasted; the little rebels have been forgotten, but they lived too. Here and there in fables and old-country anecdotes we catch the echo of a woman's voice protesting, as in the tale of some housewife outwitting her husband. *The Arabian Nights* have many such stories. Certainly feminine protest existed in old England—what about the following?

> Whistling girls and crowing hens
> Always come to bad ends.

I find it significant, both because there *were* evidently girls who whistled and because of the propaganda against them implicit in these words. We know about Aphra Behn, the seventeenth-century playwright who often protested against woman's lot, and there was, too, "Mary Astell," who wrote a long book on the subject from which I shall quote in due course.

But American women, people used to say, are a new breed. Though the United States has taken its language and many of its customs from England, American women are not like Englishwomen. They are indulged and spoiled. They behave like queens. They bully their husbands, leading them around like pet dogs. Articles in British papers point, over and over, to statistics that indicate a high incidence of heart disease and early death among American husbands. The cherished theory held by the English is that our unfortunate men work themselves into early graves to satisfy their wives' demands for luxuries: bigger and better cars, huge houses or apartments, glittering dishwashers. Then, having killed off their husbands, the harpies sit back and live the life of Riley on the insurance. Look at them, say the English—and the French, and the Germans, and the Italians—swarming over to Europe in chartered planes, thronging the shops, playing bridge in luxury hotels. As if this were not bad enough, we have the statistics relating to divorce—the American laws which grant ridiculously generous alimony most husbands must pay even when they are not the offending parties. No wonder American women own 80 percent of the nation's wealth.

Then what on earth are they complaining about? What can be the matter with the greedy creatures?

Well . . . it takes rather a long time to explain.

It all started, I think, with the comparatively recent beginnings of white America, which was founded as a colony—or, rather, as several colonies—and settled by a lot more men than women. At the outset there were not enough women to go around unless the male settlers mated with female Indians, and even then it was not so easy to get hold of Indian women as it might sound. The Indian men resisted conquest and usually fled, taking their women with them. As a result, wives were at a premium among the settlers, a situation which gave them an inflated value. As valuables, they were placed on pedestals, and the men of America got into the habit of thinking of their females as something special, something rare. Naturally this attitude did not prevent women from working. They did work, and hard, but the attitude cost the men nothing to maintain, and it had advantages that became increasingly evident as the settlements grew larger. A woman who grows up thinking of herself as a fragile treasure is not apt to put herself in danger of breaking, and on the whole, the ladies behaved much as they were expected to do. No lady on a pedestal, especially if she happens to have a fear of heights, is likely to rock it.

The longer women remained in this immobilized state the more boring they became, but to their husbands this was no drawback, since men found friends among their peers, other men, and didn't have to depend on women for companionship. Those few exceptional cases who did were the fathers of lonely pioneer families who relinquished keeping women on a pedestal: they were forced to talk to their wives as equals because there was nobody else around. But such men were in the minority, and most wives remained where their husbands placed them, in their homes, a little lonely perhaps until the children grew old enough to be companionable, but contented enough, as canaries in their cages are contented if they are well fed. However, women are not canaries. Sooner or later some of them began to think, all the more inevitably because they could read, and the seeds of thought were there in the books. Such seeds sprouted and grew up and caused trouble. It might fairly be said that literacy is the root of most of our troubles today. Certainly it had a lot to do with the revolt of the women.

The record begins in the annals of various foreigners who came to America in the early days and then went home to write their impressions of our women. It can be traced further in a study of the books that American women read; from them we learn something of what began to stir in their minds—or, in some cases, what may have kept those minds comfortably asleep. Finally, we will glance at some of the women themselves, who became aroused enough to clamber down from their pedestals and take part in the world's happenings. Today it is a truism, but a century and a half ago it was not, and it took a determined female to make her mark on public affairs. Still, there were females determined enough to do so. Women were so active in the abolitionist movement, for example, that it was sometimes thought of as theirs exclusively, though that was not true. Many of the same women campaigned as well for temperance, and did it so effectively that in the end the dries had their way and forced legal prohibition of alcoholic drinks. Not that it worked, but the fate of the Noble Experiment is another story. My point is that women brought the law about. But it was with even greater effort and clout that they turned to the franchise, on the reasonable theory that other feminist demands could be met and all their grievances as a sex obviated if only they had the power themselves to change laws. It took them years to achieve this goal, but in the end they got the vote. And if even now we do not live in the utopia they promised themselves, it is not for want of their trying.

Pedestals are definitely out.

CHAPTER 2

"All Men Would Be Tyrants . . ."

THE FIRST TWO ENGLISHWOMEN to set foot on American soil were landed at Jamestown, Virginia, in 1607. They were Mistress Anne Forrest and her maid Anne Buras, two of a shipload of five hundred immigrants sent out by the London Company to settle the country. England had claimed a share of America ever since Columbus first discovered the New World, more than a century earlier, this in opposition to Spanish claims; but the two countries had yet to confront each other on American territorial matters, and the only opponents encountered by the early settlers were Indians. The company made haste to provide more women in later ships—healthy, strong young females, most of them unmarried, destined to be wives for the men who had already arrived. One ship alone in 1619 brought ninety women to Jamestown. The men who married them were required to reimburse the company for their brides' transportation costs, and probably felt they had a bargain, since there was no other source of likely ladies for them, the enmity usually felt between Indian and settler rendering interracial marriage impracticable. John Rolfe's marriage to Pocahontas was one of the few exceptions.

It was a hard life, especially in those first days of settlement, for the people had not been wisely picked for the pioneering venture. Instead of hardy country folk who knew how to work the land, many were townspeople who knew little or nothing of clearing, digging, or hunting, and the equipment the company sent with them was equally unsuitable. The men came ashore expecting to make their fortune overnight by picking up nuggets of gold, which, they had heard, were lying around everywhere. There was no gold, and the people, miserably housed and fed, had little idea of how to improve their lot. Soon they were assailed by diseases, by typhoid and other fevers, and many died during that first winter. By 1610 only sixty of the original five hundred were left, though the company continued to augment their numbers with fresh victims.

Paradoxically, the rival Plymouth Company, whose charter gave it the right to develop the northern half of the Atlantic seaboard, considered less choice than Virginia because of the inferior soil and harsher climate, did better at colonizing. The passengers on the *Mayflower* hoped to end their voyage at Jamestown, but the ship was blown off course and arrived at Plymouth Rock in 1620 with the Pilgrims and a number of indentured servants, all of whom were far better suited than the Jamestown lot for the rigors of life in the colonies. From the beginning, too, there was a greater proportion of females in the New England settlement than in Jamestown. Of the 101 passengers on the *Mayflower,* twenty-nine were women and girls—eighteen married women, eleven girls. A boy was born at sea and a girl appeared as the ship sailed into Cape Cod Bay, but one of the women, young Mrs. Bradford, drowned about the same time, so the number was still twenty-nine. The Pilgrims' record of survival was better than that of Jamestown, but even so, by the time spring of 1621 came around in New England only four women and eleven little girls were still alive.

Overall, north and south, the shortage of English females on the Atlantic seaboard was not to disappear for a long time, as even after a century most newly arriving immigrants were of the male sex. Though rarity improved the standing of the women in some respects, colonial law was based on the English common law, according to which women had fewer legal rights than those of the men.

"By the laws of Massachusetts as by those of England a married woman could hold no property of her own," wrote Edmund S. Morgan in *Puritan Love and Marriage.* "When she became a wife, she gave up everything to her husband and devoted herself exclusively to managing his household." She was really a part of him: if he pulled up stakes and moved, she was supposed to go along without demur—as, in fact, she is expected to do today, according to common usage. Even now, when a woman marries she leaves home as a matter of course.

"Leave thy father, leave thy mother, and thy brother," sings the man in Francis Thompson's "Arab Love Song":

> Leave the black tents of thy tribe apart . . .
> And thou, What needest with thy tribe's black tents,
> Who hast the red pavilion of my heart?

What needest indeed, and where else was a woman to go, especially then? Even today it is a problem. As a girl said to me recently: "We're the only minority I know that has absolutely no homeland. Africans can go back to Africa, Jews to Israel, but where can women go?"

Yet, even with disadvantages of this sort, the career of wife or housekeeper was the least degrading course open to an English or American woman of colonial times, and many found compensation in the married state. In a wedding sermon the Reverend John Cotton of Boston outlined his ideas of the duties of a wife: to stay at home, look after the children, and manage the supplies brought home by her husband. A few exceptional housewives were trusted by their men to manage the family finances, but, as Professor Morgan wrote, even these intelligent, trustworthy females were deemed incapable of harder mental activity. The delicate little brain of a woman, if over-taxed, was likely to give way entirely. Such was the fate of Mistress Ann Hopkins, wife of Governor Edward Hopkins of Connecticut, who spent too much time reading and writing. As a result, said Governor John Winthrop in his *History of New England,* she went insane.

> Her husband, being very loving and tender of her, was loath to grieve her, but he saw his error, when it was too late, for if she had attended her household affairs, and such things as belong to women, and not gone out of her way to meddle in such things as are proper to men, whose minds are stronger, etc., she had kept her wits, and might have improved them successfully and memorably in the place God had set her.

Fortunately, there was little danger of most women in North America going insane from such a cause during the seventeenth and eighteenth centuries. Even among men literacy was not universal. Statistics quoted by James D. Hart in *The Popular Book* show that in Massachusetts and Connecticut between 1640 and 1700 the number of people who could so much as sign their names varied between 89 and 95 percent, but these figures do not include slaves, indentured servants, most hired men, *and most women.*

Indentured servants in America, often also called bondsmen or bondswomen, were people who bound themselves to work unpaid for a certain period for whoever would pay their passage out from England. Some were lawbreakers who had been given the option of coming to the colonies instead of going to prison at home. A few were "shanghaied" by ruffians for pay. But most were comparatively respectable, adventurous young people. They led a hard life. A bondsman had to obtain his master's permission to marry or work outside for pay, and if he broke the rules he was liable to an increased term of bondage. Nevertheless, some bondswomen made advantageous marriages, and it was in hopes of such a fortunate outcome that most girls sought indenture in the first place.

Hart observes a slight improvement in the general level of female literacy as time went on: "Of the few women who had official business between 1635 and 1656, 42 percent were able to sign documents; their number increased to 62 percent between 1681 and 1697." Presumably, however, few of the ladies carried their talents beyond this exercise, or were tempted by the available literature to learn to decipher it. Had they done so, they would have had a fairly wide choice among the religious books that formed their husbands' favorite reading.

"Samuel Sewall saw nothing unusual in spending part of a Saturday outing to Dorchester reading Calvin on the Psalms while his wife picked cherries and raspberries," wrote Hart. Nor, apparently, did Mrs. Sewall, intent on her holiday task, find it unusual for her husband to read Calvin while she worked.

That man was wrong who said the British Empire's downfall began when it was declared unlawful for a man to beat his wife. The real problem was introduced when his wife and daughters began to read. This is obvious when we reflect that a woman cannot very well call down on her husband's head the law against wife beating unless she knows that such a law exists, and she cannot discover that save by hearsay, which is undependable—or through reading. Colonial women had little time for study, and so unless they had been taught to read in childhood, they simply never learned. They worked cruelly hard, tending and feeding their families, helping their men at farming, and giving birth to child after child, many of whom did not survive. Life was harder for women than for men: it was commonplace for a man to be widowed and remarried twice, wearing out three women in his one lifetime. Small wonder, then, that so few women insisted on equal rights. They had no time to think of rights. As George Orwell has pointed out, we seldom get revolt among the truly wretched and downtrodden; the big revolutions are carried out by reasonably well fed people who can afford to dream of liberty. The French workers who rose against their aristocratic masters in 1779 had enjoyed some years of unwonted prosperity just before the Revolution.

To be fair to colonial husbands, it is true that if the lot of their wives was difficult, the men too were hard-worked. But most were inflexible in their ideas of how far to permit women to go, and were swift to rebuke the rare females who overstepped the mark.

The classic example of daring womanhood in the colonies was Mrs. Anne Hutchinson, that rare creature, a well-educated female. Born Anne Maybery in England toward the end of the sixteenth century, the daughter of an English preacher, Anne came to Massachusetts in 1634 with her husband William Hutchinson and joined the congregation of John Cotton, whose preaching she admired. According to the *Dictionary of National Biography,* "she was well versed in the scriptures and theology," which accomplishments were her undoing, for soon she was arguing these matters in a most unwomanly way, disagreeing with all the clergy except her favorite Cotton. "She also pretended to immediate revelation respecting future events," the article continues, and—which was doubtless even more shocking—she held meetings of women in Boston twice a week, and there preached to an audience of nearly a hundred, under pretense of telling them what the Reverend John Cotton had said in his sermons.

Women were not her only supporters. A number of men, "Antinomians" as they called themselves, also thought well of Mrs. Hutchinson; one of them was her brother-in-law, the Reverend John Wheelwright. When her admired Cotton, embarrassed by her open approval and support, made public statements disapproving of some of her views, the Antinomians retorted by trying to elect Wheelwright as his assistant.

"The agitation seriously affected the peace of the infant colony; it interfered with the levy of troops for the Pequot war; it influenced the respect shown to the magistrates and clergy, the distribution of town lots, and the assessment of taxes," the *Dictionary* author tells us. "On 30 Aug. 1637 an ecclesiastical synod at Boston condemned Mrs. Hutchinson's doctrines, and in the ensuing November the general court arraigned her for not discontinuing her meetings as had been ordered."

At Anne Hutchinson's trial she defended herself "with ability and spirit," though she was pregnant and ailing at the time and the court forbade her to sit down until she nearly fell to the ground. The defense was in vain. For heresy and various other offenses, including the fact that she had not taught her female listeners to stay at home, she was banished from the Massachusetts Bay Colony. In the spring of 1638, accompanied by her husband and family and a number of other pioneers, she moved to Roger Williams' colony on Rhode Island, where they lived for the following four years. During this interval Anne gave birth to a deformed child, or, as word had it when the news trickled back to Massachusetts, a "monster," which did not survive. The tragedy was fit punishment from Heaven visited on a heretic, said her detractors. Incidentally, the same thing was said about one of her former followers, a Mrs. Dyer, when she too produced a "monster." God is not mocked, said the righteous.

Then William died and Anne, who had never been made exactly welcome by Roger Williams, again moved, taking fifteen of her sixteen children—her eldest son being away—and the servants of the household to a Dutch settlement near Hell Gate in Westchester, New York. There they lived for another two years until 1644, when all of them were killed by Indians. Anne's fate must have seemed a grim vindication to those who had condemned her as a heretic. God is not mocked, they reminded each other back in Massachusetts. Governor Winthrop, who had been head of her judges, declared that Mistress Hutchinson's tragedy was at least in part due to her husband. William should not have allowed his wife to follow such a wayward path, said Winthrop: he was a man of very mild temper and weak parts, wholly guided by his wife; and thus was in the wrong, for the proper conduct of a wife is submission to her husband's instructions and commands; he is her superior, the head of the family, and she owes him an obedience founded on reverence. Governor Winthrop held that a husband stands before his wife in the place of God and is the "conduit pipe" of the blessings supplied by the Heavenly Father to the family.

Nevertheless, the Puritans did not think a wife should be her husband's servant or slave. One of their number, Daniel Ela, found this out to his cost when he told his wife Elizabeth, in the hearing of his neighbors, that she wasn't really his wife at all but only a servant. The neighbors tattled, and Daniel was brought to court and fined forty shillings for his offense, even though Elizabeth refused to charge him with it.

Everything considered, the Puritan wives of New England were better off than married women of ancient Rome, of the Middle Ages, or even of contemporary England. Puritan husbands were forbidden by law to strike their wives or force them to break God's laws, besides which—and this was an especially important privilege—the Puritan wife had equal authority with her husband when it came to governing the children and the servants. The writings of Judge Samuel Sewall bear witness that a wife's power was sometimes quite considerable. He noted in his diary on October 30, 1713, that his son, Sam, traveling with his wife and meeting one William Ilsly on the road, had warned the said Ilsly not to expect to stay in their house. "Daughter said she had as much to do with the house as he," noted the judge. "Ilsly lodged there." So things could not have been completely bad for *all* American women in the eighteenth century.

And they were to improve, if that is the right word, late in the century because of the Revolutionary War of 1776. War usually does have the side effect of release for women—not that most of them would welcome this way of getting out from under, but it happens. During those famous hostilities it was the privilege of wives deprived of their husbands to do men's work and maintain their families' welfare by more direct methods than were usually employed in times of peace. In July 1777 the lively Abigail Adams in a letter to her husband John reported that certain Bostonian families had attacked a coffee-hoarding merchant, forced open his warehouse, and looted it. Mrs. Adams also spoke her mind in another letter, dated March 31, to John in Philadelphia, where he was attending the Continental Congress. Loving her husband as she did, she wrote humorously, but even so, she could not have considered all of the following passage quite outrageous:

"In the new code of laws which I suppose it will be necessary for you to make, I desire you would remember the ladies and be more generous and favorable to them than your ancestors. Do not put such unlimited power into the hands of the husbands. Remember all men would be tyrants if they could . . . if particular care and attention is not paid to the ladies, we are determined to foment a rebellion, and will not hold ourselves bound by any laws in which we have no voice or representation."

Generation succeeded generation. Society expanded and diversified, until it became difficult to make any more generalizations about the American Woman, who was by this time represented by a large variety of types, as Eleanor Flexner commented in *Century of Struggle*. American women comprised all classes: indentured servants, mistresses of tobacco plantations, pioneer women on the frontier. The one condition they had in common was insecurity, for as long as the country continued to be opened up, any woman, no matter what her social position, might suddenly be uprooted if her man should decide to seek new fortunes for himself and his family. His wife would then have to undergo the same hardships that were the lot of the Pilgrim woman and the Jamestown settlers in earlier days—drudgery, loneliness, and often despair.

At least, however, American women of this era are appreciated by posterity. In the 1930s the residents of a number of states through which run westward trails erected replicas of a statue called "The Pioneer Woman," which represents a female in a sunbonnet, more than life size, apparently striding along in a high wind that molds her voluminous gingham skirts against her powerful thighs. She carries a rifle, and somewhere in the composition are two or three children clinging to her clothing. In spite of the suggested stride, the figure stands—of course—on a pedestal.

A visitor from England, touring the country from east to west, once said of the statue: "You Americans obviously think very well of that pioneer woman I see everywhere, but has nobody ever asked what would have happened to her if she had stayed at home?"

It's a good point. What lay before her was the frontier with all its dangers and sorrows, but behind her was the life of a single woman—untrained, undowered, unwanted. It is true that frontier life was uncomfortable at the very best, while at its worst the pioneers were harried, hungry, and overworked. But the pioneer woman had one compensation. If the toil was back-breaking, if childbearing turned into tragedy, as it was apt to do, at least her ego was not bruised by neglect. She was needed; she mattered. On the other hand, frontier life was, as it always is, a phase of transition that is not long enduring. With the front line moving steadily westward, new people stepped in to take up the duties of those who went on. Behind the line of progress cities grew up with houses and shops and factories and safety, and people lived in security, no longer troubled by wild beasts or hostile Indians.

In such conditions, we may speculate, the pioneer woman's importance must have faded. Her particular qualities of physical strength and endurance were unnecessary in the town, and as a result she must have lost that authority which in any case was not founded on law. Such women, no doubt, merely bowed their heads and accepted the situation. They had not expected any better: sex discrimination was a fact. And yet, in theory, girls were supposed to be equal to boys in one important matter at least. Feminist literature seldom mentions this because it weakens the cause, but in New England the education of little girls, as of little boys, was considered an integral part of the system, from the earliest days of the settlers.

Calvin had decreed that everyone should read the Bible in order to be sure of salvation. Accordingly, as soon as conditions permitted, the Calvinists of the Bay Colony founded schools for their young, where the children could learn to read Scripture; and once a child has mastered the trick of reading, there is nothing to keep his (or her) attention from straying from the pages of the Bible and lighting on less inspiring literature. Since Christian doctrine holds that females, like males, have souls to be saved, girls as well as boys were supposed to attend school. But did they?

Possibly some managed it, but the tendency in most families was to keep Daughter at home to help with the chores. Finding money for the church schools, like any other sort of financing, was not easy in the colonies, and parents who could afford to pay fees for education were expected to do so. It was yet another factor that militated against schooling for girls.

In 1642 the Bay Colony passed a Poor Law framed to provide schooling and training for the children of poor parents, and the other New England communities, with the exception of maverick Rhode Island, resisted only a little while before passing similar laws. According to this legislation, children need not actually attend classes at their town schools, but they had to be taught to read somehow, at home, if necessary. The qualification provided a welcome way out for parents who wanted to keep their daughters at home, and if even such excuse was not sufficient, there were other arguments, such as that which held that the law didn't really apply to girls. Some townsmen declared that the word "children" as used therein really meant only boys, though others took issue with this theory.

The earliest testimony on this vexed matter comes from Hampton, New Hampshire, under the date 1649—a declaration that the schoolmaster was required to teach the town's children, both male and female, to read and write and cast accounts. But did the master actually obey this directive? Possibly he ignored it. What is certain is that few primary schools in New England received girls on equal terms with boys. As for the so-called grammar schools that carried on education for some after the primary course was completed, according to Dr. Adolphe E. Meyer's *An Educational History of the Americans,* they were all but impregnable male strongholds "designed for the future masters of a world which was clearly the male's own special precinct." Only little girls who were determined to learn to read—and such little girls must have been as few then as they are now—managed somehow to do it.

"Through the efforts of the family and the school dame, or the special dalliance of a sympathetic pastor here and schoolmaster there, many a lass could and did grow up to be an educated and virtuous Puritan,'' wrote Meyer. I am not sure what is meant by ''dalliance'' in this context, but it is true that other New English lasses, less lucky in their families and friends, did not become educated at all.

The ''middle colonies'' of New York, Pennsylvania, and Delaware, though their background was more of a mixture, what with German and Dutch settlers as well as English, fell in with New England in the matter of education, for Quaker and Moravian agreed in this respect. There, too, girls were supposed to learn the three Rs in their religious schools; there, too, a considerable number of them actually stayed at home to help their mothers with housework. The settlers of the South ordered things in a different way. The South was thinly populated, and the few churches there were not dedicated to the Puritan faith, but the Anglican. Nor did the planters feel a pious compulsion to provide even the most elementary sort of education for any but their own offspring. More than half the population were servants or laborers, and as there were no towns like those of New England, no congregations had a responsibility to build schools for the children of workers. So matters went for a generation or two, until it became apparent to the wealthy planters that their social inferiors were outbreeding them, producing numbers of potential malcontents and troublemakers. It seemed advisable to take precautions, and the authorities set up workhouse schools where poor children could be trained as apprentices in various trades. A Virginia law of 1705 ruled that the boys who attended such institutions must be taught to read and write as well as work, and nearly half a century later, in 1751, a similar stipulation was made for workhouse girls.

For their own children, however, rich parents in the South engaged tutors, who lived in the house, or they provided schoolrooms for their children and those of their friends who were willing to share the cost. Higher education for boys sometimes included a Grand Tour of Europe. The daughters, like those of well-off parents elsewhere in America, were sent to finishing school to acquire, according to Merle Curti's *Learning for Ladies,* ''religious and moral habits and the gracious veneer of drawing-room culture and respectability.'' In other words, they were prepared to be ornaments to the houses they would, it was hoped, someday grace as the wives of landed gentlemen. Finishing schools advertised in contemporary journals, promising to produce accomplished young ladies who could perform on at least one musical instrument, dance, do needlework, and paint in watercolors. Some boasted of teaching more intellectual subjects: Curti quotes an advertisement that listed "chirography [handwriting], uranography [astronomy], mythology, mezzotint, calisthenics, dancing and flourishing." It sounds impressive, but the schools were usually run on a shoestring. A female seminary in North Carolina, for example, was staffed by the proprietor alone, the Reverend Gilbert Morgan, though his wife—when she had the time—did occasionally lend a hand.

Finishing academies charged large fees, but the men who could afford to pay them took pride in doing so. The forebears of these fathers—or most of them—had come to America to better themselves, and paying high prices was one method of proving their success. Sending daughters to finishing schools was a form of conspicuous consumption among the British aristocracy, and loyal colonials, especially in Virginia, were happy to follow their example.

Thus, through one system or another, many eighteenth-century American women were literate, and a few, but only a few, attained an intellectual level that surpassed that of the average man. Abigail Adams was educated by her father, a reverend gentleman named Smith who respected the mental potentialities of his daughters. New England women were practical, and some of them worked outside as well as inside the home; Curti says they were "skilled in management of estates, shops and even more ambitious projects." In business and law offices women functioned usefully, and others served as shop assistants. As long as towns kept growing larger and the economy expanded, women found work to do over and above the chores of housekeeping, but it would be inaccurate to say that all girls clamored for the opportunity to prove themselves in a man's world. Custom was opposed to such an attitude, and no matter what the economic situation might persuade them to do, their upbringing was concentrated on what were considered womanly preoccupations. They expected to marry and bring up families, but in these expectations they were not romantic. Marriages were still made with an eye for the suitable match rather than romantic love. When people spoke of love they meant respect, affection, and habit rather than sexual attraction. They were not immune to such attraction, but they had other words for it, such as "infatuation," "lust," or even "the devil's lure." But change was on the way.

CHAPTER 3

''*Robbed—by the Laws . . .*''

THE PIONEERS OF THE SEVENTEENTH AND EARLY EIGHTEENTH CENTURIES had little chance to indulge in reading for pleasure. If they knew how to read—and, as we have seen, they did not all possess this knowledge—they favored the Bible or works closely associated with Scripture. But for the next generations, most of whom lived in towns or on farms, literature—of a sort—came into its own, especially for the women. After the evening meal many a family gathered to listen as Father read aloud. At first he had only imported books with which to supplement the Bible, but as the years passed printing shops were established in the colonies and books were published in America, most of them reprints but also an increasing number of original American writings. The imports were usually of English origin, though in certain communities, especially New York and Philadelphia, there was enough demand for German and Dutch texts to make it worth the stationers' while to stock them.

Thus, as the eighteenth century continued, Father did not always choose Scripture to read from. The Americans' outlook kept broadening, and a certain frivolity crept into their tastes. There were even plays produced in the larger towns, by Shakespeare and Gay and Dryden. Backwoodsmen who didn't get a chance to see these productions had to content themselves with reading the pieces, and though New England's divines thundered against the pernicious stage, both productions and books of drama flourished in the eighteenth century. Poetry too was popular, especially the moral sort by Watts, Pope, and Thomson, but the greatest change that came over the average American's reading preference was that he—and she—developed a fondness for novels. Already fiction of a sort was in fashion: children could immerse themselves in *Pilgrim's Progress,* confident that their elders would approve. It was, and still is, an enjoyable adventure story, highly preferable, in a child's estimation, to such lugubrious tomes as *An Alarm to Unconverted Sinners,* which his elders professed to admire.

Another kind of adventure story met with even more favor—the so-called Indian Captivities, which were accounts, usually truthful, of people who had been captured by Indians and later escaped or were rescued by members of their own race. Such stories were all the more hair-raising because they were topical.

"Actually or ostensibly autobiographical accounts, often by poorly educated people, these books described the narrator's capture, a cruel march into the wilderness, the brutalities he suffered while living among the Indians, and his eventual escape," wrote James D. Hart. He cites the outstanding work of this genre, *Narrative of the Captivity and Restauration of Mrs. Mary Rowlandson,* which, first issued as early as 1682, went into a fifteenth edition in 1800. Other tales similar in nature had careers nearly as long.

But a new kind of reader began to make her desires felt in the kind of book she liked—the city woman, who had less reason than her pioneer mother to occupy herself with blood and thunder. In the softer conditions that now prevailed, women turned to the soft emotions and toyed with sentiment and the notion of romantic love. They found fuel for these gentle fires in England, from where came four novels of note in the decade of the 1740s—Richardson's *Pamela* and *Clarissa Harlowe,* and Fielding's *Tom Jones* and *Joseph Andrews,* the last-named starting out as a satire on *Pamela* but surviving as a success in its own right. Women who read these books saw themselves in Pamela or Clarissa, fell in love with the heroines' lovers, felt the same anguished need to decide between virtue and the satisfaction of sinful desires as the fictional ladies, and suffered as the heroines suffered. When Pamela won her spiritual struggle and found virtue rewarded, thousands of women who had completed their day's drudgery of housework rejoiced as if they themselves had had her good fortune, though they had never been faced with any such glamorous choice, nor were likely to be. When poor Clarissa lost a similar battle between vice and virtue, the housewives wept.

These sentimental novels lacked appeal for the young and adventurous, women as well as men, who wanted more of what they found in the Indian Captivities—danger and excitement. In 1764 there appeared in England a book that satisfied such needs as well as the longings of gentler female readers: *The Castle of Otranto,* subtitled

"A Gothic Story by William Marshal, Gent., from the original Italian." It was, indeed, the first Gothic novel, an amalgam of ghosts, ancient ruins, and supernatural terrors vaguely connected with religion, the whole mixture proving highly palatable to the public on both sides of the Atlantic. The pseudonymous William Marshal was in truth Horace Walpole, whose identity was one of the worst-kept secrets in English society, but it was the custom of the times for writers to use *noms de plume*. "The original Italian" was another figment of his imagination.

Provenance and authorship made no difference to most of the book's enthralled readers, who shuddered as they tried to follow the mysterious twists of the plot, meandering and dark as the subterranean tunnel that led from the castle cellars to the chapel. It was fun to feel appalled shock when the villainous Manfred decided to put away his wife Hippolita and marry lovely Isabella, a princess entrusted (with supreme idiocy, one cannot help thinking) to his care by her noble father. Unexplained voices thundered warnings through the stone corridors: "Beware! Beware!" Pieces of stone statuary swelled to gigantic size and one was never told exactly why. Catholic convents and monasteries, symbols of mystery to a Protestant public, played their part; one wonders what eighteenth-century English fiction would have done without Rome. Nor was virtue invariably rewarded in this life. Matilda, who never did anyone harm, met an untimely end. In the last few pages readers were treated to just the right, titillating amount of sorrow.

"Frederic offered his daughter to the new Prince, which Hippolita's tenderness for Isabella concurred to promote. But Theodore's grief was too fresh to admit the thought of another love; it was not until after frequent discourses with Isabella of his dear Matilda, that he was persuaded he could know no happiness but in the Society of one, with whom he could forever indulge the melancholy that had taken possession of his soul."

"Forever indulge the melancholy . . ." The public did not yet demand unmitigatedly happy endings to romance. Pamela's tale is a bit nearer to real life (though not very), but she too got her just eighteenth-century deserts: not unalloyed happiness, but a mixture of gall and sweetness, whereas poor Clarissa's end was pure tragedy. The women of eighteenth-century England and America enjoyed a good cry. It is impossible to be sure, but we can hazard a guess that the men preferred Sterne's *Tristram Shandy,* Smollett's *History of England,* Blackstone's *Commentaries* and Locke's *Essay Concerning*

Human Understanding, none of which appealed to most women. However, Goldsmith's *The Vicar of Wakefield* was acceptable to almost everyone of either sex, being moral, yet telling a good story. For women who wanted more lugubrious material—and their name, according to the records, was legion—there was Goethe's *The Sorrows of Young Werther.*

What hardly needs saying is that a considerable number of American women did not need fiction to stir up their sensibilities, even after the hardships of pioneer days had become a memory for the increasing number of town dwellers. Hardships of another sort were enough and more than enough to keep Jane Mecom, for one, thoroughly occupied. Born Jane Franklin in 1717, she was Benjamin Franklin's sister and favorite sib, youngest of the seventeen children of Josiah, who, having come to America from England in 1683, married Abiah Folger and settled in Boston as a soap boiler and tallow chandler. Jane's life is a vivid reminder of what society was like in the colonies of her time—a mixture of plain living and hard work, mitigated by an occasional flash of hope and pride, which in her life was supplied wholly by her brother Benjamin, the genius. In 1727, when she was seventeen, she was married, doubtless by the arrangement of her elders, to Edward Mecom, a saddler. Mecom died in 1765, by which time his wife had borne him twelve children. He must have handed down to them some fatal weakness of mind and body, for the record of their various calamities is appalling. One son, Peter, went mad before he reached maturity; another, Benjamin, later met the same fate. The other Mecom children died young, but most had already begotten their own lot of children, whom Jane was left to support.

"She was always poor and overworked, as well as harried and bereft," wrote Carl Van Doren in his introduction to *The Letters of Benjamin Franklin and Jane Mecom.* "It is a wonder that she lived at all . . . In her later years she read whenever she could find time for it."

Most of Jane's life was spent in Boston, where—with occasional help from her famous brother—she made ends meet by keeping a boardinghouse. She could hardly prosper at this, since, as Van Doren points out, most of her boarders were needy members of her own family, and he gives a staggering list of them. For example, after her daughter Sarah died, Sarah's widower came with his four small children to live with Jane. Two of these children died in her house, and one of the survivors, a boy of four, was lamed for life by a fall. A Colonel Ingersoll, whose first wife had been a niece of Jane's but was now dead, sent his two daughters to live in the house. Another boarder, Sarah Bowles, was the widowed stepdaughter of one of Jane's sisters. A woman known only as "poor Sarah" sometimes helped out by washing the dishes, but was usually too ill to leave her room. Jane's ailing, shiftless sons came to live there from time to time, and one brought his wife along. The tale of these children's various failures and early deaths is too depressing to repeat. But Jane herself lived to be eighty-two, surviving Benjamin by four years. She wrote to him on his eighty-fourth birthday: "This Day my Dear Brother compleats his 84th year you can not as old Jacob say few and Evel have they been, Except those wherin you have Endured such Grevious Torments Laterly, yous have been filled with Enumerable Good works, Benifits to your felow creatures, & Thankfulnes to God . . . I am as you sopose six years younger than you Are being Born on the 27th March 1712 but to Apearance in Every wons sight as much older." And small wonder.

Benjamin Franklin liked women, by which I do not mean that he was a wencher—or, rather, merely a wencher. Certainly he earned his reputation for gallantry; not that this was difficult in the times he lived in, with John Adams, for one, observing him with chilly disapproval whenever he went gallivanting. But Franklin was not the kind of roué who hates women for their frailty even as he takes advantage ot it. He championed the right of females to be people, arguing that their inferiority in various fields owed itself to lack of education, not to some immutable law of God. Speaking of this in *Learning for Ladies,* Curti reminded his readers that most Americans of Franklin's time held that women were by nature inferior to men and at best were "diadems in their husbands' crowns." Such people accepted without question the inferior legal status of women—a status which, admittedly, was slightly higher than that of Englishwomen, but still closely followed common law.

"In the position he took on the abilities and status of women, Franklin was in advance of his American contemporaries," said Curti. Not all his contemporaries, however: one exception was the English-born Thomas Paine, who shared Franklin's views and expressed them in an essay published in the periodical he edited, the *Pennsylvania Magazine*, for August 1775: "Even in countries where they may be esteemed the most happy, [women are] constrained in their desires in the disposal of their goods, robbed of freedom and will by the laws, the slaves of opinion, which rules them with absolute sway and construes the slightest appearance into guilt; surrounded on all sides by judges, who are at once tyrants and their seducers . . . Who does not feel for the tender sex?"

Paine was probably the first in America to plead publicly for the rights of women, and his article might have stimulated Abigail Adams when she wrote her famous letter to her husband. Paine's theme was not new in England, however. Rebellion is visible in the writings of the Restoration dramatist Aphra Behn, and in the last decade of the seventeenth century an odd little book was published under the title *An Essay in Defence of the Female Sex: In a Letter to a Lady, Written by a Lady*. The author—anonymous, of course; this was *de rigueur*—was said to be one Mary Astell, but Mrs. Astell could not be found, and her true name is still unknown. Whoever she was, she made some interesting points. To defend her sex, she said, might seem too difficult a task to attempt, considering how many great wits had strongly attacked it. But she would not yield, or admit that women are naturally less fitted than men for such argument. Nature had no part in woman's mental inferiority, which came about "through the usurpation of men and the tyranny of custom (here in England especially)," with the result that few women were fitted by education and acquired wit, or letters, to defend themselves. Asserting that great allowances had to be made for the disparity of their circumstances, she continued in the disputatious vein then popular among learned men: If women were naturally defective, the defect had to be either in the soul or the body. But according to the savants, all souls are alike, with no sex distinction. Nor according to learned physicians could the defect be found in woman's body, since the physical aspect of the mind, regardless of sex, is the same.

Mrs. Astell turned her gaze on animals other than humans, to see if there was any difference between male and female intelligence with them. Between species are great differences, of course: "An ape, a dog, a fox, are by daily observation found to be more docile and more subtle than an ox, a swine or a sheep." But between the sexes of the same species this is not true: "a she ape is as full of, and as ready at imitation as a he; a bitch will learn as many tricks in as a short a time as a dog, a female fox as many wiles as a male."

She wondered if it might not be a matter of nationality. Dutch women, she mused, manage not only their family affairs but money matters as well as Englishmen could do. She had often heard English merchants complain of their countrymen on this point: "that they breed our women so ignorant of business; whereas were they taught arithmetic and other arts that require not much bodily strength, they might supply the places of abundance of lusty men now employed in sedentary business . . ." Not to mention the advantage to be gained if women, suddenly widowed, could manage the affairs their late husbands left in confusion.

Since women are not as strong or tough as men, continued Mrs. Astell, they have to be clever. Men, with their superior strength, are contrived for action and labor. They are brave and strong and can undergo the drudgery of providing sustenance. It is the woman's task to manage and distribute this sustenance. Even though woman is usually poorly educated, can it be honestly said that she is unworthy to be man's companion? Not even man says so very often. In summary, Mrs. Astell accused men of having used their strength to steal superiority from women. In the infancy of the world, she argued, men and women were equal, partners in dominion, but men spoiled all that. "They have endeavored to train us up altogether to ease and ignorance; as conquerors used to do those they reduced by force, that so they may disarm 'em both of courage and wit; and consequently make them tamely give up their liberty, and abjectly submit their necks to a slavish yoke." In time, she continued, men's tyranny grew until it reached a height of cruelty like that found in the East, where the women, like Negroes on the plantations, are born slaves, and live prisoners all their lives. Small wonder, she said, that certain women withdrew from the society of men and became Amazons!

Education, repeated the writer, was at the bottom of this inequality. In the beginning of childhood there was no difference between the teaching of girls and boys, but at the age of six or seven the sexes were separated: "The boys are sent to grammar-school and the girls to boarding-schools or other places, to learn needlework, dancing, singing, music, drawing, painting or other accomplishments." The worst of this, added Mrs. Astell, was that girls were taught only their own tongue and perhaps fashionable French among the languages, whereas boys were taught Latin and Greek, which enlarged their capacities.

In spite of all this, if women would only use their talents wisely they could keep the flag flying. "I wish they would shake off this deep despondence . . ." wrote Mrs. Astell.

The *Defence* was a clarion call, but it is doubtful if Jane Mecom, to name only one American female, ever got the chance to read it. It must have been easier to find novels, and pleasanter to read them when time allowed—that is, unless she felt, as many preachers did, that such reading was downright sinful. Certainly, in spite of clerical prejudice, many of her countrywomen—and some countrymen too—by the early years of the nineteenth century were reading fiction with great enthusiasm. According to Hart, at this time 90 percent of adult whites in the United States were literate to some extent, and women in particular looked for more and more novels.

In spite of the Revolution and the prejudice against articles of English manufacture that it engendered, English novels did not come under a ban. The American public depended too much on them, because their own writers fell short in providing a sufficient amount of printed fodder. One popular work was Mrs. Ann Radcliffe's *The Mysteries of Udolpho,* an innocent, silly book containing much more "sensibility" than *The Castle of Otranto,* as shown by the great number of times the heroine swoons, or falls senseless to the ground, or knows no more. Like their opposite numbers in England, American readers also relished stronger meat in *The Monk,* by the Englishman Matthew Gregory Lewis, which was first published in 1796 and printed in America three years later. "Monk" Lewis, as he came to be known after his success, was only nineteen when he wrote the novel. He said he had been inspired by *The Mysteries of Udolpho,* for which he avowed great admiration, but *The Monk* was far more blood-chilling and can hardly be called innocent, containing as it does what one editor rightly called a "charnel-house atmosphere" as well as incidents of voyeurism and rape. The modern offerings found in certain bookshops near New York's Times Square are merely pallid imitations of Matthew Lewis' masterpiece.

The protests of anti-fiction American preachers redoubled with the appearance of the Gothics. It was said that novels softened the mind, unfitting it for more solid reading and polluting the imagination. It is significant that some of these blasts were aimed at male readers as well as female: in 1803 the principal commencement address given at Harvard was directed against the dangers of fiction. Nevertheless, the bulk of fiction readers were female, who like their brothers, went on reading novels unperturbed by the annoyance of their spiritual leaders.

A commentator of the time said of a popular lending library that its shelves could scarcely contain the weight of works much in demand, and he named them—*Female Fraility, The Posthumous Daughter, Cavern of Woe, Cottage on the Moor,* and so on. He mentioned "alluring, melting, irresistible titles . . . *Delicate Embarrassments, Venial Trespasses, Misplaced Confidence.*" Everyone wanted them, he said, from girls of thirteen to matrons of three score. His word is borne out by a letter from the book peddler "Parson" Weems, he who invented the story of George Washington and the cherry tree, to his publisher, who was urging him to sell the works of Jonathan Edwards: "I wrote to you, begging for sweet prosperity's sake that you wd send no more of such books, but send rather, 'fine sentimental Novels.' "

All this novel reading must have played its part in changing American women's attitude toward sexual matters. According to Page Smith's theory in *Daughters of the Promised Land,* women in colonial America from 1620 to the second half of the eighteenth century were unprudish and matter-of-fact about sex. In 1744 Dr. Alexander Hamilton of Maryland paid a visit to Philadelphia and reported afterward that he hadn't seen one prude in the place. Within the next fifty years, however, the popular attitude, according to Professor Smith, underwent a striking alteration. He calls as one witness Médéric Louis Elie Moreau de Saint-Méry, a Frenchman who came to America in the last decade of the century for a protracted visit. Moreau de Saint-Méry complained that the girls of Philadelphia were ridiculously prudish; that all American women, in fact, had this fault, and went to ridiculous extremes to maintain propriety. In their speech, he declared, they divided their bodies into two, as if "from the top to the waist is stomach; from there to the foot is ankles." Ladies would not let doctors touch their bodies, and could not bring themselves even to describe certain ailments to their medical advisers. One young woman referred to her ulcerated breast as a pain in the stomach.

Professor Smith theorizes that this change in manners derived from a change in American family arrangements. In the newly appeared middle classes the women, no longer married off arbitrarily by their elders, had to find husbands for themselves. Because they were painfully anxious to meet the requirements of the men, they formed themselves into what they considered to be the stereotype of the sort of girl a man wanted to marry, affecting delicacy and innocence in their speech and behavior.

This interpretation may be correct, but I think the new prudishness owed itself to another influence as well. Even in the late eighteenth and early nineteenth centuries America was not an independent microcosm, cut off from Europe. On the contrary, in spite of the difficulties of transport, between 1790 and 1820 immigration from Europe increased rapidly, and even before 1790 there had been a constant influx of immigrants. Such new arrivals from England, France, Germany, and the Netherlands brought with them their own customs, and American usage inevitably reflected such imports. There was a time lag resulting from the conservatism of the immigrants, who tended to cling to the old ways. If any culture, be it yeast or civilization, is transplanted, the transplants are slow to change at the outer limits. While the center, or nucleus, steadily develops, and the development in time is transmitted to the outer periphery, there is always this lag. Visitors from the Old World to the New were often amused by the old-fashioned ways that prevailed among Americans: the prissy-mouthed misses of the United States still obeyed the dictates of an earlier generation in Europe.

Not all travelers agreed in their conclusions about American women. When Alexis de Tocqueville came to America in 1831, he, unlike his compatriot Moreau de Saint-Méry, saw no undue prudishness among the females. On the contrary, he was impressed by the youth of the girls who stepped out from under the care of their mothers long before they reached marriageable age.

"An American girl scarcely ever displays that virginal softness in the midst of young desires or that innocent and ingenuous grace which usually attend the European woman in the transition from girlhood to youth," he wrote. "It is rare that an American woman, at any age, displays childish timidity or ignorance. Like the young woman of Europe she seeks to please, but she knows precisely the cost of pleasing. If she does not abandon herself to evil, at least she knows that it exists and she is remarkable rather for purity of manners than for chastity of mind."

In no way can that passage from *Democracy in America* be interpreted as a description of prudery. De Tocqueville thought that part of the difference between these young women and those of his own country could be explained by the fact that America was a Protestant nation. Protestant countries that had retained or acquired the right of self-government had a tradition of freedom which was "infused into the domestic circle"; in the United States, Protestantism combined with great political liberty, and young women were surrendered early and completely to their own guidance, even more so than in England. He confessed that it took some getting used to.

"I have been frequently surprised and almost frightened at the singular address and happy boldness with which young women in America contrive to manage their thoughts and language amid all the difficulties of free conversation," he admitted. But they did manage. An American woman, even in early youth, was always mistress of herself. He wondered if this method of education might not be more satisfactory than that of the French, where women were carefully given a reserved, retired, almost conventual education, then were suddenly abandoned without guide or assistance to cope with democratic society and all its irregularities. American women were not taught virtue on the basis of religion alone. Their mentors sought to arm a woman's reason too. Admittedly, such an education is not without danger. "It tends to invigorate the judgment at the expense of the imagination and to make cold and virtuous women instead of affectionate wives and agreeable companions to men," said de Tocqueville, but he thought that such an education was indispensable in a democracy.

All this carefully nurtured independence was irrevocably lost to an American woman, he observed, when she married. Public opinion in America, where the people were at once puritanical and commercial, led them to require such abnegation on the part of their females. A married woman was carefully circumscribed within the narrow circle of domestic interests and duties, and was forbidden to step beyond it. She knew it; she entered her new state voluntarily and freely. Nor was it only the strength of public opinion that influenced her in taking the step. That "cold and stern reasoning power" that was so carefully trained in her sufficed to show her that a spirit of levity and independence in marriage is a constant subject of annoyance, that the amusements of the girl cannot become those of the wife, and that a married woman's happiness is in her husband's home. Such an austere attitude was bound to stand her in good stead through the almost inevitable financial vicissitudes of marriage—for fortunes in America, though easily made, were as easily lost, yet wives never thought of deserting their husbands for this reason.

"It would seem that their desires contract as easily as they expand," said de Tocqueville admiringly. He found it even more praiseworthy that women took it for granted that they should accompany their husbands on perilous ventures in the wilderness. American husbands always took their wives along and expected them to share in the privations that attended such expeditions. De Tocqueville declared that he had often met young women, brought up in every comfort of large New England towns, who had been set down, without any intermediate stage, in comfortless hovels in the forest.

"Fever, solitude, and a tedious life had not broken the springs of their courage," he reported. "Their features were impaired and faded, but their looks were firm; they appeared to be at once sad and resolute."

CHAPTER 4

Angel or Ass

NOT ALL THE EARLY NINETEENTH-CENTURY WRITING that American women read was fictional. Three British women and one American had a considerable effect on thoughtful females in the States: Mary Wollstonecraft of England, Judith Sargent Murray of Gloucester, Massachusetts, the Scots-born Frances Wright, and her sometime friend, the English Mrs. Frances Trollope, mother of the future novelist Anthony Trollope. Mary Wollstonecraft, Judith Murray, and Frances Wright were all vigorous activists, but Frances Trollope was merely a commentator of the scene as she saw it. All, however, in their separate ways affected the thinking of American women. Mary Wollstonecraft would have been amazed to learn to what an extent her best-known work, *A Vindication of the Rights of Woman,* was to have on this country. It has become the Bible of American feminists.

Who knows what drives some women to rebel while others remain unmoved? Mary's life was of a sort to fill her with resentment against the fate that made her female, it is true, but hundreds of other young women in similar circumstances did not fight against their destiny as she did. Still, there it is—she did. She was born in 1759 to parents who, though not actually poverty-stricken, managed badly enough to live in a constant state of insecurity. Her father, a heavy drinker, was often surly and violent, especially to his wife. That lady adored and spoiled her son Ned, but paid little attention to the other children. Ned accepted his mother's adulation but never helped with family problems. Mary's sister Eliza made a disastrous marriage, and, worst of all, Mary's beloved friend, Fanny Blood, came to grief through a man. Fanny too was the daughter of a drunkard, but she had a better education than Mary, and early in their friendship she helped the younger girl, training her in reading and writing so that later Mary was able to teach and write professionally. Fanny's husband was another selfish man. After a short, unhappy marriage she died of child-bed fever.

After a variegated career as governess, paid companion, proprietress of a short-lived school, and author of a book, *Thoughts on the Education of Daughters,* Miss Wollstonecraft at the age of twenty-nine decided to follow a literary career. Her publisher, Johnson of St. Paul's Courtyard, encouraged and helped her, and by the end of 1788 had published three more books from her pen. She lived in London and often dined at his house, where she met Thomas Paine and other literary lights.

A Vindication, her most famous book, appeared in 1792. In spite of its difficult style—like many of her contemporaries, Mary took Dr. Samuel Johnson for a model—it is an impassioned, indignant, absorbing volume. The ideas it propounded startled a world in which the inequities assailed by the author were accepted as part of God's natural order. In the dedication she warned the reader that her main argument was based on the principle that if women were not educated to become men's companions, knowledge and virtue could not progress.

The book contains attacks on a number of male writers—Milton, Swedenborg, Rousseau, and a popular clergyman named Dr. Gregory—all of whom, Mary declared, denigrated women, each in his own way. She scored such "heterogeneous association" as "fair defects," "amiable weaknesses," and so on. "If there be one criterion of morals, but one archetype for man," she wrote, "women appear to be suspended by destiny, according to the vulgar tale of Mahomet's coffin; they have neither the unerring instinct of brutes, nor are allowed to fix the eye of reason on a perfect model. They were made to be loved, and must not aim at respect, lest they should be hunted out of society as masculine."

Women, she continued, had to look up to man for every comfort. "In the most trifling dangers they cling to their support, with parasitical tenacity, piteously demanding succour; and their *natural* protector extends his arm, or lifts up his voice, to guard the lovely trembler—from what? Perhaps the frown of an old cow, or the jump of a mouse; a rat would be a serious danger. In the name of reason, and even common-sense, what can save such beings from contempt; even though they be soft and fair?" The world would hear no more of such infantile airs, she wrote, if girls were allowed to exercise and not kept in close rooms. If fear in girls, instead of being cherished, were treated in the same manner as cowardice in boys, they would quickly get over it.

Rousseau had written: "Educate women like men, and the more they resemble our sex the less power will they have over us." Exactly, said Mary, "I do not wish them to have power over men, but over themselves." Scornfully she quoted another man's description of the perfect woman, who treated her husband with respectful observance and tenderness, studying his humors, overlooking his little mistakes, submitting to his opinions, giving soft answers to hasty words, complaining as seldom as possible. "Such a woman ought to be an angel—or she is an ass," commented Mary.

A Vindication shows that Mary Wollstonecraft had a lively, original mind. She dared to say, for example, that parental affection is probably the blindest modification of perverse self-love. But the most startling suggestion in the book is that women should have representatives in the government, instead of possessing no direct share in its deliberations: "Let woman share the rights, and she will emulate the virtues of men."

Soon *A Vindication* and its attractive author were the talk of literary London. Mary made money and promptly spent most of it on her sisters and brothers. In 1792 she went to Paris, intending to study French and at the same time find out what was happening over there. Then the war between England and France caught her in the capital, and she could not get away. Instead she met and fell in love with the American novelist Gilbert Imlay, author of a slushy novel, *The Emigrants*. Her biographer Camilla Jebb is hard put to it to excuse what happened next. We are not quite so pained today as she was by the fact that Miss Wollstonecraft lived with Imlay without benefit of clergy, but Miss Jebb felt impelled to soften the blow for her public. She said that no one could read Mary's letters without being convinced that she considered the bond between Imlay and herself absolutely sacred and lasting, but "It still remains an open question why she should have thought it right to place herself . . . on the same level as women of an altogether different type." In extenuation she reminds us of Imlay's bad influence, the anarchic ideas rife in the atmosphere, and the difficulties faced by aliens like these lovers who might wish to contract marriage abroad.

William Godwin, who later married Miss Wollstonecraft, was to offer another excuse. Mary refused to marry Imlay, he said, because she was in debt and marriage would have made him liable for her financial responsibilities. Still, poor Miss Jebb felt forced to admit that in one of Mary's novels is disturbing evidence that she simply believed she was doing the right thing in not marrying Imlay. "She propounds a theory of marriage far from immoral, but certainly not conventional. There is also the fact which in common honesty must not be ignored, that her marriage with Godwin was only legalised within five months before the birth of their child."

However, all this is looking ahead. Mary gave birth to Imlay's daughter in France in 1794, and named the infant Fanny after her dear dead friend. She seems to have been quite happy and confident at that time, but soon a change came over Imlay. The political situation was now less tense, and he was able to travel back and forth between England and France. He availed himself of this freedom and spent so much time away that, when little Fanny was eighteen months old, Mary shouldered the child and followed her lover to London, where she discovered that he had another mistress. It was a great shock. Even her extraordinary strength of mind could not stand up against the conventional idea of how a woman should behave in these circumstances. As Goldsmith said:

When lovely woman stoops to folly
And finds too late that men betray,
What charm can soothe her melancholy,
What art can wash her guilt away?

The only art her guilt to cover,
To hide her shame from every eye,
To give repentance to her lover
And wring his bosom, is—to die.

Mary did indeed try to die, though the account of her attempt is vague. Did she throw herself into the Thames, only to be rescued? Whatever her method, it was unsuccessful and she survived. Once the crisis was over, she was comforted by her many loyal friends, and soon regained a more characteristic courage. She must live for Fanny's sake. She went back to work and wrote more books. In due course she entered a close relationship with William Godwin, political philosopher and essayist, and in 1797 they were married. A child was born, as Miss Jebb correctly asserted, five months after the wedding day, and this event killed Mrs. Godwin; she died soon afterward of puerperal fever. The child, also named Mary, survived and grew up to marry the poet Shelley and to write *Frankenstein*.

By one of those coincidences not uncommon in the world of ideas, Mrs. Judith Sargent Murray, of Gloucester, Massachusetts, published in 1790—the same year that saw the emergence of *A Vindication of the Rights of Woman*—an article expressing similar ideas. In the *Massachusetts Magazine* for March-April, under the title "Equality of the Sexes," Mrs. Murray appealed for equal rights for females in education. She asked if people were looking at sex differentiation as it actually was or as they assumed it to be. Too many merely inherited beliefs that upon examination proved ridiculous.

"Is it upon mature consideration we accept the idea, that nature is thus partial in her distributions? Is it indeed a fact that she hath yielded to one half the human species so unquestionable a mental superiority?" she asked, and argued that this superiority—if it existed—could be traced rather to differences between the education given to boys and that of girls. Boys' education continued the advantages which began almost immediately after birth. Yet could anyone seriously claim that a boy of two is wiser, has better judgment, than a girl the same age?

"But from that period what partiality! How is the one exalted and the other depressed, by the contrary modes of education that are adopted! The one is taught to aspire, the other is early confined. As their years increase, the sister must be wholly domesticated, while the brother is led by the hand through all the flowery paths of science . . . Is it reasonable that a candidate for immortality, for the joys of heaven, an intelligent being, who is to spend an eternity in contemplating the works of the Deity, should at present be so degraded, as to be allowed no other ideas, than those which are suggested by the mechanism of a pudding, or the sewing of the seams of a garment?"

But there was an important difference between Mrs. Murray's outlook and that of Miss Wollstonecraft. Mary Wollstonecraft was angry and not hopeful, while Mrs. Murray, as befitted a denizen of the brave new world, was confident of better things to come. She was sure that something could and would be done to remedy the inequities of the educational system in America, and her optimism was well founded. After all, Thomas Paine and Benjamin Franklin were on her side, and she had another ally in Dr. Benjamin Rush, professor of chemistry at the University of Pennsylvania and a physician as well. In 1787 Dr. Rush had spoken out for a broader base in female education. His recommendations were founded on the hardly feminist notion that women should be trained so that they might teach their sons "the principles of liberty and government." Still, it was better than nothing, and all these male supporters of the cause had influence. When it came to education, Americans then as now were receptive to suggestions for improvement, and eight years after the publication of Mrs. Murray's article she was able to produce a progress report.

"Female academies are everywhere establishing," she wrote with gratification, "and right pleasant is the appellation to my ear."

It is true that a number of girls' schools were springing up in the general proliferation of educational institutions that accompanied that of the population. However, step by step with them came criticisms of their standards. It was rumored that the curricula of female academies sounded a lot better than they were in practice, and Dr. Rush must have been disappointed with the results in at least one respect. He had prophesied that if girls were encouraged to read biographies and travel books they would stop wasting their time on sentimental poetry and novels; yet, in spite of having free choice and plenty of access to uplifting literature, they continued to read sentimental poetry and novels—as did their parents, their brothers, and their neighbors. Most of this literature still came from England: if we look at the list of America's favorite books during the first two decades of the nineteenth century we might be excused for forgetting all about the War of 1812. Nobody seemed to hold a patriotic prejudice against Byron—*Childe Harold* and *The Giaour*—or the rhymer and romancer Sir Walter Scott. We find a few exceptions. Americans eagerly read Washington Irving's *History of New York* and Isaac Mitchell's American Gothic novel *The Asylum, or Alonzo and Melissa,* and James Fenimore Cooper's reputation was on the rise, but still Byron and Scott led all the rest. Admittedly, these preferences were not entirely voluntary. The lack of a copyright agreement between Britain and the United States made it more profitable for American publishers to pirate English books, on which they didn't have to pay royalties, than to print American works, on which they did.

For women, the importance of education in America can hardly be overestimated, but in the short run it was probably the textile factory rather than the girls' school that made more difference to females. Eleanor Flexner is of the opinion that the true beginning of women's liberation can be pinpointed in Pawtucket, Rhode Island, in 1790, when Samuel Slater harnessed water power to run a spinning mill and so in the course of the next twenty years revolutionized the textile industry. Until the mill was invented, women had spun and woven all their cloth at home, a domestic chore like pig killing or bread baking. Then the first power-driven loom was set up in Waltham, Massachusetts, and everything was suddenly different. Women were released from at least one form of drudgery. Furthermore, textile making, which quickly became America's first large-scale industry, offered girls (and children too, unfortunately) a chance to work outside the house and make good money. Hundreds of young women started going out to work, becoming financially independent of their menfolk. They had to work long hours, but so did houseworkers, and as breadwinners they achieved a higher position in society than their mothers had ever dreamed of. Many subsidiary freedoms, too, accompanied the change. As Eleanor Flexner has said in *Century of Struggle*, if it was proper for a girl to work in a textile mill—which few disputed—other social taboos had to be reconsidered.

Another profession opening to women was teaching. In Northern states the local governments were contributing to the upkeep of free schools, and teachers were needed for all of them. In a predominantly agricultural society most able-bodied men worked on the land, so teaching was mainly the province of the women. At first it was considered enough if the teacher could impart the simple fundamentals of education, and few women were qualified to go beyond these limits until Mrs. Emma Willard, another New Englander, questioned the system. As little Emma Hart, Mrs. Willard had shown a talent for mathematics, and her father, in spite of the generally held belief that such studies might hurt the tiny female brain, encouraged the child to go ahead and learn more about the science.

Grown up and with her brain unimpaired, Miss Hart married Mr. Willard, headmaster of a Vermont boarding school for boys. She too was a teacher, but of girls. Wishing to introduce her pupils to new studies—mathematics, geography, and history—she applied for permission to sit in on the examinations held at her husband's school so that she might get an idea of the teaching methods used on the boys. This was refused, so Mrs. Willard devised her own methods of instruction. She also did a lot of hard thinking, with the result that in 1819 she presented to Governor De Witt Clinton of New York, during a session of the state legislature in Albany, a paper entitled "An Address to the Public . . . Proposing a Plan for Improving Female Education," which set out her theories and proposed reforms with detailed plans for a girls' seminary in Albany.

Clinton was in favor of the project. He tried to persuade legislators to approve it altogether, but they met him only halfway, agreeing to grant Mrs. Willard a charter for her school but refusing her the necessary funds. Possibly they felt that Albany, which already possessed one female academy, was adequately provided for. Instead, the proposal was picked up by the neighboring town of Troy, where the citizens agreed to subsidize Mrs. Willard's school, and in 1821 it opened as the Troy Female Seminary. The girls were duly taught not only the usual domestic sciences but mathematics, geography, history, and the "natural sciences," which included physiology, a staggering innovation for female students. Any mention of the human body was considered the height of indelicacy, and Emma Willard's biographer, Alma Lutz, has written of the course, "Mothers visiting a class at the Seminary in the early thirties were so shocked at the sight of a pupil drawing a heart, arteries and veins on a blackboard to explain the circulation of the blood, that they left the room in shock and dismay." It is difficult to believe that the diagram of a heart, for instance, could carry sexual connotations, but evidently it did. In the physiology textbooks at Troy Female Seminary, paper was pasted over diagrams that pictured the body or details thereof. Still, the seminary not only survived but flourished, and other schools were structured along similar lines, so that girls were at last able to study, among other subjects, Mrs. Willard's favorite mathematics.

An amiable egotist, the English Captain Frederick Marryat, author of *Mr. Midshipman Easy,* visited the Albany Female Academy in 1837 and noted in his *Diary in America:* "Conceive three hundred modern Portias, who regularly take their degrees, and emerge from the portico of the seminary full of algebra, equality, and the theory of the constitution! The quantity and variety crammed into them is beyond all calculation . . . This afternoon they were examined in algebra, and their performance was very creditable. Under a certain age girls are certainly much quicker than boys, and I presume would retain what they learnt if it were not for their subsequent duties in making puddings, and nursing babies. Yet there are affairs that must be performed by one sex or the other, and of what use can algebra and other abstruse matters be to a woman in her present state of domestic thraldom."

Caddishly, he also told what happened at the next day's examination, which he attended. This time the girls were examined in French, and whenever a girl was stuck Marryat whispered the answer, which she quickly used. Perhaps to make up for this betrayal, he added: "It must be acknowledged that American women are the *prettiest* in the whole world."

Captain Marryat was only one of a rather large lot of Old World intellectuals who crossed the sea in the aftermath of the War of 1812 when things became more friendly, to witness how democracy was making out in the Western Hemisphere—a mixed crew that included de Tocqueville, Mrs. Trollope, Captain Basil Hall, and Harriet Martineau. This is not to say that they all arrived together, of course; they did not.

Mrs. Trollope's visit, which was to be extended for some years, began on Christmas Eve in 1827, when the ship *Edward* sailed into the mouth of the Mississippi and she disembarked with her friend Miss Frances Wright, a young French painter named Auguste Hervieu, and three Trollope children, Henry, Cecilia, and little Emily. Anthony and another boy had been left in school at home. The strongminded Miss Wright, a fascinating woman who deserves to have a section to herself, and will get it, was a close friend of General Lafayette. No stranger to America, she was returning to the States after a visit to her native land, Britain, to look at the tract of land she had acquired in Tennessee, where she intended to bring together blacks and whites and educate them in common schoolrooms. Opponents to abolition were always saying that blacks were naturally inferior to whites, with brains incapable of the same intelligence, and that slavery, for this reason, was their right and natural state. Hoping to disprove such arguments, Frances had sent her sister Camilla ahead to get things started at Nashoba, as the Tennessee place was called.

Hervieu, who like many others had been swept off his feet by the force of Miss Wright's personality, hoped to teach art to the children of the Nashoba school. It is not quite clear what Mrs. Trollope was meant to do in the community, but she was sure that America would be a good thing for her, and Miss Wright was glad to include in her group such an enthusiastic supporter. Mrs. Trollope had blithely left her husband in charge of the family farms, though he was an inveterate bungler. She meant to be a pioneer in the New World, side by side with wonderful Miss Wright. She would bring up Henry, Cecilia, and Emily in the healthy, forward-looking surroundings of Tennessee, and when they had all struck roots and were flourishing, no doubt Mr. Trollope and the boys could join them. As for slavery, she was thoroughly in agreement with Fanny Wright and the other abolitionists.

Most of the English probably felt the same about slavery; at least all the other visitors to America indicated as much. Britain had outlawed the institution domestically in 1811, and in 1817 declared it illegal for an Englishman or English ship to take part in slave trading anywhere in the world. The Trollopes and their companions were much moved when, in New Orleans shortly after their arrival, they saw a genuine live slave—a black girl—sweeping the steps of a house. They paused to converse with the poor thing. "It was the first slave we had ever spoken to," wrote Mrs. Trollope in *Domestic Manners of the Americans,* "and I believe we all felt that we could hardly address her with sufficient gentleness." The girl's cheerful demeanor puzzled them, however: surely she should have been more visibly bowed down by the misery of her situation.

Another experience awaited Mrs. Trollope in New Orleans. "The first symptom of equality that I perceived, was my being introduced in form [i.e., with due ceremony] to a milliner . . . in the very penetralia of her temple, standing behind the counter . . . She was an English woman, and I was told that she possessed great intellectual endowments, and much information; I really believe this was true." This young woman, Mary Carroll, later gave up her millinery store and opened a "philosophical bookshop." She was a great admirer of Frances Wright.

Mrs. Trollope was less pleased with another phenomenon encountered in New Orleans: the social ostracism suffered by pretty "quadroons" at the hands of the proud Creoles. Her own snobberies and prejudices were different. Daughter of a clergyman of modest means, Frances Trollope was intelligent and quick-witted but incorrigibly insular, and her book infuriated American readers, but is undeniably funny even now.

She was disgusted to learn, en route to Memphis on the steamboat, that most American men chewed tobacco and spat it out all over the place. At Memphis, where it had been raining for several days, the party had to climb uphill to the hotel through deep, slippery mud. All in all, her first few days in Tennessee discouraged Fanny Trollope with the New World, though Frances Wright, who was made of sterner stuff, never admitted that she felt discomfort. Memphis was not much of a settlement, Mrs. Trollope felt. The weather continued dreadful, and she could not get used to the glumly silent men who crowded in to meals, ate in a tremendous hurry, and exhibited the frightful table manners she had already observed aboard the *Belevedere:* "The total want of all usual courtesies at the table, the voracious rapidity with which the viands were seized and devoured, the strange uncouth phrases and pronunciation, the loathsome spitting, from the contamination of which it was absolutely impossible to protect our dresses . . ."

At last, much to Mrs. Trollope's relief, the time came to move on to Miss Wright's settlement at Nashoba, and her friends could hardly wait to see it, but water-logged roads delayed them and the coach broke down. When they finally got there, Frances Trollope's dismay and disappointment were total. In a clearing hacked out of the forest, a few log cabins floated like islands in a sea of mud, and that was it. Miss Wright's sister Camilla and her husband Richeson Whitby shivered with ague as they greeted the newcomers, and looked miserably thin and ill. They explained that the damp climate was at fault. A few black children sat around listlessly, for there were no classes as yet; the experiment had not begun. The lodgings and food were dreadful, and Mrs. Trollope quickly decided that Nashoba was out of the question. After a few days she departed the settlement, returning to Memphis with the children and Hervieu, who had switched his allegiance. They moved on from there to Cincinnati, which Hervieu had heard of as a fine, up-and-coming city. The Nashoba settlement failed soon afterward, and Fanny Trollope's friendship with Miss Wright remained unrevived.

At least Cincinnati was better than Memphis, thought Mrs. Trollope, even though pigs swarmed in the streets or were butchered in the surrounding woods, spoiling one's walks. She acquired a house for her group, and immediately discovered the chief drawback to living in a slaveless district in America: nobody would work for her in the kitchen. Only with the greatest difficulty could she get "help," as she had to call it, for it was petty treason in the Republic to call any free citizen a servant. "The whole class of young women, whose bread depends upon their labour, are taught to believe that the most abject poverty is preferable to domestic service," she wrote indignantly. Hundreds of poor girls worked in the paper mills or other factories for less than half the wages they would have received in service because they considered their equality compromised by housework. Nothing but the wish to buy pretty clothes would induce them to submit to such labor. A later, gentler visitor to America, Harriet Martineau, tried in *her* book *Society in America* to soften Mrs. Trollope's ill-tempered remarks such as these. American girls who were too proud for domestic service, she said, might seem mistaken in their dislike of such work because they deprived themselves of a respectable home and station, etc.; "but this is altogether their own affair," she reminded her readers.

Still, Mrs. Trollope's vexation is comprehensible. It was hard to manage a house and large household in a strange land without help. She had to find out what to do with the garbage (leave it in the middle of the road for the pigs to clean up), where and how to market (downtown, very early in the morning, since everything was gone by eight o'clock), and how to cook on the strange stove, which must be stoked with wood. She was delighted, therefore, when a girl turned up at last and announced, "I be come to help you." But her difficulties were not over. The girl simply laughed when Mrs. Trollope asked how much she expected for a year's wages.

"Oh Gimini! you be a downright Englisher, sure enough," she said. "I should like to see a young lady engage by the year in America! I hope I shall get a husband before many months."

And she had arrived with no clothes save what she stood up in, a most unsuitable yellow dress embroidered with red roses. The Trollope girls helped their mother supply her with the underclothes Mrs. Trollope considered decent, and they also made the young lady a proper dress for work. The girl never thanked them, for this or other favors. Instead, she called them "grumpy" when they refused to let her borrow their clothes. She knew lots of young lady helps, she declared, whose old women—that is to say, mistresses—didn't mind lending things, and when Mrs. Trollope refused to advance her the money to buy a silk ball gown, she gave notice. Reflecting on the experience, Mrs. Trollope wrote that she could not possibly give an adequate idea of the sore, angry pride that seemed to torment "those poor wretches" of girls. Another one who worked for the Trollopes for a while must have been naturally gentle and kind in the beginning, said her mistress, but her good feelings had been soured and her gentleness turned to morbid sensitiveness by having heard thousands of times that she was as good as any other lady. She deeply resented the fact that she had to eat in the kitchen, away from the family.

"I guess I know that's 'cause you don't think I'm good enough to eat with you. You'll find out that won't do here," she said.

"I found out afterwards that she very rarely ate any dinner at all, and generally passed the time in tears," wrote Mrs. Trollope, mystified. "I did everything in my power to conciliate and make her happy, but I am sure she hated me."

Mrs. Trollope was not always unkind about American women. She found many of them pretty, though, she declared, they didn't know how to use their voices, and she considered them an unhealthy lot. Even the fashionable and admired among them did not know how to hold themselves or move gracefully: they lacked what she called *tournure*, or were, in other words, flat-chested. No, it was not the women she minded so much, not even the habit they had in Ohio of referring to all females save herself as ladies—"the lady over that way takes in washing," for instance, or "that there lady, out on the Gulley, what is making dip-candles," whereas they always referred to Mrs. Trollope as "the English old woman." No, it was not the women or not even the servant problem that made Cincinnati a disappointment. It was just that she found the society so dull. Captain Marryat, when he visited Cincinnati eight years after her departure, was told by an unnamed lady that poor Mrs. Trollope was no judge of the town's society, because nobody who was anybody had cultivated her acquaintance. After all, the lady explained, the woman had arrived from nowhere, traveling without her husband but in company with some artist. How could one know her?

It seems likely that Mrs. Trollope described Cincinnati accurately, if without charity. Very likely there *was* no conversation worthy of the name, as she complained, and one can see that the parties she attended were not really exciting, with the ladies always herded together at one end of the room and the gentlemen at the other—though, she added, to be fair one must remember this was the rule all over the States. The gentlemen spat, talked of elections and fat-stock prices, and spat again. The ladies looked at each other's dresses and talked of "Parson Somebody's last sermon on the day of judgement, on Dr. T'otherbody's new pills for dyspepsia" and so on until tea was announced, upon which everyone started to work on the food—a staggering amount of hot cake and custard, hoecake, johnnycake, waffle cake, and dodger cake; pickled peaches and preserved cucumbers, ham, turkey, hung beef, apple sauce, and pickled oysters. Soon afterward they all went home, no doubt to troubled slumbers. But even worse was the ball Mrs. Trollope attended at a hotel, for there, much to her astonishment, the gentlemen had their supper in one large room while the ladies were served with a buffet collation in the ballroom, strolling about with their plates until the sweetmeats were brought, which they sat down to eat in chairs ranged against the walls, dressed up but hardly festive-looking in the circumstances.

Most of the ladies, good churchgoers that they were, thought the theater a sinful place, so, though there was a theater in town, it was poorly attended. On one occasion a couple of dancers visited town and gave a performance, and though this was most respectable of its kind, the ladies walked out on it and the gentlemen muttered under their breath. No concerts, no dinner parties, and only half a dozen public balls a year, at Christmas time—which left nothing for the ladies to do but go to church, which they did *en masse*. Dressed in their finest, they went in throngs to chapel and meetinghouse, on every possible occasion. Gentlemen as a whole did not, save for the young sprigs who went to stare at the girls. The ladies, said Mrs. Trollope, were as much influenced by their religious sects as were those in Roman Catholic countries, with one important difference: the Protestant priests of America, not being celibate, were intensely admired by the ladies, because they were the only men they knew who possessed rank and distinction. Frances Trollope observed this phenomenon more and more clearly as the revival season approached, when itinerant preachers gathering in the town had their pick of places to stay, since they were cordially invited by the highest-ranking ladies. The hostesses held meetings to honor the guests, and invited crowds to join in the festivities and the public confessions that accompanied them. At one of the revival meetings at the principal Presbyterian church, Mrs. Trollope was astonished and horrified by what went on. There was a hell-fire sermon first and then a hymn during which frightened young girls, sobbing and trembling, made their way to the "anxious benches." The priestly supporters of the speaker wandered among them, whispering, and the girls became hysterical, falling on their knees and crying "Oh Lord!" "Oh Lord Jesus!" and "Help me, Jesus!" It was a frightful sight, said the Englishwoman. It was not simply a matter of the lower orders indulging in emotion, she reminded her readers; the congregations in general were very well dressed. She concluded that these excesses were the direct result of boredom. With no card games, no billiards, and no theater, the women of Cincinatti had to find release somewhere.

As part of her sociological studies, Mrs. Trollope visited a local school for girls on the occasion of their annual public exhibition. It is clear from her description that Emma Willard's theories had caught on even out there in the Middle West. Much to the visitor's surprise, the "higher branches of science" were included in the curriculum and one sixteen-year-old had taken a degree in mathematics, while another was examined in moral philosophy. "They blushed so sweetly, and looked so beautifully puzzled and confounded," she wrote, "that it must have been difficult for an abler judge than I to decide how far they merited the diploma they received." But she was skeptical of the value of such studies, which she doubted would survive the wear and tear of half a score of children and no help. Captain Basil Hall, after paying a call on a Boston high school for girls at about the same time, had similar misgivings. The young ladies worked away at algebra, he said, in a surprisingly rapid manner. "The only question is, whether or not this be the fittest study for misses?"

Mrs. Trollope jotted down some random comments on the less fortunate women of America, the wives and daughters of manual laborers, the true slaves of the soil, as she called them. Almost all of them lost every trace of youth and beauty before reaching the age of thirty, due to their lives of hardship, privation, and labor. Even the young girls looked pale, thin, and haggard. One never saw among them a single plump, rosy, laughing face like those of English cottage girls. This tragic picture is somewhat alleviated by Mrs. Trollope's sparkling, malicious description of pleasantries among young Americans. No nice American girl would mention anything so indelicate as, for example, a *shirt* in the presence of a gentleman, which fact should explain the following passage:

"A young lady is employed in making a shirt, a gentleman enters, and presently begins the sprightly dialogue with 'What are you making, Miss Clarissa?'

" 'Only a frock for my sister's doll, sir.'

" 'A frock! not possible. Don't I see that it is not a frock? Come, Miss Clarissa, what is it?'

" ' 'Tis just an apron for one of our Negroes, Mr. Smith!'

" 'How can you, Miss Clarissa? why is not the two sides joined together? I expect you better tell me what it is.'

" 'My! Why then, Mr. Smith, it is just a pillow-case.'

" 'Now, that passes, Miss Clarissa! 'Tis a pillow-case for a giant then. Shall I guess, Miss?'

" 'Quit, Mr. Smith; behave yourself, or I'll certainly be affronted.'

"Before the conversation arrives at this point, both gentleman and lady are in convulsions of laughter. I once saw a young lady so hard driven by a wit, that to prove she was making a bag, and nothing but a bag, she sewed up the ends before his eyes, showing it triumphantly, and exclaiming, 'There now! what can you say to that?' "

Unfortunately Mrs. Trollope's comments were not always confined to her journal. She was too witty to be guarded, and her occasional *bon mots* inevitably were picked up and repeated, to the rage of the mocked.

In March 1830 the family set out from Cincinnati for fifteen months of travel through the States, for Mrs. Trollope wanted more material for her projected book about America before going back to England. They visited Wheeling, Baltimore, Philadelphia, Washington, New York, and Niagara, and everywhere they went, even in the halls of government, men spat. They also drank immoderately. Mrs. Trollope decided that it was the fault of the women. If they would only make themselves charming, cultivated, and particular, she said, men would not dare enter parties "reeking with whiskey, their lips blackened with tobacco, and convinced, to the very centre of their hearts and souls, that women were made for no other purpose than to fabricate sweetmeats and gingerbread, construct shirts, darn stockings, and become mothers of possible presidents . . ."

American women were lazy too. They must be, she said; how else was one to account for the strange custom so common to the Atlantic cities of young married people living indefinitely in boardinghouses? Or perhaps, again, it was the fault of those extraordinary men. "I can hardly imagine a contrivance more effectual for ensuring the insignificance of a woman, than marrying her at seventeen, and placing her in a boarding-house. Nor can I easily imagine a life of more uniform dulness for the lady herself; but this certainly is a matter of taste . . . I always experienced a feeling which hovered between pity and contempt, when I contemplated their mode of existence.

"How would a newly-married English woman endure it, her head, her heart full the one dear scheme—'Well ordered home, his dear delight to make?' " (Miss Martineau, as usual, came forward later with an explanation of the curious custom, and soothing words to accompany it. It was simply a matter of scarce domestic help, she said.)

Giving her wit its head, Mrs. Trollope described a day in the life of a hypothetical lady "of the first class" in Philadelphia, wife of a senator or some equally important man. It is morning. In her handsome house the lady rises, dons a costly silk dress, and descends to her parlor, neat, stiff, and silent. Breakfast, brought in by the footman, consists of fried ham, salt fish, and coffee. As she and her husband eat, he reads the newspaper, with another waiting under his elbow. After breakfast he bustles off to work, and the lady puts on a snowy white apron and washes the dishes. At eleven she doffs the apron and drives to the Dorcas Society, where she spends some hours sewing and chatting with other ladies about church and mission matters. About three o'clock she returns home, puts on an apron—a scalloped black silk one this time—inspects the kitchen and the parlor to see that all is well, and sits down, work in hand, to await her spouse . . . "He comes, shakes hands with her, spits, and dines."

Though Mrs. Trollope was never succinct, she managed for once to sum up her feelings concerning Americans in two sentences, near the close of the book: "I do not like them. I do not like their principles, I do not like their manners, I do not like their opinions."

CHAPTER 5

Bold Blasphemer

> Miss Wright stands condemned of a violation of the unalterable laws of nature, which have created a barrier between the man and the woman, over which neither can pass without unhinging the beneficent adjustments of society, and doing wanton injury to the happiness of each other.

ONE WOULD LIKE to be sure that Frances Wright and her co-editor Robert Dale Owen reprinted that passage from the *Louisiana Focus* in a spirit of mischief, but it seems unlikely. Like many other reformers, she lacked a sense of humor. But she had everything else: intelligence, beauty, generosity, ardor, and courage. We should not be too critical.

How is she to be explained? Where did she get her courage and the rest of it? Without cynicism I suggest that her chief advantage was simply money. A penniless Fanny would not have been well educated or self-confident; her intelligence would have been concealed until it withered away. But with money she had all the backbone she needed, and her talents flowered. Out of all the women I am discussing she seems never to have suffered from the pedestal syndrome. Late in life she married a man who should have known better than to try to make her behave according to his ideas of what was proper in a wife, but he did try, so she simply dissolved the marriage. Why not? She could afford to.

Born in Dundee, Scotland, in 1795, Frances was the elder daughter of a rich man. He was evidently an enthusiastic liberal in politics, but as he died when she was two and a half years old, he could hardly have affected her development. As his wife died at the same time, he left three orphan children: Frances and Camilla and a boy who died young. Frances a ward of the court, was reared in England by relations of her mother, and Camilla joined her there after a few years. But Frances found the English household too conservative and as soon as she reached her majority, at eighteen, she took Camilla with her and returned to Scotland, which she found more congenial. One of her great-uncles was professor of moral philosophy at the University of Glasgow, and Frances became interested in kindred subjects. By the time she returned to the land of her birth she had abandoned orthodox religion, and considered herself an Epicurean, or materialist.

The early 1800s were stirring times for rebels like Frances Wright. She was fascinated by the thought of the new republic in America, and made up her mind in advance that everything there was splendid. In 1818, despite criticism from her relations, she and Camilla sailed, unchaperoned, for New York. There they stayed with friends of friends and made a lot of acquaintances, especially Irish refugees, and Fanny wrote a play, *Aldorf,* about a fourteenth-century rebellion in Switzerland, which was acted by an English cast and got good notices. In the spring of 1819 the Wright sisters traveled in New England and the "middle states," but avoided the South because they disapproved of slavery. Returning to England in 1820, Frances settled down to writing a book on her experiences. It appeared a year later as *Views of Society and Manners in America,* and in it she spoke at some length about the position of American women:

"The deference that is paid to them at all times and in all places has often occasioned me as much surprise as pleasure," she asserted, and went on to say that this was true in *all* classes—which might have surprised a few readers in America, but could not have failed to gratify them. She was startled, not unpleasantly, by the liberty enjoyed by American women. Only one thing was lacking in their lot, she felt: educational facilities to compare with those she had known at home.

Frances was admired for her book, and as a result she met all sorts of prominent reformers in London. She became friendly with the aged Jeremy Bentham, the philosopher, and dedicated her next book, on Epicurus, to him. She also made the acquaintance of General Lafayette, who had long been her hero. For him she developed such fondness that her biographer, William Randall Waterman, called it an infatuation, though he was sixty-three and she only twenty-six. It may have been a purely filial feeling—she always signed her letters as if she were his daughter—but when the Wright girls came to make extended visits at La Grange, his house in France, the general's relatives objected to their presence. Frances' suggestion to put an end to their carping was that Lafayette should declare herself and Camilla his legally adopted daughters, but he never did this.

Miss Wright's appearance was striking, and she was generally admired. It was a time when the statuesque was the ideal. Let Mrs. Trollope describe her as she appeared in 1828 at a lecture in Cincinnati:

"Her tall and majestic figure, the deep and almost solemn expression of her eyes, the simple contour of her finely formed head, unadorned, excepting by its own natural ringlets; her garment of plain white muslin, which hung about her in folds that recalled the drapery of a Grecian statue, all contributed to produce an effect, unlike anything I had ever seen before, or ever expect to see again."

Fanny usually wore her hair short in defiance of fashion. The eldest Trollope boy, recollecting the first time he ever saw her, said she was dressed for riding in Turkish pantaloons. Considering the date, this is an interesting item. (As far as I know, nobody has ever described the appearance of Camilla.)

In 1823 the sisters went to La Grange, and there they stayed six months while Fanny worked on a biography of Lafayette, until her hero, who had been involved in an unsuccessful military conspiracy, decided that he had better leave the country for a while, and accepted an invitation from President James Monroe to come to the United States in 1824 for a state visit. His family, who had been making more and more pointed remarks about the length of the Wrights' stay, suddenly turned pleasant again and urged the sisters to go along with Papa and keep an eye on him, so the Wrights followed General Lafayette to America and spent the winter of 1824–25 near him in Washington.

In the spring the general traveled south, and Fanny and Camilla went after him by a roundabout route, pausing at two communities that had been founded in Economie, Pennsylvania, and Harmonie, Indiana, by a German utopian named George Rapp. An English philanthropist, Robert Owen, had recently bought Harmonie from the Rappites, intending to try out an experiment in his own brand of communism there, and Frances' attention was caught by the idea. Perhaps her enthusiasm was great enough to outweigh her feelings for Lafayette. Nobody seems certain, but when the general went back to Europe the Wright girls did not come to the ship to see him off. In a letter written to Fanny early in 1826 Lafayette referred to an unhappy interview with her that took place in Philadelphia, and perhaps at that time they had agreed to part. The Duke of Saxe-Weimar, who in 1829 published a record of his trip to America, spoke ill-naturedly of Fanny and her relations with Lafayette soon after Bunker Hill celebrations in Boston in 1825. He said:

"I am told that this lady with her sister, unattended by a male protector, had roved about the country, in steamboats and stages, that she constantly tagged about after General Lafayette, and whenever the General arrived at any place, Miss Wright was sure to follow the next day; as little notice had been taken of this lady in Boston, a literary attack was expected from her pen. She is no longer young, and is of tall stature and masculine manners."

Fanny, who at that time was thirty, never showed the slightest perturbation at such gossip. She seems not to have cared at all about public opinion. She was preoccupied with the task of finding suitable territory for her own utopian experiment, then of stocking it with slaves and white people who were to work together until the slaves were ready to take their free place in the world. In Washington she met Robert Owen and interested him in the idea, and he invited her to return to New Harmony, as he had rechristened the Rappite-built town of Harmonie. First, however, she found the land in Tennessee and named it Nashoba, an Indian word meaning wolf. She also bought a few slaves and placed in the community with them various whites who were willing to work there, including Camilla and Richeson Whitby.

Everything went awry in Nashoba from the start. It was not only that the place was full of malaria—Frances herself fell gravely ill of it and had to leave America a year later for a protracted convalescence in England—but the slaves did not appreciate the full philosophical theory behind their hoped-for emancipation: they would not work hard unless they were pushed in the old Southern way. One of the whites, James Richardson, took one of the mulatto girls as a mistress. Earnestly believing the marriage tie to be wrong, Richardson proceeded to proclaim their cohabitation in what he thought was an honorable manner. Whitby was a weak reed, but at least he and Camilla did get married quite legally, which is not what the community's detractors claimed. Nashoba was called a brothel, and in the outside world tongues wagged furiously. The experiment was finished soon after the scandal reached its height, and Frances, wiser and poorer, was some years winding up Nashoba's affairs and settling the slaves in the West Indies, leaving Whitby in charge of the territory in Tennessee. But now she could accept Owen's invitation, and she went to New Harmony, where with his son Robert Dale Owen she edited a paper, *The New Harmony and Nashoba Gazette* or *Free Enquirer,* which treated of philosophical questions.

On the Fourth of July, 1828, Frances delivered the patriotic address of the day in New Harmony, and did it so well that she decided to go on and give lectures. Women did not ordinarily speak in public, but this was no deterrent to Fanny Wright; it was a challenge. Her appearance in Cincinnati mentioned by Mrs. Trollope was the occasion of one of these lectures, at which the speaker treated of many subjects, including religion—she was still opposed to it—and education, but what interests us most is that she also had a good deal to say about the position and treatment of American women. Frances knew far more now than she had in early days when she saw everything in the country through rose-colored spectacles. She felt that the failure to educate women ("provide for their mental needs") left them helpless, at the mercy of people—especially the clergy—who would prey on their ignorance and credulity. Naturally this kind of statement did not endear her to the clergy, but then they were not predisposed in Fanny's favor in any case. As for education, she said in one of her most famous lectures:

> Until women assume the place in society which good sense and good feeling alike assign to them, human improvement must advance but feebly. It is in vain that we would circumscribe the power of one half of our race, and that by far the most important and influential. If they exert it not for good, they will for evil; if they advance not knowledge, they will perpetuate ignorance. Let women stand where they may in the scale of improvement, their position decides that of the race. Are they cultivated?—so is society polished and enlightened. Are they ignorant?—so is it gross and insipid. Are they wise?—so is the human character elevated. Are they enslaved?—so is the whole human race degraded. Oh! that we could learn the advantage of just practice and consistent principles!

But Miss Wright did not demand only equal education: she inveighed against the law that deprived married women of their own property and declared the wife one person with her husband. She called it a system that inflicted "absolute spoliation, and allows of absolute robbery, and all but murder" against the female who swore away at one and the same moment her person and her property, and often her peace, her honor, and her life. In the *Free Enquirer* of April 29, 1829, Fanny wrote:

> I would ask every father not absolutely dead to all human feeling how he can permit his daughters blindly to immolate all their rights, liberties, and property by the simple utterance of a word, and thus place themselves, in their tender, ignorant, and unsuspecting youth, as completely at the disposal and mercy of an individual, as is the negro slave who is bought for gold in the slave market of Kingston or New Orleans.

Even more startling was the fact that Miss Frances Wright should advocate birth control, arguing that America would not long be the land of plenty if big families, especially among the poor, became the fashion. People should not have more children than they could afford to feed, said Miss Wright. This argument, especially as it came from an unmarried woman, shocked people and made it easier to believe that she actually said in her lectures—as, admittedly, she did—that the marriage tie was mischievous, inefficient, and hypocritical. But she did not advocate doing away with marriage altogether, for she realized that this measure would never be accepted by the masses. Instead, she argued that more liberal divorce laws should be introduced, so that unhappily married people might be set free. Not that this suggestion softened the inevitable criticism: it was at this time that the *Louisiana Focus* concentrated, or focused, its spotlight on Miss Wright. A few weeks later she began to be pestered by planned disturbances during her public appearances. In Louisville, Kentucky, her lecture was interrupted by the cry of "Fire!"—though there was no fire. In Baltimore, sensing a hostile feeling in the audience, she started her lecture by telling them that as she understood that her hearers were all American gentlemen, she had confidence in their attention and courtesy. Nobody interrupted that lecture, nor did anything untoward happen in Philadelphia, where she next appeared.

New York, she felt, would be a real test. Wearing a Queen Mary ruff and a dark-colored jacket, and accompanied by a group of Quaker ladies who sympathized with her views and took this occasion to demonstrate their feelings, Miss Wright gave her address to New Yorkers on January 4, 1829. In the next day's issue, the *Commercial Advertiser* reported:

> Her voice, which filled the room without apparent effort on the part of the speaker, is both strong and sweet. We recollect no female whose

recitations in this city have been celebrated, at all comparable to this lady, in this particular . . . For an hour and a half she held the attention of her audience enchained, excepting that attempts were made to applaud which were frequently suppressed by the majority, from a wish not to interrupt her at length succeeded, and towards the conclusion she received several distinct and thunderous rounds of approval . . .

The same paper less than a week later, however, turned on Fanny Wright after her third lecture, in which she attacked the clergy and said that she intended to publish her paper in New York. They called her a bold blasphemer and a voluptuous preacher of licentiousness. The outcry was joined by other papers. On January 10 the *Evening Post* noted with aggrieved astonishment and alarm that the lessees of the Park Theatre had agreed to let it for six nights to Frances Wright to lecture in. "Have they considered," asked the *Post,* "what may be the consequences of the displeasure of the people? Suppose the singular spectacle of a female, publicly and ostentatiously proclaiming doctrines of atheistical fanaticism, and even the most abandoned lewdness, should draw a crowd from a prurient curiosity, and that a riot should ensue, which should end in the demolition of the interior of the building, or even in burning it down, on whom would the loss fall?" What about the insurance policy? After all, the building was insured against fire only if a theatrical exhibition was being held; would the policy cover a loss incurred because of Miss Wright's lectures?

Oddly enough, several attempts *were* made to burn the hall down, but nothing came of them but a lot of smoke, and Fanny Wright's lectures attracted more and more crowds. On January 28 the *Post*'s worst fears were realized and the *Free Enquirer,* as its truncated title now proclaimed it, opened offices in New York, complete with Robert Dale Owen and the rest of the staff.

Next, Miss Wright proposed to lecture in Boston. The *Boston Gazette* said that this would be all right so long as she didn't question the marriage laws. ". . . we confess we do not feel predisposed to relish the masculine eloquence of this bold and forcible female," said the editor in his issue of July 22, 1829. "We shall not be gratified by her visit to the city. We get on very well as we are . . ." And though he said that she could come if she liked—"we shall listen or not as we desire"—Frances found it strangely difficult to hire a hall; somehow or other they were all engaged. She did at last get hold of an empty theater. Curiosity brought a lot of people to hear her there, but the editor of the Boston *Courier*, who was evidently among their number, said that he was not impressed by her talk. His chief objection, he wrote in the July 30 issue, was that Miss Wright was doing what only a man should attempt. Women must not assume the prerogatives of men; they had their own place in society, and that place was the home. He saw no threat to the clergy in Miss Wright's lectures, but the Boston clergy were more timorous. The Reverend Lyman Beecher, father of Harriet Beecher Stowe and Catherine Beecher, was shocked into giving a series of lectures on "Political Atheism."

In New Harmony some months earlier, Frances Wright had made the acquaintance of a French gentleman, William Phiquepal, or, to give him his full name, Guillaume Sylvan Casimir Phiquepal D'Arusmont, born in France in 1779. In spite of his seniority to Fanny—and the undeniable fact that he was unpopular among most gentlemen of her acquaintance—Miss Wright found his company agreeable. Perhaps he brought back memories of her happy days in France. At any rate, early in 1830 she announced her engagement to him.

The marriage did not take place at once, however; the "Free Enquirers" had other fish to fry, and busied themselves with the reform of the status of the working man, a better form of government, and universal education. In this last, the guardianship of the state would be complete: parents could visit their children at suitable hours but would not be allowed to interfere in any way with the school's routine. On these points generally the Free Enquirers, or as some opponents called them, the Fanny Wright Party, ran into trouble, especially when the New York Working Men's Party, organized under their direction, polled nearly a third of the votes in the November election of 1829 and sent a candidate to Albany. The New York press, almost to a paper, attacked Fanny Wright in whatever way it could, settling at last on the financial arrangements she had made for Nashoba and, later, to settle her slaves in Haiti. Doubts were cast on her honesty and motives regarding the whole affair, but these did not disturb this experienced campaigner; she thought it best to leave the scene because she was doing harm to the working men's cause. Therefore, after a final burst of lectures, she went to Europe in 1830. Camilla accompanied her. Camilla's baby had died, her marriage was practically ended, and she was in a state of depression and debilitation.

The sisters arrived in France during the summer, just in time to see the overthrow of Charles X and the triumph of Lafayette in the July Revolution. Frances renewed her correspondence with the general, writing in her first letter: "I need not say how I long to reach you and yet perhaps it is as well that I should not be seen at your side just at this crisis." She spoke of her concern for Camilla, but her sister was getting better, she assured him, and she trusted she would soon be able to embrace her old friend.

Camilla did not recover, but died in February 1831, leaving Frances lonely and, for perhaps the first time in her life, uncertain as to her future. She had planned to go back to America with Camilla; now she wrote Owen that she needed several more months of rest. But before her European stay came to an end, in July 1831, she married Phiquepal, who then resumed his family name and was known henceforth as D'Arusmont. Theirs was what we would call a civil ceremony: they were married at the mayor's bureau in the presence of a few friends, among them Lafayette.

Mr. Waterman, Miss Wright's biographer, seems a little puzzled as to why she, of all people, consented to undergo a ceremony for which she had such little patience, but he claims that in this she was not really as inconsistent as some people alleged. She was thoroughly aware that an ideal relation of the sexes was impracticable as society was then constituted. Also, she may well have remembered the furor resulting from the Nashoba residents' attempts to do away with the institution, and behaved accordingly. Marriage was still a necessity. But she was careful to avoid, as far as was within her power, the lamentable consequences to married women whose property passed into their husbands' keeping. She retained control of her property, and maintained the right to divorce in case things should go wrong.

For some years Frances D'Arusmont and her husband lived quietly in France. She brought over some of her fortune, and with Lafayette's help D'Arusmont got an appointment as director of an experimental agricultural school. The couple had a daughter, Frances Sylva, a year after their marriage. Fanny seems to have seen less and less of the general, perhaps, her biographer hazards, because she disapproved of his conduct during the July Revolution or perhaps because she was so busy at home. D'Arusmont, who handled her business affairs, grew angry at the record of Robert Dale Owen's careless way in the past of dealing with Frances' money, and as a result her friendship with Owen came to an end. Nevertheless, she was still on good terms with his father, and in 1834, during a short visit to England, at Owen's request she gave a few lectures in favor of rational education, an action that angered D'Arusmont. She was not writing to him often enough, he complained in a letter to her; if she did not mend her ways, he could come over to England and fetch her back. One would have thought that this was not, repeat *not*, the way to deal with Frances Wright . . .

The D'Arusmonts returned to the United States late in 1835, expecting to make a short visit in connection with Madame's property interests. They came in by way of New Orleans and paused at Nashoba, where Richeson Whitby was in charge of the remnants of the colony, and still receiving an annuity bequeathed to him by Camilla. They got to Cincinnati in February 1836, and there the mischief started. Frances had really not intended to go back to the lecture circuit, but she saw so many things going wrong with the country that she couldn't help herself. She had to, she simply had to tell people what was wrong with the American banking system. In May she began lecturing, and for the next three years she continued doing so throughout the States, speaking on such subjects as chartered monopolies, slavery, and the "Nature and History of Human Civilization, considered in the Past, the Present, and the Future." It was during this last-named series that she declared that during the development of the earliest civilization, which with its priest-king and hereditary castes benefited the few at the expense of the many, the subjugation of women first took place—"the first master measure employed for the more certain enslavement of the species." This situation, she implied, had never really been remedied.

At some point during these three busy years, with Frances lecturing, writing for the papers, and even editing a small one herself in Philadelphia, she and D'Arusmont parted, and ultimately, thanks to her foresight in preparing the way, were divorced. She was living alone in Cincinnati when she slipped on an icy pavement, fell, and broke her hip. This accident seems to have been fatal, though her death was slow: she never recovered, and nearly a year later, on December 13, 1852, she died.

Perhaps as her biographer says, Miss Wright's greatest contribution was to the intellectual emancipation of women, though she certainly did not confine her activities to this one exercise. She showed what the feminine mind was capable of. After Fanny Wright, it was very hard for any man to argue that women were delicate little things who must be protected.

CHAPTER 6

America: Paradise for Women?

IT WILL HAVE BEEN NOTED that there is a wide divergence between Frances Wright's impressions of American women and those of the other Frances, Mrs. Trollope. Miss Wright's sturdy independence may have colored her opinions: in any case she showed unfailing faith in the intelligence of those of her sex who came to hear her speak, whereas Mrs. Trollope was uncompromisingly scornful of most females in America. Granting her obvious prejudice, was this really the way it was? Were American women, those spoiled, adored, pampered princesses we have always heard about, truly neglected to such an extent that English women, of all people, found it in their hearts to pity them? It seems that this picture did bear some resemblance to the truth, if we are to believe the quieter accounts of Harriet Martineau and Basil Hall.

Miss Martineau, a writer on philosophical and religious subjects, came to the States in 1834 for a visit that was to last two years. She needed a rest, she explained in her introduction, and had selected America because she knew the language and there would be no extra difficulty on that account—for the thirty-two-year-old Miss Martineau was deaf and carried an ear trumpet. Her book, *Society in America,* is less belligerent and more thoughtful than Mrs. Trollope's, and, as I said earlier, she attempted occasionally to correct some of the other lady's severer descriptions. In the following passage, for instance, she sounds almost as if she *liked* Ohio:

"I travelled by waggon in the interior of Ohio. Our driver must be a man of great and various knowledge, if he questions all strangers as he did us, and obtains as copious answers. He told us where and how he lived, of his nine children, of his literary daughters, and the pains he was at to get books for them; and of his hopes for his girl of fourteen, who writes poetry; which he keeps a secret, lest she should be spoiled."

This gives a far more amiable impression than Mrs. Trollope's style, but in another and important respect the ladies were in complete agreement. Miss Martineau too thought the lot of American women was hard. "Throughout a prodigious expanse of that country, I saw no poor *man,* except a few intemperate ones," she wrote. "I saw some very poor *women;* but God and man know that the time has not come for women to make their injuries even heard of."

The subject of women's rights was never very far from Miss Martineau's thoughts, and her American experience helped her to clarify her general theories. She noted striking similarities between the legal positions of women and slaves, but there were differences as well. Like slaves, women were politically nonexistent; unlike slaves, they were taxed if they had property. (Slaves, of course, had no property.)

The government, she noted, could divorce women from their husbands, and could fine, imprison, even execute them for certain offenses, though women had no voice in it. She felt that such a government was not, therefore, truly democratic, since its powers were not derived from the consent of all the governed. As governments varied from state to state, there were consequent variations in their treatment of women: in some states women had the right to half their husbands' property, but in others they had only one-third. In some states a woman on her marriage had to turn over all her property to her husband, but in others she retained a portion of it. In either case the law was undemocratic. Yet two of the "most principled" democratic writers on government—the American Thomas Jefferson and the English James Mill—had accepted this state of affairs, falling into disgraceful fallacies and indirectly advocating despotism over women. Jefferson had written in a letter (*Correspondence,* Vol. IV, p. 295) that even if America were a pure democracy in which all inhabitants met together to transact their business, the following would have to be excluded from their deliberations: infants (minors), women, "who, to prevent deprivation of morals, and ambiguity of issue, could not mix promiscuously in the public meetings of men," and slaves, who had no rights of will or property. Miss Martineau scoffed at all this: women in America, like slaves, had no rights of will or property, and it was nonsense to talk as Jefferson did about their morals and so on.

"As if there would be more danger in promiscuous meeting for political business than in such meetings for worship, for oratory, for music, for dramatic entertainments," said Miss Martineau.

James Mill in his *Essay on Government* was equally culpable, but in another way. He had argued that women did not have to vote, since they were almost all represented either by their fathers or their husbands. But no person's interests are or can be identical with any other person's, wrote Harriet Martineau, according to the true democratic principle, while his "almost all" glibly ignored all women who had neither husbands nor fathers, and even those who possessed such connections had to be protected by law against them.

Miss Martineau heard other arguments against women's rights which do not sound quite as unfamiliar today: that a woman's special duties might interfere with her political activity, and that women wouldn't bother to vote even if they could. She retorted that as for the woman who might not have time to vote, she ought at least have the right to make up her own mind. Those who doubted that females would take the trouble to vote if they could, she said, should remember New Jersey, where in the late eighteenth century, thanks to an ambiguity in the law, women were permitted to vote as men did, and vote they did until the law was rephrased and they were excluded from the polls.

Throughout her travels in America, from North to South, Harriet Martineau kept these topics in mind even during lighter moments, such as when, during a tour of the Great Lakes, her steamboat touched at the new settlement of Milwaukee and seven young women came to call on the new arrivals. They were the entire female population of Milwaukee, of which the total population was four hundred souls. She was shown an appeal in the brand-new local paper for more ladies to come on out and be married. Next, she went South. "Cincinnati is a glorious place," she said flatly.

But the Southern states were not glorious at all, since the slave system cast a shadow everywhere. Many white women, she said, admitted to her privately things that they would never have said in public about the way they lived, in fear and shame. In Mobile a lady confided that she and her family suffered in mind, body, and estate from the licentiousness of white men among the Negro women. Miss Martineau asked if the Negro men ever tried to retaliate. Oh yes, said the lady, indeed they did. Only a short time earlier a white boy and girl had disappeared on their way home from school. Later the severed head of the little girl was found in a plantation creek not far from the city—evidence, said the whites, that the child had been violated by

Negroes. Shortly afterward, two young women who rode out from town in that direction dismounted and were seized by a couple of slaves belonging to the plantation. They got away safely, but when the news reached Mobile everyone there decided that the slaves must be the same men who had killed the schoolchildren.

"The gentlemen of Mobile turned out; seized the men, heaped up faggots on the margin of the brook, and slowly burned them to death." None of this story had ever appeared in the papers.

"I charge the silence of Mobile about this murder on its *fears;* as confidently as I charge the brutality of the victims upon its crime," wrote Harriet Martineau.

In New England she viewed the textile mills, which were much larger than they had been during the visit of Mrs. Trollope a few years earlier. Lowell, for instance, in 1818 was a settlement of two hundred souls, and had then boasted one small mill with twenty hands, but in 1832 when Miss Martineau saw it, five thousand employees held mill jobs, of which three thousand eight hundred were female. It was not so much, she said, that females were better suited to the work, but that so many young men were emigrating to the West, for example to Milwaukee, that they left behind them a serious overpopulation of women. Miss Martineau tried but could not get dependable figures on this overpopulation: the statements made to her, she said, were so incredible that she withheld them. Suffice it to say that there were many more women than men in from six to nine states of the Union. Obviously, the mills were a godsend to these surplus girls and their families. In pre-mill days they would have been just that—surplus—and with nothing to do but live in poverty as best they might, since it was not the custom in America for women (except slave women) to work out of doors, and, as Mrs. Trollope often noted, young women did not want to go into domestic service. Even if there had been enough openings for so many, they would probably have been stubborn about that, and until the mills grew up there was much silent suffering from poverty. But the mill factories introduced employment, relief, and—what was no doubt most important for proud young Americans—self-respect. For the first time, large numbers of the nation's girls were able to be independent of men. They looked happy and busy, and dressed remarkably well.

At the Waltham Mills near Boston five hundred hands were employed, girls earning from two to three dollars a week besides board, and little children a dollar. Most girls lived in company houses that accommodated six to eight each. When there were sisters they often brought their mother to keep house for them and their companions, in a house built by their own earnings. These girls could save enough out of their board to clothe themselves and still have money left at the end of the week. Miss Martineau noted admiringly that some had managed to clear off the mortgages from their fathers' farms or to educate their brothers at college. Many were rapidly saving up to be independent. She saw a whole street of houses built by the girls' earnings, some with piazzas and green venetian blinds, neat and prosperous-looking, and she was told that many of the girls had collected "private libraries of some merit and value." She repeated that they all looked like well-dressed young ladies, and added a remark to which we shall return: "The health is good; or rather (as this is too much to be said about health any where in the United States), it is no worse that it is elsewhere."

But one thing about the mill communities, she thought, could be improved. Space in the New World was almost unlimited, and the factory girls, as she had seen, could build churches and houses, buy libraries, and educate their brothers in the learned professions. Why, then, did they not allow themselves more room? They had no private apartments, and sometimes they slept six or eight in a room, even three in a bed.

Though the married women of the Northern states were liable to be fully occupied by housework—domestic service being so uncertain—those women who did not marry often worked for their living. One might almost say, with Miss Martineau, that in the North work was the rule for the unmarried female, and idleness, or "vacuity," the exception. In the South, however, girls were brought up to pity all females (except, again, slaves) who had to work, and they talked endlessly of marrying early. "A more hopeless state of degradation can hardly be conceived of," the writer said severely, "however they may ride, and play the harp, and sing Italian, and teach their slaves what they call religion."

The Southern lady of the house was really a slave like the blacks she owned. She had to oversee everything, carry a huge bunch of keys—for everything must be locked up—and give out whatever was wanted for the household. How much better off was the village milliner in the North, or the artisan's wife who swept her own floors and cooked her husband's dinner, than the planter's wife with twenty slaves to wait on her. The Southern lady's sons migrated because work was out of the question for them and they hadn't the means to buy estates. Her daughters had no better prospect than to marry like their mother, to toil as she did. Yet, said Harriet Martineau, some planters' ladies were among the strongest-minded and most remarkable women she had ever met. This was understandable, for women who have to rule over a barbarous society, even one as small as a plantation, who have to make and enforce laws, provide for all the community's physical wants, and regulate their habits must be strong and thoroughly disciplined. On the other hand, those Southern ladies who shrank from their responsibilities became lamentably weak in character—selfishly timid, humblingly dependent, languid in body, and with minds of no reach at all.

It hardly needs saying that, like Mrs. Trollope, Miss Martineau viewed with dismay the system by which the quadroons of New Orleans were maintained as a reservoir of sex for the local gentlemen. The average young man of means, she said, while still unmarried, usually selected a girl from the quadroon group and set her up in a pretty little house in a certain quarter of the town. When the time came for him to marry, he was expected to settle the house and furniture on his mistress, say good-bye, and leave. A few liaisons of this sort lasted a lifetime, but not many interfered with a man's marriage.

"Every Quadroon woman believes that her partner will prove an exception to the rule of desertion. Every white lady believes that her husband has been an exception to the rule of seduction," declared Miss Martineau, and she added that the system degraded white women most of all. Not that she wished to imply any stain on the white woman's purity: on the contrary, there were obvious reasons why they should be pure beyond a doubt. With more men than women in their society, most of them married young, and—thanks to the slave women—few men made attempts on their virtue.

Life in the South was exceedingly hard on women, thought the observer, and not only because of its sexual mores. In a society that spared its wives a share in the men's engrossing concerns of life, there was no wholesale confidence and sympathy, and women sank to be merely ornaments of their husbands' houses. The kind politeness, the gallantry with which Southern wives were treated by their husbands, was insufficient to loving hearts. These same gallant husbands greeted with horror any idea of their women's having to work, and were eager to keep them in unearned ease, which Miss Martineau considered "the deepest insult which can be offered to an intelligent and conscientious woman." The very tone of conversation adopted by these gentlemen toward ladies was an added insult: no man would dream of talking so to any other man, as if he were a mindless, childish creature.

It came as a surprise to the visitor to learn that Americans, of all people, were not free from the foolishness of snobbery. One might have expected the spirit of democracy to prevent such a weakness, but it did not. A schoolgirl prattled to her of the delightful "set" she belonged to at school, saying that it was a shame how grocers' daughters were creeping in everywhere, so that no set was safe. In Philadelphia the ladies of Chestnut Street had nothing to do with those of Arch Street, though it seemed to the puzzled Miss Martineau that both lots were equally charming. It was hard to find the reason for this schism. One informant explained that it was a question of generation; that the fathers of the Arch Street ladies had made their families' fortunes, but the Chestnut Streeters owed their comfortable circumstances to their *grandfathers,* which fact put them one rung up on the ladder. But there was another theory: Arch Street ladies, it was said, rose on their toes only twice before curtsying, whereas the ladies of Chestnut Street rose thrice.

Looking back from a resting place in the East over all her travels and observations in America, Miss Martineau caught up on her journal and indulged in some random thoughts. I shall cull a few of those that have to do with women, because they are so revealing both of conditions in the United States as they were when she witnessed the daily life of the country, and of the meeting—which often seemed a collision—between the philosophies of Old World and New World femininity.

We will start in New York, where her friends assured Harriet Martineau that ladies had a wonderful life. The rich merchants of New York outfitted splendid houses uptown and there installed their wives. Every morning these self-denying gentlemen got up early, snatched breakfast, and rushed off two or three miles to their countinghouses, where all the long summer's day they bustled about in the heat, dust, noise, and traffic of Pearl Street. They came home almost too tired to eat or speak. Meantime, their wives had had the whole day to water their flowers, read the latest English novel, visit friends, and go shopping—"paying, perhaps, 100 dollars for the newest Paris bonnet."

On the American woman's voice: "A great unknown pleasure remains to be experienced by the Americans in the well-modulated, gentle, healthy, cheerful voices of women. It is incredible that there should not, in all time to come, be any other alternative than that which now exists, between a whine and a twang. When the health of the American women improves, their voices will improve. In the meantime, they are unconscious how the effect of their remarkable and almost universal beauty is injured by their mode of speech."

Americans preferred the word "lady" to "woman" and used it almost exclusively, which sometimes had a strange effect, at least according to English opinion. We have seen how the usage irritated Mrs. Trollope. Miss Martineau was not irritated, but she was startled by a prison warder's reply when she asked him, during a visit to a Tennessee prison, if there were any women in jail: " 'We have no ladies here at present, madam. We have never had but two ladies, who were convicted of stealing a steak.' " And she quoted a lecturer discoursing on the characteristics of women: " 'Who were last at the cross? Ladies. Who were first at the sepulchre? Ladies.' "

The longest portion of these musings of Harriet Martineau deals with the "vaunted chivalry" of American men toward women. The consideration shown to women—ladies, if you will—was, in her opinion, greater than was rational or good for either party. Of course it was a good thing for gentlemen to be polite on stagecoaches, where Americans could show Europeans a thing or two about manners, but they overdid it. All men, no matter how old or sick or tired they might be, were expected as a matter of course to give up the best places in the coach to any and every lady passenger, no matter how young and well and hearty *she* might be. On one occasion, in Virginia, she saw five gentlemen riding on top of the coach, where they had neither handhold nor resting place for their feet, so that a young lady who was slightly delicate could lie down at her ease inside. Utterly ridiculous, said the Englishwoman indignantly; the young lady's parents should have hired her a private vehicle if she was as delicate as all that—or, better still, kept her at home. (I feel bound to agree. Pedestals are clumsy things to travel with.) Besides, all this doting was lamentably bad for female behavior. Like the spoiled children they were, the ladies carried on in a blush-making manner.

"Screaming and trembling at the apprehension of danger are not uncommon," wrote Miss Martineau, "but there is something far worse in the cool selfishness with which they accept the best of everything, and usually, in the south or west, without a word of acknowledgement." Observe, "in the south or west." It was not lost on her that in those mill towns of New England, where men were few and women independent, the women behaved much better in public and on the road.

America a democracy? Not where women were concerned. Women were either downtrodden, i.e., denigrated in law and underpaid in the marketplace, or placed so high that they became useless ornaments. Though Miss Martineau did not use it, the image of a chamberpot on a pedestal comes vividly to mind.

Trenchantly, she summed up the matter: all the while the American woman's intellect was confined, her morals crushed, her health ruined, her weaknesses encouraged, and her strength punished, she was told that her lot was cast in the paradise of women—"and there is no country in the world where there is so much boasting of the 'chivalrous' treatment she enjoys."

Strong words, and she did not stop there. What men really meant when they boasted, she said, was that the American woman got the best place on stagecoaches. Gentlemen gave up their seats to her. Orators acclaimed wife and home: a woman's husband wouldn't dream of letting her go out to work, and he toiled to indulge her with money. She was free, but only to get her brain turned by religious excitements. Like the slave, she was given indulgence instead of justice. In our language (obviously not Miss Martineau's), the American woman was being sold a bill of goods.

In Harriet Martineau's opinion, the American woman's intelligence was confined by the education she received. Never mind those courses in chirography and uranology I have mentioned; Miss Martineau brushed all that aside as window dressing. Girls' education was poor in America, she insisted, because they had none of the objectives in life for which better teaching would fit them; as long as they were excluded from the objectives for which men were trained, they would avoid true intellectual activity. In plain truth, marriage was the only course left open to them. She was willing to admit that in many ways marriage in America was not so bad: women got a better deal there than in England, since the couple's property was more evenly divided, "but it is still the imperfect institution which it must remain while women continue to be ill-educated, passive, and subservient; or well-educated, vigorous, and free only upon sufferance." In some states, Louisiana and Missouri for example, a widow automatically inherited her late husband's property, and even elsewhere the marriage property laws were superior to those of England, except in Massachusetts, which had copied the faults of English law—and she said that every person she met in that state was ashamed of it for that reason.

But enlightened property laws were not enough to keep American women from frustration. The greater number of them were occupied with wifely and motherly duties—"the sole occupation of women in America," she wrote rather rashly, forgetting for the moment and in the heat of exposition her own comments on New England's mill-factory girls. If they had not that, i.e., their wifely and motherly duties, they had nothing, she continued. Yet, in the United States just as everywhere else, it was not every woman who was fitted to be a wife and mother. In proof of this, if it needed proving, Miss Martineau too spoke of that phenomenon, the boardinghouse.

"The more I saw of boarding-house life, the worse I thought of it; though I saw none but the best," she wrote. True, it was often the only way out for couples, especially newly married ones, because it was so difficult to get domestic servants. Also, for people who had no houses or furniture and no way of acquiring them, a boarding-house was convenient and economical. Even so, no sensible husband, if he knew the facts, would expose his domestic peace to the fearful risks involved of leaving his wife prey to such complete idleness. As soon as their men had gone to work, elegantly dressed ladies repaired to the common drawing room and settled down, there to sit for hours doing nothing but staring out the windows or gossiping with one another, with any gentleman of the house who happened to have no business, or with visitors. Silly ladies often told each other the most private matters in these surroundings, and many a business secret was disclosed.

Turning to other snippets of memory, Miss Martineau said she was often asked a question she considered significant because it showed such a large difference between family manners in England and America. It concerned Jane Austen's *Pride and Prejudice*. Was it possible, people asked her, that the Bennet family would really behave that way? Would a foolish mother like Mrs. Bennet be permitted to spoil her two youngest daughters as she was supposed to have done? Surely the sensible older daughters, Jane and Elizabeth, would take the case into their own hands rather than let their younger sisters run wild! And in America, Miss Martineau admitted, this was true. The superior minds of the family would take the lead, whereas in England nobody would dream of questioning a mother's authority. In

England, parents valued authority as a right, but in America a parent would rather not possess it. An American mother of her acquaintance mentioned, merely in passing, an incident illustrating this difference. The woman's eldest daughter had recently been married, and two or three of the younger children refused to attend the ceremony because they were angry at their new brother-in-law for taking her away.

"What children in England would have dreamed of absenting themselves in such a way?" said Miss Martineau, half scandalized, half admiring.

At another point she said that she had found a prevalent idea in America that English ladies concerned themselves very little with household affairs. They got this strangely mistaken impression from the fashionable English novels deluging the country at the time. Many otherwise intelligent people believed all Englishwomen to be like the countesses and duchesses they read about, and were surprised to hear that they too had to do the shopping, keep accounts, and even cook a meal once in a while. Once they had been convinced of this, they were more than willing to talk about housekeeping, and from many a comfortable chat she discovered the following:

"All American ladies should know how to clear-starch and iron: how to keep plate and glasses: how to cook dainties: and, if they understood the making of bread and soup likewise, so much the better. The gentlemen usually charge themselves with the business of marketing; which is very fair."

But women's spare-time occupations seemed trivial. Some went in for good works, and more for religious activities of one kind or another. All were probably ineffective busy-work. Then too, though all American ladies were more or less "literary," whatever that means, thinkers among them were rare though readers were plentiful. The ladies preferred to be spoon-fed with ideas rather than think them up for themselves. Miss Martineau found more intellectual activity among women who didn't read so much. Though all educated girls were taught drawing and watercolor painting, artistic talent was hard to find. "Natural philosophy" was not pursued to any extent by women. There was some pretension of "mental" and moral philosophy, but the less said about it the better. Altogether, it was a sad state of affairs. No mean moral philosopher herself, Harriet Martineau thought she had the explanation: American women were better educated by Providence than by men.

"They are good wives; and, under the teaching of nature, good mothers. They have, within the range of their activity, good sense, good temper, and good manners. Their beauty is very remarkable; and, I think, their wit no less. . . . One consequence, mournful and injurious, of the 'chivalrous' taste and temper of a country with regard to its women is that it is difficult, where it is not impossible, for women to earn their own bread.''

All this was bound to end soon, since many women had to go out to work despite all that prejudice and chivalry could do to prevent it, but the lot of the poor female breadwinner was sad. With the exception of factory jobs, there were only three resources for working women—teaching, needlework, and keeping boardinghouses or hotels. The scanty reward for female labor in the States remained the reproach of the century.

We have a few somber hints from Mrs. Trollope, and something a trifle more definite from Miss Martineau, about the health of American women in the nineteenth century. Miss Martineau thought American women a sickly lot, and seems to have encountered few exceptions, though she had kindly words for one group of bouncing, athletic New England girls. Not long before she came to the States a popular book was published there—*Principles of Physiology,* by a Dr. Combe. If it had not been for the influence of this book, she was convinced, she would have found the situation even worse, for Dr. Combe recommended plenty of fresh air and soap and water, and people were beginning to follow his suggestion, whereas before, she said acidly, these commodities had been neglected. Even as things were, much remained to be done. In private houses, bathrooms were a rarity. In steamboats—and Miss Martineau, after two years of travel, knew a lot about them—there were very limited accommodations for washing; in fact, if you weren't in a private stateroom there was nothing at all. She said that she could not imagine how the ''ladies of the cabin'' (those who traveled without staterooms) could be expected to enjoy any degree of vigor or cheerfulness after a voyage of four or five days during which they could only wash their hands and faces. There should be a public demand for bathrooms, or at least washing closets, in every boat making trips of longer than twenty-four hours.

In all hotels except the first-rate ones the same thing was true: they offered no accommodation for washing. One could not wonder at it, since the ordinary public did not seem to understand how necessary cleanliness is to health. The only Americans (with a few honorable exceptions) who appreciated such truths were the Creoles of Louisiana, in whose houses a guest always found a large pan or tub of fresh cool water in a corner of his room, morning and night. Living as they did in a torrid climate, they appreciated soap and water.

The American excuse for avoiding fresh air was always the climate, but Miss Martineau did not accept this. She admitted that in a new, raw country the "environs" of the city did not tempt one to go out for walks, but some rare ladies managed to get exercise in spite of this. Reluctant walkers need only think of India, where the indefatigable English ladies, rather than go without healthy outdoor effort, got up very early in the morning and went out before the sun grew strong. Many American women, when taxed by Miss Martineau with sedentary habits, claimed that they got enough exercise running their houses, but she was not mollified. Everyone would feel the better for getting out of the house, she insisted, especially those overheated American houses. She had the deepest mistrust of anthracite coal fumes.

"Young ladies who dry up their whole frames in the heat of fires of anthracite coal, never breathing the outward air but in going to church, and in stepping in and out of the carriage in going to parties . . ." No, it wouldn't do. "It made me sorrowful to see children shut up during the winter in houses, heated by anthracite coal up to the temperature of 85°; and to see how pallid and dried the poor little things looked, long before there was a prospect of their speedy release from their imprisonment. Some, who were let out on fine days, were pretty sure to catch cold . . . The burning of anthracite coal affected me unpleasantly, except where an evaporation of water was going on in the room. I suspect that some of the maladies of the country may be more or less owing to it."

One proof of the dangers of lack of exercise, she held, was that distortion of the spine was more common among American than European women. The feeling of vigorous health was almost unknown among American ladies: friends spoke quite blithely of so-and-so having a "weak breast" or "delicate lungs" with hardly more gravity than English people used in referring to a common cold. One American woman of Miss Martineau's acquaintance declared complacently that she could not walk a mile. Possibly it was not all a matter of fresh air, cleanliness, and exercise; possibly it was also a question of diet. "I should like to see hot bread and cakes banished," she said; "diminution in the quantity of pickles and preserves, and also in the quantity of meat eaten." (It was the custom in many houses to eat meat three times a day.) "I should like to see the effect of making the diet of children more simple."

Moreover—though she touched on this topic very delicately, so that one must read the passage over several times to get its meaning—there was a considerable amount of secret hard drinking done by ladies. Unlike their men, they could not be intemperate in public, which made it all the worse. They drank, she thought, because of that ever-present "vacuity": they were bored because they had nothing to do.

It is a pity that we have no statistical evidence to support what both Englishwomen had to say about the health of nineteenth-century American women, but a few of their remarks have significance even without statistics. Both spoke more than once of the pale complexions of American girls and women. In spite of their beauty, the English ladies could not help comparing those sallow faces with the rosy countenances they saw all around them at home in England, but it is possible that this pallor was not as indicative of ill health as they concluded. The English are island people, growing up within reach of salty sea breezes. The air is comparatively chilly and it keeps faces chapped and glowing, whereas most of the American ladies seen by Mrs. Trollope and Miss Martineau lived inland. They were continentals, with continental complexions. However, it is significant that the three Trollope children who accompanied their mother to America and lived for months in Ohio suffered and ultimately died of tuberculosis—or, as it was then called, phthisis—and that the other Trollope sons, who stayed in England, never had the disease.

It is pleasant to report that Captain Basil Hall, R.N., reporting on *his* visit to Lowell, spoke of "the healthy and cheerful look" of the girls. In his *Travels in North America,* covering the years 1827 and 1828, he told how he was awakened at six in the morning by the bell that called the people to their work and, looking out the window, saw "the whole space between the 'Factories' and the village speckled over with girls, nicely dressed, and glittering with bright shawls and showy-colored gowns, all streaming along to their business, with an air of lightness, and an elasticity of step, implying an obvious desire to get to their work."

But Hall was surprised by the absence of women from any form of merrymaking in America. At a great stock show at Brighton, near Boston, where he expected something like a county fair in England, he was disappointed to find no girls or women visible anywhere in the whole place. It made him feel ill at ease with what he described as the cruel spectacle of such crowds of people, on a fine sunny day and in as pretty a little valley as ever was seen, with no women amongst the crowd. He wandered about seeking signs of life and merriment, but could find none, only groups of idle men smoking cigars and gaping about, hands in pockets, or looking listlessly at the cattle, or following one another in quiet, orderly crowds, glad of the smallest excitement to carry them out of themselves—and not a woman to be seen. There were parties of men "hard at work with the whisky or gin bottle," and companies working away at hot roasts and meat pies—ordinary enough signs, an Englishman might think, at any county fair, but it was peculiar to note the absence of talking or laughing or any hilarity at all.

"I felt my spirits crushed down, and as it were humiliated," wrote the captain, "when, suddenly, the sound of a fiddle struck my ear, literally the very first notes of music I had heard, out of a drawing-room, in the whole country. Of course I ran instantly to the spot, and what was there?—four men dancing a reel!"

The whirligig of time . . . Nowadays Americans accuse Englishmen of neglecting *their* women.

CHAPTER 7

A Natural Right

In the 1820s and 1830s, library and bookshop statistics tell us a lot of Americans were reading Irving, Scott, and Byron, and though it is impossible to break down these statistics further into age groups and their tastes, we can be sure that among Byron's readers was a large proportion of girls and young women, sighing and palpitating over his poems. Perhaps part of his popularity with the females was due to his reputation for wickedness, but the verse itself was romantic enough to attract them. Of course, not all his adorers were American. In 1821 Fanny Kemble, an English child of twelve at school in Paris, fell madly in love with Byron, and if this seems a long way off from our subject, it is not really, for Fanny was in time to cross the Atlantic and become an outstanding American woman. In the Paris school's drawing room she was drowsing one afternoon after tea when one of the bigger girls teasingly put an open book on her lap, pointing to the following lines:

> It is the hour when from the boughs
> The nightingale's high note is heard.

"Oh, it's Byron!" cried Fanny, looking at the title. "Oh, do let me have it—oh, do let me read just a little more!"

The other girl consented, and Fanny ran off with her prize to her room. But there her roommate lectured her severely: Byron, she said, was not proper reading for little girls. Fanny surrendered, read no more of the enchanting poems, and carried the book back to the friendly big girl.

She was a romantic. Her immediate love of Byron's work was characteristic of her impulsive, enthusiastic nature. She came of a stage family so aristocratic in their world and so illustrious that no word was ever breathed to impugn their respectability. Mrs. Siddons was her aunt, and her father, Charles Kemble, was considered the best Shakespearean actor of all time. Her mother, *née* Marie Therese de Camp, had been an actress from the cradle. With all these influences around her, Fanny, oddly enough, viewed the idea of a stage career with abhorrence. She meant to be a writer. But the fates are stubborn, and Fanny did, after all, go on the stage. It happened thus: Charles Kemble, as actor-manager of the Covent Garden Theatre, was caught in a depression that hit England in the late 1820s and found himself on the verge of ruin. Something new and startling was needed to bring the public to Covent Garden, and the Kembles hit on the idea of putting Fanny on. They told her to learn the part of Juliet as fast as possible. As soon as she had done so they shoved her into the spotlight to act that famous tragic role, and—as happens so seldom in real life, though often in Hollywood romances—she became a hit overnight.

After that success the Kembles simply couldn't afford to let their talented daughter throw away her new career. They were still worried about their finances in 1832—they were always worried about money, more or less—and Charles decided to take her on tour in the United States, where many Thespians vastly inferior to the Kembles had made their fortunes. So reluctant Fanny, "one of the finest actresses England ever produced," according to a biographer, Margaret Armstrong, obediently went to America, scribbling faithfully in her diary along the way. This journal was published in 1835, soon after her marriage, and it is not—to understate the case—very revealing, because her husband was a conservative type who insisted on so many excisions that the reader wanders through page after page of passages like this: ". . . and . . . waiting for us when we returned from . . . Dined with . . . and called on Mrs. . . . who is not well, poor lady."

However, between such blanks the author gave a vivid picture of the America she saw as she moved with her father from one city to another and looked with cold eyes at the native women. Few met with her approval; she was young and intolerant. She assured her readers that she had not read Mrs. Trollope's book, but her early impressions were remarkably similar to that lady's, demonstrating the same patriotic pride in things English, the same criticism of things American.

She thought the women on Broadway very gaily dressed, with a pretension to French style and a more than English exaggeration of it. They walked with a "French shuffle," as if their feet hurt, which they probably did. Fanny complained of the high cost of French dresses, silks, and embroideries, and blamed it on the extravagance of American women—quite extraordinary, she said, considering their average income: they would readily spend up to sixty dollars for a bonnet just to wear sauntering on Broadway. Even worse, she saw a woman riding in a black velvet beret. "Only think of a beret on horseback!"

To do the girl justice, she did not brag. We would not be able to know, merely from reading her account, that she was even more of a smash hit in America than she had been at home. No doubt she was too indifferent to the stage to talk about it. Instead, she continued to chatter about American people: "The women here, like those of most warm climates, ripen very early, and decay proportionately soon. They are, generally speaking, pretty, with good complexions, and an air of freshness and brilliancy, but this I am told is very evanescent; and whereas, in England, a woman is in the full bloom of health and beauty from twenty to five-and-thirty; here, they scarcely reach the first period without being faded, and looking old." She adds, in what might almost be a rephrasing of Mrs. Trollope and Miss Martineau, that though the climate is often blamed for the ladies' ill looks and ill health, she thinks that it is more likely due to the "effeminate" way they are brought up—little exercise, rooms like ovens during the winter, and early marriage.

Traveling by stagecoach to Philadelphia, she was irritated by a number of young ladies in high spirits, who talked with "the national nasal twang." They were all pretty, two especially so, with delicate complexions and beautiful gray eyes. "How I wish they could have held their tongues for two minutes," wrote Miss Kemble. Soon after the coach started, one of them complained of being dreadfully sick, which appeared to Fanny Kemble to be a most frequent ailment among American females, who must all have had particularly bilious constitutions. "I never remember travelling in a steam-boat, on the smoothest water, without seeing sundry 'afflicted fair ones' who complained bitterly of *sea-sickness* in the river," she said.

A few weeks later she announced that the lot of married women in the States was unenviable. They were either house drudges and nursery maids or, if they appeared in society, comparative ciphers. It was the young girls, the "chits," who led society—girls who in England would be sitting in pinafores, knowing their place. Musing that it was rare to find married ladies "at home" in the morning, she decided that this was due to the total impossibility of having a housekeeper. American servants steadfastly refusing to obey more than one mistress, the lady of the house had to look after everything in person, and simply didn't have time to get dressed and receive visitors before noon.

Presumably she never had time to look after her daughters either, wrote Miss Kemble waspishly, because they were—she used the word advisedly—*hoydenish.* Girls of any age from ten to eighteen laughed, giggled, romped, flirted, and screamed loudly, without restraint, in public. They ran in and out of shops and hung about the streets, and they apparently played truant a good deal, because Fanny was always meeting groups of the chits at times when they should have been in class. In England, she told herself, girls that age would still be in the nursery under the strictest discipline: what could their mothers be thinking of? Not only did they run around the streets and make nuisances of themselves in the shops, but they went into society far too young, often by themselves, putting themselves forward without their mothers, aunts, or any other kind of chaperon. Certainly they had self-possession, the visitor reflected, but they had gained this quality at the expense of charm. Shyness was unknown to them; it seemed to be unknown to any American regardless of sex or age. However, something could be said in the young misses' defense, she discovered—or, if not defense, at least explanation. When she imparted these views to a male American, he replied seriously: "You forget the comparatively pure state of morals in our country, which admits of this degree of freedom in our young women, without rendering them liable to insult or misapprehension."

She had to admit that he was right, and so must we. Nice girls were safe in America as long as men felt that they were *truly* nice. The trick was to convince potential wolves of one's virtue, and the noisy, carefree manners of the virginal hoydens evidently carried this necessary conviction. Of course there was the other side of the coin, the reservoir of ladies of easy virtue, but nice girls were not supposed to know anything about them. Without indulging in such murky afterthoughts, Fanny admitted that she had seen many pushy, mannerless American girls marry and settle down into excellent wives, forsaking society and devoting themselves to household duties exclusively. What more could anyone ask of a girl?

For herself, Miss Kemble was as careful as possible of appearances. She listened attentively when a clergyman of her acquaintance gave her a sermon about waltzing, and was speedily convinced that he was right. She promised never again to waltz, except with a woman or her brother. "After all," she said to her journal, " 'tis not fitting that a man should put his arm around one's waist, whether one belongs to any one but one's self or not." The clergyman had made an impression: he was convinced, he said, from conversations he had heard among men that waltzing was immoral in its tendency.

"I am married, and have been in love," he added, "and cannot imagine anything more destructive of the deep and devoted respect which love is calculated to excite in every honorable man's heart, not only for the individual object of his affection, but for her whole sex, than to see any and every impertinent coxcomb in a ball room, come up to her, and, without remorse or hesitation, clasp her waist, imprison her hand, and absolutely whirl her round in his arms."

"So," wrote Fanny, "farewell, sweet waltz, next to hock, the most intoxicating growth of the Rhineland!"

By the end of the year the Kembles and Fanny's chaperon, Aunt Dall, were seasoned travelers, having been to Philadelphia, West Point, and various other cities. Now they were on their way to Baltimore. Fanny could talk from firsthand experience of the horrors of the ladies' cabin aboard any large steamer in winter. It was generally crammed to suffocation with women, she said, who were strewn in every direction, though most of them naturally huddled around the stove, which made the atmosphere unbreathable. Some ladies sat lazily in rocking chairs, "cradling themselves backwards and forwards, with a lazy, lounging, sleepy air, that makes me long to make them get up and walk." Others, of course, managed even on fresh water to be very sick. There were usually about a dozen children, some naughty, some sick, all squalling, others happy, romping and riotous. "A ladies' cabin on board an American steamboat is one of the most overpowering things to sense and soul that can well be imagined," she concluded.

In Washington, where she was presented to President Jackson, Miss Kemble was told of an Indian school that for a while flourished in Massachusetts. The purpose of the institution was to convert young Indian men to Christianity, but several of the students fell in love with, and married, American girls—by which she seems to mean *white* American girls—and took them away to live in the woods, after which the school fell apart. It must have placed the wretched wives in a horrible situation, reflected Fanny, when the men returned to their savage ways of living. Thanks to the censor, the diary of 1833 reveals little of her personal life, but it is evident that she was giving considerable thought just then to the position of married women. There was good reason for this: she had promised an American that she would marry him and live in the States.

Was her decision due to what she might have called a *coup de foudre?* Probably. She was a romantic after all, and Pierce Butler had courted her enthusiastically, hanging about the theater from the first time he saw her perform in Philadelphia, following the Kembles on tour, and sending masses of flowers everywhere she lodged. Her biographer Margaret Armstrong thinks that Fanny married Butler in sheer reaction to the stage life she hated, most especially after her beloved Aunt Dall died in June 1834. It seems likely. In any case she turned over her share of the tour's earnings to her father and married soon after Aunt Dall's death, returning with Pierce to Philadelphia and leaving Charles Kemble to go home alone.

It was not a happy marriage. The Butler money came from rice and cotton, grown on plantations in Georgia. As a lively young Englishwoman of her time, Fanny was opposed to slavery, but she knew little about it. She did not even know—she claimed later—that plantations in the South were worked by slaves. Butler had represented himself as a young Philadelphian of means, which, strictly speaking, was true: an older family connection was managing the estates in Georgia at that time, and when Fanny did come to understand the situation it was too late. However, she was evidently aware of the facts when Harriet Martineau visited Philadelphia, since they discussed the question. Fanny admired Miss Martineau, unaware that her new friend did not really like the outgoing, radiant ex-actress. When they discussed abolition, Fanny assured Harriet that she knew, because her husband had told her so, that the slaves on the Butler plantation were happy and carefree, that they loved their masters, and didn't want to be free. Even so, she was revolted by the concept of slavery and often said so.

There were other troubles too in the marriage, some of which are set forth in Pierce Butler's petition for divorce from his wife on the grounds of desertion. That the document is dated 1849 indicates how long the unhappy pair endured their unhappiness before they could bring themselves to take such a distasteful step. Divorce was considered even worse than a miserable marriage, though by 1849 the Butlers had been estranged for years, but, as we shall see, Fanny had additional reasons for resisting such a solution.

Butler's petition is fascinating. In it he set forth, in illustration of his wife's faults, accusations of "peculiar views" entertained by his wife on the subject of marriage as an institution: "She said that marriage should be companionship on equal terms—partnership, in which, if both partners agree, it is well; but if they do not, neither is bound to yield—and that at no time has one partner a right to control the other." With indignation plainly mounting, he quoted from one of Fanny's letters on obedience, which he claimed from her as a natural right. Fanny reminded him that obedience did not enter into their marriage contract (they had been married in a Unitarian church), and declared that it was not "in the law of her conscience" to promise obedience to any human being, who was by definition fallible like herself. Pierce Butler felt that this outlandish argument spoke for itself, proving as it did that Mrs. Butler's opinions regarding the duties of a wife toward her husband were peculiar and impracticable.

Worst of all, however, was Mrs. Butler's attitude toward "the painful subject of difference, slavery." Butler alleged that after their marriage, and not before, Fanny had declared herself to be in principle an abolitionist, and her opinions on the subject were frequently expressed in a violent and offensive manner. However, he was telescoping the story, which gave a false impression. Fanny did not evince these strong emotions until after she had visited the Butler property in Georgia, five years and two children after she was married. In the meantime she found life in Philadelphia supportable, if not happy. To be sure Pierce neglected her, but that was the custom of American husbands, and she could not blame him if she was homesick for England. The first child, Sally, was born in 1835, and Fanny wrote then to Miss Martineau that she was sorry not to have had a son, since the lot of women is seldom happy, "owing I think to mistakes in female education . . . One item alone—the tight stays, tight shoes, tight garters, tight gloves, tight waistbands, tight armholes and tight bodices, of which we are accustomed to think so little—must in many ways affect health. American women soon lose their looks and health; they never go out without veils, they pinch their pretty little feet cruelly and, of course, cannot walk."

The second Butler baby, also female, was named Frances.

By now Pierce Butler and his elder brother had inherited the land in Georgia, and in 1838 Pierce with his family set out to visit their rice plantation on Butler's Island. Fanny, of course, kept a journal of the whole adventure, starting with their departure on a cold winter's day in December. With them went the two children and Margery, their nurse. It was a long, complicated journey by railroad, steamboat, and, at the end, rowboat.

Even an abolitionist might have expected more beauty in a sun-drenched plantation of the deep South. On a flat expanse of yellow, muddy land beyond the muddy, sandy, sedgy shore stood a steam rice-mill and the house, as well as the cookhouse and the slaves' shanties. The house had only six small rooms, of which one was occupied by the overseer, but before Fanny could see the interior the party was mobbed by slaves who came pelting down to the wharf to welcome their owners, jostling, yelling, and pawing the newcomers until Pierce shouted for the overseer to drive them back. Safe indoors, Fanny looked around. Certainly Butler's Island was not sinfully luxurious: nothing about it would have reminded a modern spectator of anything in *Gone With the Wind.* The furniture had all been made on the spot—wooden bathtub, rough pine table, and wooden chairs and benches. Clothes were hung on wall pegs. Of course there was no plumbing, but twice a day the tide washed out the drainage ditch nearby. The whole place was lower than water level and was surrounded by mud dikes. Here, struggling to make the family comfortable with the help of untrained slaves, Fanny lived for half a year.

In time she managed a few changes. She would not accept what her husband told her, that the blacks just naturally smelled bad: she persuaded her servants to wash, and detected an immediate improvement. She took walks and talked to people. Appalled by the primitive conditions she found in the "infirmary" for the workers, she persuaded Pierce and the overseer to build more rooms onto it. The women, soon detecting that she was sympathetic, came to complain to her when they felt themselves ill-treated, in hopes that she would act as intermediary with Massa. Fanny was distressed by many of the facts that she learned in this manner: woman workers in the field had to go back to work three weeks after giving birth, for example. We would not consider this much of a hardship today, but ideas were different then, and Fanny was sincerely shocked. Up to the age of twelve, children did not work in the fields, but they helped by looking after the babies and bringing them to the mothers for feedings. Many women complained to Fanny that their health suffered from having to go back to work so soon, and she put it all down in her journal and her letters to friends. Margaret Armstrong has condensed much of the excited, repetitive reports: how the slaves were permitted once a month to attend church in a nearby town—not elsewhere, as mixing with slaves from other estates was considered dangerous; nor could they be baptized, most of them being Baptists, without the express permission of the overseer, which was not always given.

What really horrified Fanny was the mode of punishment by beating, even though there were certain restraints. For example, the head driver, a black, might inflict only three dozen lashes, but he could order a man or woman to be tied up for flogging so that only the toes touched the ground. A simple driver was allowed only a dozen lashes, and sometimes he delegated the job, because it gave more point to a lesson if a woman was flogged by her own husband or father. The head driver could banish a troublesome hand to a remote settlement in a swamp infested with rattlesnakes. And so on. In remote places like Butler's Island the owner was lord of life and death, but the Butlers, being model proprietors, had never wished to flog any of their possessions—dogs, horses, or slaves—to death.

"It was a simple code," wrote Margaret Armstrong. "Island life was simple. Pierce answered Fanny's questions frankly enough: he and his overseer were naively proud of their administration."

Fanny tried to put in a word now and then for some woman who had complained. She learned better when one of the women was flogged for telling tales out of school. She was shocked at first to discover that the overseer slept with slave women even when they didn't want him. The shock did not last, but her disgust did, and she often remonstrated with her bored husband on this subject. Pierce grew less and less pleased with his meddlesome wife. Later they moved to the other Butler estate, on St. Simon's Island, where cotton instead of rice was grown and where Fanny found a certain amount of white society, but Butler slaves were still there, still following her about with their appalling stories.

In May 1839 the family left the South and returned to Philadelphia. As things turned out, Fanny never went back to Butler's Island, but she had seen and recorded enough to make her even more abolitionist in sentiment than she had been before, and though she refused to publish her journal then, as many friends urged her to do, she did not refrain from other outright speech. In his statement Pierce complained of what happened in 1840 in Philadelphia, when his wife received a letter from "a perfect stranger" asking her to write something to be printed and sold at an antislavery fair to be held in that city. Pierce was provoked, and, he said, his feeling was changed to the deepest pain and mortification when he found that his wife actually intended to comply with the request. "I entreated her not to do so," he wrote. "I represented to her the shameless indelicacy on the part of the abolitionists in attempting to enlist the wife of a slave-owner."

But Fanny did it, and not for the last time. A year later when they were staying in London she published another antislavery article, which made him even more indignant. Fortunately for his peace of mind, or what remained of it, Pierce Butler, unlike Fanny's close and confidential friends, was not aware of the seethingly angry journal she had kept during her sojourn in Georgia, and was not to learn of it until she published it in 1862, well after their divorce. But already he felt very ill-used by his strong-minded wife, and he found plenty of sympathy, for it was his conception of marriage and its attendant duties, not Fanny's, that best expressed the ideas of his class and time. In *Woman as She Should Be,* a little book by the Reverend Hubbard Winslow, published in 1838 in Pierce Butler's own Philadelphia, we find a chapter on "Female Defects" which tells us, in part:

> A low estimate of female pretensions is certainly not the fault of the present day. Women are, perhaps, sometimes in danger of being spoilt; but they cannot complain that they are little valued. On the contrary, their powers are often too highly rated. Their natural defects are overlooked; and the consideration in which they are held, the influence they possess, and the confidence placed in their judgment, are in some instances disproportionate with their true claims.
>
> This, perhaps, is the cause of their occasionally aspiring to situations, and intruding upon offices, for which they are not fitted. They are betrayed into an overweening conceit of their own powers, and are not unwilling to put them to the proof. And the indulgence with which their efforts are in general treated prevents their consciousness of failure, even when they are unsuccessful . . .
>
> It is, indeed, fair that [woman] should be spared the severity of criticism; but she should not presume upon that indulgence. Nature has assigned her a subordinate place, as well as subordinate powers; and it is far better that she should feel this, and should not arrogate the superriority of the other sex, whilst she claims the privileges of her own.
>
> The character of woman, though inferior, is not less interesting than that of man.

In England, where the Butlers had gone for a long visit, Charles Greville, no mean diarist himself, observed the Anglo-American pair and wrote of them in his private papers. Fanny he had known in the days of her youthful triumphs onstage. In his diary in December 1842 he noted:

"I have been seeing a great deal of Mrs. Butler, whose history is melancholy, a domestic tragedy without any tragical events. She went to America ten years ago in the high tide of her popularity and when she was making a fortune. Then Pierce Butler fell in love with her and she fell in love with him . . . She gave up her earnings to her father, she left the stage, married and settled in America. And now after wasting the best years of her life in something like solitude near Philadelphia, with two children, whom she is passionately fond of, what is her situation? She has discovered that she has married a weak, dawdling, ignorant, violent-tempered man, who is utterly unsuited to her, and she to him, and she is aware that she has outlived his liking, as he has outlived her esteem and respect . . . With all her prodigious talents, fine feelings, and lively imagination, she has no tact, no discretion. She has acted like a fool, and he is now become a brute; the consequence is she is supremely and hopelessly wretched. She sees her husband brutal and unkind to her, ruining himself and his children by his lazy, stupid management of his affairs, and she lives in perpetual terror lest their alienation should at last mount to such a height that their living together may become impossible, and that then she shall be separated from her children for whom alone she desires to exist. Among the most prominent causes of their disunion is her violent and undisguised detestation of slavery, while he is a great slave proprietor. She has evinced the feeling (laudable enough in itself) without a particle of discretion, and it has given deep offense."

All this was true. Fanny had no discretion; Pierce held the whip hand and knew it. Little by little, he became villainous. Thanks to the law as it then stood, it was in his power to separate her completely from her children: he had full control over his offspring. Knowing this, Fanny did her utmost to hold out, but after the Butlers returned to America her husband embarked on a campaign designed to force her to let go and leave him. He gave up the house and made the family move to a boarding house. He kept Fanny and the children short of food. Though he was caught by an outraged husband with the man's wife, *in flagrante delicto,* his legal powers were unscathed. His next step was to force Fanny to give up her friends, even to stop writing letters to them. Fanny submitted to all of it, even when Pierce hired a new governess who was probably his mistress, and little by little took from his wife's hands all semblance of authority over the children. The governess even selected their clothes. Still Fanny persisted, until the day she realized that all this was harming the children. Then she returned to England and left the way open for Pierce to sue her for desertion. It was in 1845, and Sally would not be twenty-one until 1856. Then she would be free to choose reconciliation with her mother—if she wished. While Fanny waited, she filled her life. She gave dramatic readings, she wrote and published, and she made money. In 1856 Sally had her birthday and chose to join her mother; so did little Frances when her turn came two years later.

After Sally's marriage to Dr. Owen Wister of Philadelphia, who might be called the grandfather of "The Virginian," as his son wrote that classic book, Fanny Kemble spent a good deal of time in Philadelphia, where she would be near her daughter, and little Frances went along. Pierce Butler could still have made trouble for Fanny, but by this time he had no time for old quarrels. His affairs were going downhill with the rest of the South, until in 1859 he had to undergo what Miss Armstrong called the last, most humiliating expedient for a Southern planter: he had to sell his slaves to pay his debts. The people Fanny had known and tried to fight for were now put up at auction. So-called families were kept together, but a family was defined as consisting of a man, a woman, and their children, so there were separations, with parents parted forever from their married children, grandparents from the grandchildren, and brothers from sisters. Sweethearts, of course, were usually parted. According to Margaret Armstrong:

"The receipts were satisfactory. The men, women and children who had worked for Pierce Butler all their lives brought him a total of over three hundred thousand dollars . . . When it was all satisfactorily over Pierce bade his former slaves a kind farewell and presented each of them with a dollar in four new twenty-five-cent pieces."

The Civil War affected Fanny deeply, especially when, during the summer of 1861, she stayed in Switzerland with Frances. Out of the United States she always felt very American, and she was upset and angry at England's attitude toward the North-South struggle. It was maddening to be told by her English compatriots that the Southerners were cultivated gentlemen, worthy of sympathy, whereas the Northerners were just factory-owning money grubbers. Her biographer thinks that it was the defeats of 1862 that stirred her up and decided her at last to publish the journal from Georgia. Mrs. Stowe's novel had shown people what slavery was—"*Uncle Tom's Cabin* had won more converts than a million abolitionist speeches." It was no time now for scruples about Pierce. Fanny dug out her manuscript and published it in both America and England in 1863.

In England, *The Georgia Journal* was a sensation, though prudish people said it was indelicate and improper, and wouldn't let their daughters read it. Extravagant estimates have been made of its impact, such as that the book played a great part in the preservation of England's neutrality, but it is impossible to gauge these things, as Mrs. Armstrong wisely remarks. The critics lined up for or against the *Journal* according to the papers' policies. No matter: practically everyone read the "horrid story" and found it interesting. In the States the *Journal* had a similar reception, with criticism sharply divided between Southern and Northern periodicals. Some critics who approved of it declared that it would rival the famous *Uncle Tom's Cabin* in popularity and longevity, but they were mistaken. *Cabin* was a novel with an exciting plot and lots of picturesque detail, whereas Fanny would have scorned to produce any such mixture of truth and romance. Her book had only the normal life span of a topical report, but it is, nevertheless, a valuable social document. And, when one pauses to think of it, that is a considerable achievement for a woman who in early life prided herself on being a perfect lady and obeyed all the conventions. This was the girl who gave up waltzing because it was condemned by a clergyman as improper. This was the young woman who wondered anxiously about the morals of American misses—and was possibly the most aggressively respectable actress to perform in Shakespearean drama—but it was also the woman who discovered that being good and getting married does not necessarily mean that one lives happily ever after.

Fanny's natural vigor of mind and body and a keen sense of justice came to the rescue when her dream of sweet domesticity was smashed. Instead of submitting to fate and settling for a soured, ruined life, she stepped forth to become a fighter and reformer. It was an extraordinary transformation.

CHAPTER 8

The Fanny Wrightists

THE NEIGHBORS MUST HAVE DECLARED, often and often, that the Grimké sisters should have known better. They were brought up right and their mother was a lovely woman, so how did it happen? What was all this treasonable talk about the wickedness of slavery? And with their own father a slave owner—Judge Grimké, who owned plantations like any other gentleman. After all, Sarah and Angelina were Southerners too, members of one of the best families in Charleston, South Carolina: their maternal grandfather was the richest man in the state, and on the distaff side of the family were the names of two governors. It was strange, that was all, just strange, that out of a family of thirteen fine children those two girls had become freaks and traitors—abolitionists. Probably, the neighbors would have speculated, it was a case of too many brains: all that family had brains, and with Sarah and Angelina things had gone wrong on that account, which goes to show that brains never do a woman any good.

What no neighbor could understand—Sarah and Angelina did not themselves understand it clearly—was that they had been caught up in a new movement, invisible but strong nevertheless, of women trying to get out of the mold into which American culture had confined them. Intelligent women read and ingested ideas, and sooner or later began to apply certain principles, hitherto monopolized by their men, to themselves. Abigail Adams had prophesied this development half-jestingly, now it was becoming a fact. The abolition of slavery was a sign of the new philosophy. The men who complained so bitterly that abolition was the invention of a lot of nosy women understood only about half the situation. Women did indeed sponsor abolition, but it was not a wholly disinterested sentiment. Whether or not they realized it, they were acting out of deep sympathy. To use a word that later became part of America's vocabulary, they were projecting, and the cause served as a dress rehearsal for the coming struggle for their own liberation.

Sarah was the sixth Grimké child, born in 1792; Angelina, the thirteenth and last, did not appear until 1805. Slaves were all about the house during their childhood, and slave children were their playmates. Most children of their class did not question the system, but Sarah was horrified when at the age of four she saw a black woman whipped. As an adolescent, indignant at the law that forbade anyone to teach blacks to read, she secretly broke it by tutoring her waiting maid. Her father scolded her severely when this misdemeanor was discovered, but he appreciated her intelligence and once said that if she had been a boy she would have made an excellent jurist. Sarah managed to study a number of subjects not usually taught to girls by sharing her brother Thomas' lessons in natural science, mathematics, geography, and Greek, but even the usually sympathetic Thomas protested when she wanted to learn Latin with him. He appealed to their father, who agreed that this was out of the question. When Thomas was sent off to Yale and then went on to study law, Sarah tried to widen her horizons and asked if she too could not read law. Judge Grimké, however, would not hear of such an *outré* proceeding.

At thirteen, when Angelina was born, Sarah felt a special responsibility for the baby and used to mother her. She felt even more sympathetic with the child after Angelina fainted because one of her playmates, a little slave boy, was terribly beaten. For herself, however, Sarah did not yet seek freedom. She obediently "came out" at the proper time and attended the regulation balls and parties, but she was not tempted to marry any young man in her set; the life of a married woman in Charleston, looking after a household of slaves, seemed anything but enticing. Nor did she attract suitors, in spite of her father's wealth. She was not pretty, and word soon got around that she had peculiar ideas. With the "season" behind her, Sarah turned to religion like many another spinster before her. She was nearly twenty-seven when her father fell seriously ill and went to consult a famous surgeon in Philadelphia, taking Sarah with him. The surgeon, a Quaker, arranged for her to live in a Quaker boardinghouse during her father's stay in the hospital. After a few months the judge died and Sarah returned to Charleston alone. A party of Quakers happened to be traveling in the same boat, and she made friends with one of them, Israel Morris. Afterward she corresponded with him on the subject of his religion.

Slavery worried Sarah even more after she got back to Charleston, and her brother Thomas confessed to sharing some of her doubts. He was in favor of the plan proposed by the American Colonization Society, to send all the blacks back to Africa, but the other adults in the family had no patience at all with her ideas. They must have felt relieved when, in 1821, she resolved to leave them and go to Philadelphia, to live as a Quaker. It would look peculiar, they argued half-heartedly, but Sarah had inherited money from her father and could do as she liked.

In Philadelphia she lived with the Israel Morrises and attended their meeting, as Quaker houses of worship were called, becoming a Quaker herself in due course, but even then she did not find complete happiness. She longed to partake of a form of freedom unique to the sect: alone among religious houses in America, the Quakers permitted certain woman to officiate as ministers, but to achieve such a dignity, Sarah had to be approved by a committee. A few other female members of the meeting, including Mrs. Lucretia Mott, had succeeded in becoming ministers, but Sarah had taken the wrong side in an intramural struggle, and she was a convert too; these were marks against her. Time and again the recommendation was withheld, until she felt embittered. When Israel Morris' wife died, he asked Sarah to marry him and help bring up his eight children. Though she loved him, she turned him down because she had such a strong dislike of woman's place in marriage. A difficult female, Sarah Grimké, who questioned the very laws of nature and lived according to her principles.

In the meantime Angelina, grown up, decided that she too was strongly opposed to slavery. A direct, vigorous girl, she tried to persuade her minister to speak out for abolition in his pulpit. Not surprisingly, he refused. Angelina was seeking another way to fight for what was right when in 1827 Sarah came home on a visit. The sisters talked at length about these matters, and after Sarah had gone Angelina did some more thinking. As a result, in 1829 she too went to Philadelphia and became a Quaker. For a while she meekly accepted such work as the meeting gave her to do, but Angelina was not as self-abnegating as Sarah, and after a bit life palled. She thought she would enjoy being a teacher if only she had better training. She went to Hartford and talked to Miss Catherine Beecher, who encouraged her in this ambition, but the Philadelphia Quakers put a stop to her plans, saying that she had better take a place at their infant school instead. Though disappointed, Angelina was not too downcast, because she had an admirer among the congregation, and unlike sister Sarah, she had no objection to marriage. (Angelina was pretty, Sarah was not.) However, her lover died of cholera during an epidemic that also killed Thomas Grimké, and both women felt that they had reached an impasse.

According to Gerda Lerner's *The Grimké Sisters from South Carolina:* "They had come North and found freedom from slavery, but no freedom for themselves. Their feelings were dead, their intellects stifled. . . . They had reached the limit of freedom their age permitted to women. They were spinsters, aged forty-three and thirty, alone, without training and occupation and purpose—by the standard of their day, their lives were over."

But rebels like the Grimké sisters would not accept such a lot. Following Quaker custom, they had read no newspapers since coming to Philadelphia, with one exception, *The Friend,* a weekly of which the meeting approved. *The Friend* carried little news, and the sisters knew that they were ignorant of much that went on in the world. In 1833 they started reading everything they could find that would give them an idea of current events, and were speedily immersed in accounts of the controversy raging among abolitionists as to what was to be done with freed slaves: Should their liberation be gradual or immediate, and should they be colonized in Africa or kept in America? Sarah and Angelina began reading a Boston paper, *The Liberator,* and liked it, noting that its editor and publisher was William Lloyd Garrison. They discovered that the American Anti-Slavery Society had just been founded on their doorstep, in Philadelphia; they learned too of exciting events at the Lane Theological Seminary in Cincinnati.

Theodore Weld had started out as a revival preacher, had gone on to battle for temperance, and then interested himself in manual-labor schools like Lane, where poor students could work their way through. He had helped organize Lane Theological Seminary and then enrolled there as an undergraduate, for he intended to get a degree in theology in order to aid the cause of abolition. An able man, he soon became leader of the student body and arranged a series of debates among them on colonizationism versus immediatism. Some of the students, stirred up by these discussions, evidently rejected the idea of colonization in spite of—or perhaps because of—the fact that their president, Lyman Beecher, was in favor of it.

A number of seminary professors joined their ranks, and there were demonstrations. The moving spirit throughout was Theodore Weld. When he and his followers organized schools for freed slaves within the boundaries of the town, citizens complained to the seminary's board of trustees, and they in turn complained to President Beecher. Weld came close to being expelled, and most of the school went out on strike to show their sympathy with him.

Stimulated by this sort of news, the Grimké sisters began to attend antislavery meetings in Philadelphia. Of course the elders objected, and Sarah meekly desisted, but Angelina did not, and she was still attending meetings in 1834 when mobs rioted against the abolitionists, both in New York and Philadelphia. Angelina read an article written by Garrison on the subject and wrote an emotional letter to him, saying how much she agreed with his sentiments and imploring him to stick to his guns. Gratified, Garrison promptly published the letter in his paper, prefacing it with a glowing description of Angelina, Sarah, and the late Thomas Grimké as good abolitionists all. The publicity displeased the Philadelphia meeting and they rebuked Angelina, but she would not retract any part of her letter, and soon afterward, as an added act of defiance, she wrote an article for the American Anti-Slavery Society, "Appeal to the Christian Women of the Southern States." She was also contemplating a new venture, for the Anti-Slavery Society had asked her to go to New York as a missionary for the cause. She hesitated a little: conscience told her to go, but Israel Morris' sister Catherine tried to dissuade her. Angelina couldn't leave Philadelphia, said Catherine, without a certificate from her meeting. If she went without it she would probably be disowned.

Such repeated interferences from the Quakers seemed to Angelina too much to be borne, and even the long-suffering Sarah agreed. Sarah had a grievance of her own: at a meeting she had started to speak aloud, after the fashion of Quakers when the spirit moves them, only to be cut off rudely and peremptorily by the presiding elder, Jonathan Edwards. It was intolerable. Why should they not face the calamity of being disowned? Sarah declared that she too would be a missionary and in October 1836 they went to New York without asking permission. The Quakers did not disown them until some years had passed. It did not matter by then.

They met Theodore Weld in New York, in charge of the project. He immediately started them in a training course with thirty-eight male abolitionist agents, many of whom were experienced in the work already. Weld intended to send the Grimkés, as soon as they were ready, to address groups of women at meetings in private houses, and to encourage them to make their opinions known by various means such as petitioning the government. But some of the other men doubted the wisdom of such procedures. They argued that the sisters would be accused of "Fanny Wrightism" if they spoke in public, even if they spoke only to women, but Weld was impatient with these objections, and Angelina and Sarah agreed with him. When he pronounced them adequately trained, they held their first meeting. So many women wanted to hear them that no house could be found large enough to hold them all, and they had to use the session room of a Baptist church.

Angelina and Sarah were a tremendous success. More and more women attended their lectures, until Angelina grew impatient with the stuffy church rooms they used. Why, she asked, must they hide themselves away? What was the sense of this convention that kept women off the ordinary public rostrum? Women in the Bible had played a part in civic and religious affairs quite openly, she reminded her associates. The president of Oberlin College—a spin-off from the late Lane Seminary troubles, open to both sexes and all colors—actually offered her a job as assistant teacher in his Female Department. A year earlier Angelina would have been tempted; now she had other commitments and could not accept.

In May 1837 the Grimké sisters attended the Anti-Slavery Convention of American Women in New York, and in an article written for the occasion Angelina sounded her first published note of feminism: "Women ought to feel a peculiar sympathy in the colored man's wrong, for, like him, she has been accused of mental inferiority, and denied the privilege of a liberal education."

The Grimkés' New England tour took them first to Boston, where they made the agreeable discovery that Bostonians saw nothing reprehensible or even particularly strange about them. In spite of (or perhaps because of?) the archaic property laws of Massachusetts, Boston was used to women busying themselves with public affairs, and nobody so much as mentioned Fanny Wright in connection with the Grimkés. (I say "perhaps because of . . . the archaic property laws" because of Miss Martineau's declaration that everyone she met from Massachusetts was ashamed of them. Possibly Boston's women were trying to compensate for their state's backwardness. It would be like them.) It seemed natural that a few men dropped in at the women's meetings and listened to what the sisters had to say, and as the tour went on more and more men came, until at Roxbury there were thirty men among 250 women in the audience. As the meetings continued, the numbers mounted. In Boston on a return visit of the Grimké sisters there were fifty men among 550 women at the gathering, after which nobody bothered to count the males in such large mixed audiences.

It would be too much to expect that all of New England would approve of this newfangledness, however, and Angelina, especially, was soon the object of attack by—of all people—Miss Catherine Beecher, who wrote a long article on slavery in which she criticized the younger Miss Grimké. Ostensibly the criticism was based on Angelina's preference for radical abolitionism over colonization, but Catherine went on to assert that women should not join abolition societies: such activities were contrary to the divine law that women should be subordinate to men. Their influence should be confined to the domestic and social circle, said the head of the Hartford Female Seminary. And women should certainly not present petitions to Congress, she added: that was man's work. Angelina retorted that as the right of petition was the only political right possessed by women, they should exercise it whenever they were aggrieved: it was woman's right to have a voice in the laws and regulations that governed her.

Sarah too had begun to pay attention to women's rights, especially those of working women. Foreign visitors might well approve the arrangements they witnessed in the mill towns, but Sarah did not. She questioned the rate of pay for girls and children in the mills, and pointed out in her talks that men automatically earned far more for the same labor.

The first definite angry reaction to all this provocative behavior was manifested early in July in Amesbury, Massachusetts, where the sisters were lecturing. Two men interrupted Angelina in the middle of her address, to challenge some of her statements about slavery. They said they had recently visited the South and found that the conditions there were not at all as she described them. Members of the audience objected to prolonged argument at that time, so a debate was arranged between the three disputants, and it took place a few days later. Angelina routed her opponents, but the mere fact that a woman had engaged in a public contest shocked a number of people, including the editor of the local paper, who declared that the event was too indelicate to be reported.

The incident gave to Nehemiah Adams, a Congregational minister with strong pro-South tendencies, the chance he had been looking for. On July 26 he published a statement, "Pastoral Letter of the General Association of Massachusetts to the Congregational Churchmen under their care," attacking the Anti-Slavery Society members for using churches in which to debate "perplexed and agitating subjects." He warned churches against the danger of public speaking by women, which threatened the female character with widespread and permanent injury. Women should not so far forget themselves as to "itinerate" in the character of public lecturers and teachers, he said. Instead, they should pay attention to their appropriate duties and influence, as clearly stated in the New Testament. A woman's strength, declared Adams, comes from her dependency and weakness. He continued:

> But when she assumes the place and tone of man as a public reformer, our care and protection of her seem unnecessary . . . and her character becomes unnatural. If the vine, whose strength and beauty is to lean upon the trelliswork, and half conceal its clusters, thinks to assume the independence and the ever-shadowing nature of the elm, it will not only cease to bear fruit, but fall in shame and dishonor into the dust.

It may be possible to imagine to some extent the excitement that ensued over this botany lesson, but unless we remember how small the literary American world was at that time we do not get the full effect. Hundreds of people, male and female, hastened to defend Angelina. The Quaker John Greenleaf Whittier wrote a poem:

> So this is all—the utmost reach
> Of priestly power the mind to fetter!
> When laymen think—when women preach—
> A war of words—a "Pastoral Letter."

Sarah promptly issued a series of articles, *Letters on the Equality of the Sexes,* elucidating many of the Grimké ideas, in which one particular passage became famous among feminists: "I ask no favors for my sex. . . . All I ask my brethren is that they will take their feet from off our necks, and permit us to stand upright on that ground which God designed us to occupy." She demanded equal educational opportunities and pay for women, and, addressing the sex, urged them to realize their own dignity and worth. They did not need men, she wrote, to help them in their affairs. Why need it be the custom to ask ministers to open proceedings at women's meetings? Again, why did so many women and girls consent to spend their time in sewing circles, earning money to supply ministerial students? They would do better to work for the advancement of the education of their own sex. Reform would benefit men as well, since they would find women as equals much more valuable than as inferiors.

The New England tour proceeded and autumn approached, signaling its end. Feeling between pro- and anti-Grimkés ran higher, until even convinced abolitionists began to question the value of all this insistence on women's rights at the expense, they argued, of the original cause of abolition, for which the sisters had been enlisted. Angelina, unrepentant, retorted that she was glad if they could make a break in that wall of public opinion that lay in the way of women's rights, but Theodore Weld was on the side of the critics, and he remonstrated with the sisters by letter. He argued that his job was to promote antislavery organization in the North and collect signatures on petitions to Congress pertaining to slavery—and only slavery. The Grimkés were off on another tack entirely, he complained.

Angelina replied, "Can you not see that woman could do and would do a hundred times more for the slave, if she were not fettered?"

Here Angelina hit on a fundamental principle neglected by Weld: that activists must be equal, not "tolerantly suffered inferiors." Weld did understand this when it came to the blacks, and insisted that when they fought in the abolitionist cause they must be treated as equals, but he did not apply the same principle to women. Their cause was not as important to him—not then. However, to avert criticism of the sisters he excused their speaking in public by saying that they were Quakers and accustomed to that sort of thing, which sidestepping irritated Sarah and Angelina. Angelina protested that their feminism was not at all due to the Quakers, who regarded women as equal to men only on the ground of spiritual gifts, not on that of humanity. In the end a compromise was reached; the Grimkés agreed not to speak on women's rights if they were appearing on the abolitionist platform, but they maintained the option to write and speak for feminism at any other time they wished.

The Grimkés duly continued to fulfill their abolitionist speaking engagements, addressing larger and larger audiences—thanks to the advertisement afforded them by the Nehemiah Adams pastoral letter. The tour was to end in November, but before that Sarah fell ill with bronchitis, and Angelina had to do all the talking. Then, after the final day, Angelina contracted typhoid and was gravely ill for many weeks. During her convalescence through the winter months, letters went back and forth between the sisters and Theodore Weld. Weld helped Angelina rearrange her writings to be published as a book, and along the way she fell in love with him, and he with her. The news of their engagement startled their friends; Weld grew quite irritated when some of them called him a brave man.

They were married in Philadelphia in May 1838, in a characteristic ceremony. Many Negroes were among the guests, and the bride and groom had rewritten the marriage service according to their principles. Weld, indeed, made a little speech denouncing the law that gave the husband control over his wife's property, which shows that he had embraced feminist ideas after all, while Angelina promised to honor her husband, to prefer him above herself, and to love him with a pure heart. Naturally, nothing was said about obedience. A black minister prayed, followed by a white minister, and Sarah felt moved to a prayer of thanksgiving. William Lloyd Garrison read the marriage certificate aloud.

The honeymoon too was unconventional. Three days after their wedding the Welds attended what was to have been the first of a series of antislavery sessions in Philadelphia's brand-new Pennsylvania Hall, which had been built through the efforts of the reformers. Angelina was to speak, but she had hardly begun when a mob burst in, and when they were thrown out they heaved bricks through the windows. They were all stirred up over a rumor that the antislavery people were promoting "amalgamation," or integration. Above the crash of breaking windows Angelina spoke on, simply raising her voice, but the disturbances continued for two days more, and the hall, which had cost forty thousand dollars, was burned to the ground. The abolitionists carried on with their meetings in other buildings.

Later, Weld with his wife and sister-in-law retired to a little farmhouse on the Hudson. There for the first time in their lives the sisters found themselves faced with housework. Fortunately they didn't have to cook much because they were all enthusiastic converts to what was known as the Graham diet, conceived by that Sylvester Graham who invented Graham crackers and other health foods. Graham was almost totally vegetarian, and the Weld household believed his regimen to be as healthful as possible as well as easy to manage—one hot meal in the week, and apples, pears, rice, and molasses the rest of the time.

Thus the duties of housekeeping scarcely impeded Sarah and Angelina in their new venture, an antislavery pamphlet composed of damning facts from Southern newspapers, entitled *American Slavery as It Is*. It was immensely effective and sold better than any other pamphlet on the subject yet written—100,000 copies in the first year alone. Harriet Beecher Stowe was to draw upon much of the material for *Uncle Tom's Cabin*. Next, the Grimkés concentrated on a campaign to persuade women to sign petitions against slavery. This activity, like housework, was new to them, though they had often recommended signature collecting when they stood on the platform. Now they saw what it was like for the women who actually did the work. On the whole, they enjoyed the experience. It gave them the chance to talk to people woman to woman, and their enthusiasm must have put many a hitherto neutral housewife on the path toward women's rights.

In December 1839, Angelina gave birth to a nine-pound boy. Her second son came along in January 1841, and the Welds' only daughter was born in March 1844. It was one hazard that Angelina, brave as she was, could not escape; childbearing ruined her health. The specific trouble was never named, for, abolition apart, the Grimkés were daughters of the South and observed the accepted rules of modesty. The biographer thinks it most likely that Angelina suffered from prolapse of the uterus, for which in those days there was no treatment. Whatever the trouble, for the rest of her life Mrs. Weld, though her spirit never faltered, was an invalid.

However, like the confirmed reformers they were, the three continued to labor for various causes. They ran a school for a while until it became obvious that they were losing all their money in the enterprise. Then they joined the Raritan Bay Union, a utopian community in New Jersey, and under its aegis they conducted another school. An endearing description of them has been given by an observer who attended a party at the Raritan Bay commune in its heyday. He was impressed by Sarah and Angelina, both gray-haired and wearing bloomers, and by Theodore Weld dancing with immense enthusiasm, whirling his partner round and round the room, his long white beard floating as he turned.

The school at Raritan Bay lived on, even after the utopia disbanded, until it was brought to an end by the Civil War. The Welds and Sarah had always opposed violent methods of settling disputes, but they came around to the idea that the war was inevitable, and they lived through it to see the end of legal slavery in the United States. Not that everything was perfect afterward, as one had hoped.

Of course it was not: no reformer is ever completely satisfied, nor ought to be. But the Grimkés had accomplished more than they realized, and for a cause that seemed to them only secondary—women's rights. Sarah died in 1875, Angelina in 1879. Weld lived on to 1895. None of the three saw the results of what they had furthered with only a portion of their attention, the fight for women, but even as things were, they had little to regret. They had lived fully, busily, unselfishly, and to effect within their own span. Man on his deathbed can hardly ask for more.

CHAPTER 9

A Woman in the Nineteenth Century

THE LEGEND THAT WAS MARGARET FULLER has almost been forgotten except for one popular story—that Carlyle, on hearing that she had said, "I accept the universe," replied, "Gad! she'd better!"

Yet in her day she was noteworthy, and taken seriously by contemporary thinkers and writers. She was strong-minded enough to break many of the rules of convention without suffering condemnation. Or, at least, *much* condemnation.

She was born in Cambridgeport, Massachusetts, in 1810, the first of a large family. Her mother, busy with wifely and maternal duties, depended on her husband in all other matters. He was Timothy Fuller, described by Margaret Fuller's biographer, Margaret Bell, as an arrogant, self-assertive lawyer, a man of substance and influence in the community. For some reason the fact that his firstborn was a girl did not turn him against the baby. He started immediately to train and educate her, chiefly in the classics, as other scholarly men, if they were ambitious, might have trained their sons. As soon as the infant could talk she was taught Horace and Ovid, though her father did not insist on Greek until she was somewhat older.

By the time she was seven Margaret was familiar with Shakespeare, Molière, and Cervantes, but she knew few children outside her family, and those she met considered her a freak. She was a little older when Timothy, while correcting some of her English-Latin translations, noticed that she was very near-sighted, whereupon he stopped her intensive reading at once and sent her to an ordinary school. At first she had no idea of how to play with her classmates. She was not a pretty child, being unusually tall for her age and fat, but the fond father saw nothing wrong with her appearance. In 1826 when the Fullers gave a reception for the President, John Quincy

Adams, standing next to Timothy in the receiving line was poor sixteen-year-old Margaret, tightly laced and bulging in a dreadful pink dress that her father had selected.

This sight stirred a friendly neighbor to pity: she took Margaret in hand and taught her how to dress. Miss Fuller was an apt pupil, and soon acquired a dashing style all her own, developing a graceful, dignified carriage. She had a number of admirers, among them Frederick Henry Hedge, a Harvard student who later became an eminent divine. Hedge said to a friend, "That girl could do anything if she tried. Her face fascinates me, and how she can talk!"

Talk was Margaret's great talent. If, when we read her works today, we wonder how she became so popular, it we groan at her overweighted sentences and classical allusions dragged in by the scruff of the neck, we should remember that this popularity was due to her conversation rather than her writing. She was aware of this herself, and often said that she was far happier speaking than writing. In her day conversation was an important social grace, and Margaret had a lovely voice, a ready wit, and a lively imagination to help her hold her own in company.

Even the esteemed Mr. Fuller could not change the custom of the times, and girls were not admitted to university classes, so Margaret's formal education was cut off early, though for a time she attended a coed school with several clever boys—Oliver Wendell Holmes was cramming there for Harvard; Richard Henry Dana was another student. Her spare time was taken up helping her mother with the children that kept coming, but she managed to study and ride out with friends, while in the evenings there were parties and good talk. She was fascinated to hear of four young Unitarian ministers in Boston who had decided that churches were becoming too narrow and were determined to reform them. The leader of the group was Ralph Waldo Emerson of Concord, and Margaret longed to meet him, even though everyone said he was shy.

A more immediate ambition was to go to Europe, but Margaret was nearly twenty-six before she found the courage to ask her father if she could. The chance came when she published her first article in *The North American Review*. Timothy, who was ailing, nearly burst with pride. "My dear," he said to Margaret as she tended him, "I have been thinking of you in the night, and I cannot remember that you have any faults."

It seemed the right moment to ask him about Europe, and he readily consented. But suddenly he died, and everything changed for the

Fullers. He left no will, so theoretically his wife had no authority over family affairs; this passed to his nearest male relative, a brother named Abraham, who had no sympathy with the late Timothy's ideas. Uncle and niece quarreled over Margaret's next sister, the fifteen-year-old Ellen, for Abraham thought she should leave school and Margaret did not. Margaret won the argument. She was just getting ready for her European trip when the family found that Timothy had left much less money than they had hoped for. Margaret changed her plans, and told Emerson—who had at last become her friend—she must forget Europe and start to work for her living, teaching school and writing on the side, until she could earn her way by her pen.

Emerson and his wife advised and encouraged her. There was the Temple School, said "Waldo," shortly to be opened by his friend and co-philosopher Bronson Alcott, who would doubtless need assistants. Alcott had already acquired the services of Miss Elizabeth Peabody. Emerson was sure he would welcome Margaret too as a teacher, so she was introduced to Bronson Alcott and the arrangement was made. These two women were charter members of the Symposium Club, founded by Emerson, Alcott, and their friends, who met once a month for conversation. Mockingly, the public came to call the group the Transcendentalists, and the name stuck.

For a time the Temple School, run on unorthodox lines, was successful. Margaret was impressed by Alcott's teaching methods, and encouraged him to publish a book of conversations he had held with some of the children, but it proved an unfortunate move; a number of parents were scandalized by the infants' and Alcott's remarks about religion. Because it grew increasingly obvious to Margaret that nobody would ever earn a steady salary working for Bronson Alcott—he was too much of a visionary—she took the precaution of acquiring private pupils and tutoring them in her free time. This was fortunate, because affairs at the school soon reached a crisis when Alcott insisted on admitting a little mulatto girl to class, and would not give in when parents furiously demanded that he get rid of her. Child after child was whisked away, until the Temple School was forced to close down.

At least Margaret had her pupils, and as a teacher in various schools around New England she earned enough during the next few years to support herself and help her family, but a more successful project was her "Conversation Class" of twenty-five women who met and talked under her guidance. Margaret had great attraction for women and girls. Though afraid of her brilliance, they thought her wonderful. Moreover, she became editor of the *Dial,* the Transcendentalists' magazine, making a respectable job of it, though people were startled at the idea of a woman doing such work. Margaret Fuller was the first American editor to recognize the excellence of Hawthorne's writing.

Engrossed in economic struggle, she said little and wrote less about women's rights, though she was doing much thinking on the subject. Other trends of the day, such as utopianism, did not tempt her: when a number of Transcendentalists moved out to Brook Farm, Margaret was not one of them. She said that utopias were immature, though admittedly it was fun to play at farming. In fact, all her life was fun at that time, with one important exception—she was not getting anywhere toward becoming a self-supporting writer, and she needed money more than ever for her relatives. Her brother Eugene was at college, and Ellen, having finished her education, had fallen immediately into marriage with the penniless poet Ellery Channing; the couple were chronically hard up.

Margaret suddenly decided on a change. All her life she had suffered from blinding headaches and symptoms of what she called nervous fatigue, always when she was forcing herself to do something uninteresting. Now, declaring that her health demanded such action, she gave up her job at school and left the *Dial,* to settle down to her own writing. First, however, to celebrate this break for freedom, she took a trip out West with two friends, early in 1842, and later published an account of her travels, *Summer on the Lakes* (1843). It was no chatty travel book like those of Mrs. Trollope or Harriet Martineau—Margaret Fuller could not have written in the vernacular even if she wanted to. Everything she saw in the frontier country called forth from her overstocked brain a classical parallel or evoked some memory of obscure myth or legend. This happened especially when her interest was caught by the Indians who visited the earnest little trio from the East. Margaret simply had to compare these aboriginals with the races of ancient Egypt or the Far East.

To prepare the book she had to look up references, so she requested permission to read in the Harvard Library. It was an unusual idea, letting a woman in, but the university library did not dare refuse the renowned Miss Fuller, and she duly got her reading privileges. As the first woman ever to do so, she was resented by Harvard undergraduates who had to accept her presence among them in the reading room. As it happened, their grudging attitude was grist to her mill, since she was writing her book on woman's position.

Few persons were better qualified to talk about it. From early childhood Margaret had seen her mother subjected to the status of favorite breeding animal, patiently accepting the commands of her husband as if she had no mind or will of her own. It was true that Mrs. Fuller did not seem to resent her position; according to her lights, Timothy Fuller was a model husband and father. But under his domination, Margaret saw, she lost whatever scrap of independent intelligence she had ever possessed, and his death left her helpless, an untrained slave who had lost her master and could not cope with the world. The benevolent despot was supplanted by a far firmer tyrant, her brother-in-law Abraham, who would have bullied the whole family if Margaret had not defied him.

Not because this was an extraordinary situation, but because it was commonplace, Margaret was deeply interested in it, and her book *Woman in the Nineteenth Century* (1845) embodied her thought on the female dilemma generally. She had in mind not only the legions of quiet women like her mother, but females like herself, intelligent and educated, who could not compete with men, even inferior men, in breadwinning or in gaining recognition, because of their sex. That the fault lay not in femininity itself but in convention made no difference to the harsh fact that woman was victimized. Margaret discussed the situation thoroughly. As always, her style was awkwardly pedantic, but her ideas were not. Like certain modern writers, she tried the effect of changing the sex of subjects of well-known quotations. Instead, for example, of "Frailty, thy name is woman," she wrote: "Frailty, thy name is man." And for "The Earth waits for her Queen," Margaret wrote: "The Earth waits for its King."

There, she said at the end of her demonstration, it didn't really make all that much difference, did it? Both statements were equally valid. It was time to consider the position of women in America, which was markedly similar to that of the country's slaves. Of course, she wrote, men would not care to discuss these similarities: they did not wish to see their wives stirred up. Margaret imagined a conversation between such a man—the irritated trader, she called him—and a reformer like herself, presumably abolitionist as well as feminist. The trader cries:

"Is it not enough that you have done all you could do to break up the national union, and thus destroy the prosperity of our country, but now you must be trying to break up the family union, to take my wife away from the cradle and the kitchen-hearth to vote at polls, and preach from the pulpit? Of course, if she does such things, she cannot attend to those of her own sphere. She is happy enough as she is. She has more leisure than I have—every means of improvement, every indulgence."

The reformer asks him if he has inquired of his wife whether she is indeed satisfied, and he replies that he hasn't, but he knows she is. She is too nice a woman to want to make him unhappy or to step out of her own sphere. "I will never consent to have our peace disturbed by any such discussions," he adds.

The reformer protests that it is not for him to consent or deny; that is for his wife to decide, and he demands indignantly, "Am I not the head of my house?"

"You are not the head of your wife," replies the reformer. "God has given her a mind of her own."

The argument continues, with the Margaret-reformer winning every point, as is to be expected, until finally, dropping the Platonic form of dialogue, the text becomes a straight essay. The woman question, Margaret pointed out, was much in the public mind; one had only to look at the morning papers to believe it. This was natural, she said, since nobody could espouse the antislavery cause without thinking of women as well as enslaved Africans. To take one example, in the matter of property a woman was not much better off than a slave. The widow whose husband had died intestate did not take his place as head of the family, and she inherited only a part of his fortune, even if she herself had brought it to the marriage—"as if she were a child, or ward only, not an equal partner." And there were many worse cases—innumerable instances of men living on their wives' earnings, refusing to work and wasting what the women brought in. If such a man's wife should in desperation take her children and leave him, he could follow her from place to place and threaten to take the children away—as he could do in law—until the poor harried woman consented to pay him off.

"I have known such a man come to install himself in the chamber of a woman who loathed him, and say that she could never take food without his company," wrote Miss Fuller. Then there were men who stole their children when their wives were at work, took them into dissolute company, and deliberately exposed them to danger, moral and physical, in order to blackmail the mothers, who in spite of having borne and reared the children did not have equal rights to them.

Perhaps because of all this power, men felt toward women as they did toward slaves. The attitude is obvious, said the writer, in contemptuous phrases often heard, like "Tell that to women and children." Most men looked on women as beings lower than themselves, creatures with inferior reasoning powers, who must be kept out of mischief by constant, unimportant activity such as housework. In all except these simple matters, men felt, their women could not be trusted to manage things for themselves; they must be supervised, or they would muddle everything. Which was why reformers believed that woman's lot was unlikely to improve until she had the vote. Those who opposed votes for women would protest that the franchise was unnecessary, since every man is privately influenced by the women in his life—wives, sisters, or female friends—and they could trust him to carry out their wishes, or, if this was not enough, a woman could always write articles, couldn't she? To give them the vote would spoil them. The beauty of home would be destroyed, the delicacy of the sex violated, the dignity of halls of legislation degraded by any attempt to let the ladies vote. Such duties were inconsistent with those of a mother. "And then," wrote Margaret, "we have ludicrous pictures of ladies in hysterics at the polls, and senate-chambers filled with cradles."

Yet, she continued, if for argument's sake we accept the questionable proposition that woman, a creature too delicate to vote, should be kept safe and cloistered at home, as nature intended, we are faced with the fact that home is not necessarily all that safe and pleasant. It may be dull there, but it is not really as quiet and comfortable as men profess to believe. A woman may be spared excitement, but she does not escape drudgery. "Not only the Indian squaw carries the burdens of the camp, but the favorites of Louis XIV accompany him in his journeys, and the washerwoman stands at her tub, and carries home her work at all seasons, and in all stages of health." People who think women physically incapable of taking part in government affairs forget the Negresses working in plantation fields, or seamstresses at their killing labors. It is not as easy as men make it sound, either, for an educated woman to find freedom through writing, as up until recently there has been as much opposition to females writing as to their speaking in public.

One more argument against women's suffrage remained: that the sanctity of the home would be invaded if women interested themselves in these matters. But the woman who votes, or even speaks in public, is not going to leave home more often on such errands than she already does to gad about at balls, the theater, revival meetings, or gatherings to promote religious missions.

Woman in the Nineteenth Century was finished, and on the eve of publication Margaret took an important step toward the independence she had correctly described as rare for women to achieve. The wife of Horace Greeley, who had recently founded the New York *Tribune*, met Miss Fuller and quickly fell under the spell Margaret cast on so many females. At home she talked and talked about wonderful Miss Fuller until Greeley agreed to meet her and see for himself how brilliant she was. He too was impressed, so much so that he invited her to be literary editor on the paper. Margaret accepted, though it meant she must leave New England and the family to live in New York. Only the thought of her health made her waver, but the Greeleys said she was to live with them in their house far from the city center, in a wooded ravine at Turtle Bay, close to the East River. So it was arranged.

Her relationship with the Greeleys was pleasantly informal. Greeley, never a man to mince words, spoke his mind freely when his new literary editor did not behave as he thought she should. He felt that she ought to spend a regular number of hours every day in the office, like the rest of the staff, unless she was out on a story. Her casual ways distressed him, and when she explained that she could write only when she was in the mood, he nearly exploded. What kind of way was that to run a newspaper? Sometimes when he wanted a book review for a certain issue, Margaret told him that she was still thinking about what to say and had not yet begun writing it. He retorted that she spent too much time sitting around talking with a lot of women, when she could perfectly well have been writing her review. As for those famous headaches, she drank too much tea; that was the core of the matter. Nevertheless, they remained friends, and Margaret in time learned to take a more professional attitude toward her duties.

When *Woman* appeared it had considerable critical success, was much discussed, and sold well. Her first royalty check came to the considerable—for that time—sum of $85. Margaret became the lioness of New York's literary circles. It must have been a happy time, for she had fallen in love and believed herself to be loved in return. James Nathan from Hamburg, younger than she by a few years, called on her nearly every day to wander with her in the wood (because the Greeleys did not like him). He was romantically good-looking; he played the guitar and sang to Margaret and paid her delightful compliments. But at times he was moody, and stayed away and wrote her unpleasant letters until she too was plunged in gloom. Still, the brighter moments made up for the bad ones, until he announced one day that he must return to Hamburg for a time, for business reasons. He would need money, he said, and Margaret might help by persuading Greeley to buy travel articles from him. Desolate at the thought of losing him, Margaret nevertheless promised to do her best with Greeley, even if she had to rewrite Nathan's pieces.

He had been gone for some months and had sent more articles than letters when Margaret got the chance to go abroad with friends, first to England and then to travel on the Continent. Her improved financial position made it possible to do it, and her excited happiness was dimmed only slightly by Nathan when he heard the news and wrote angrily to ask how, without her help, he could now sell his articles to the *Tribune*. He felt that she owed it to him to stay in New York. Fortunately, Margaret was not besotted enough to agree, since soon after she arrived in Edinburgh she received another letter from Nathan announcing that he was engaged to a Hamburg girl. The news was not as painful as it might have been. What with the flurry of arranging her affairs and making sure that her mother and sisters and brothers could get along in her absence, the feeling she had nurtured for Nathan had somehow ebbed, and she had no time to tend a broken heart. After all, there were more important things to think about, including the fact that at the age of thirty-six she was fulfilling the ambition that fate had defeated ten years earlier. In the end the remnants of her grand passion were dissipated in a quarrel with Nathan over her letters, which he refused to return because they might someday be valuable.

In London, Margaret met Carlyle and other famous literary figures, and was soon immersed in English life. The town was full of talk about European politics. One evening Giuseppe Mazzini was presented to her, and she was thrilled, for she had long admired his revolutionary activities and his attempts to unify Italy under a republican government. Mazzini had been a political exile for a long time, but soon, he hinted, all this would be over, for he hoped to return to Rome in the near future. Margaret remembered this when, with her American friends, she moved to France and then to Germany. At that point the others announced they were going home, but she went on to Rome to settle for a bit and write articles for the *Tribune* about the political situation. There she met Giovanni Angelo Ossoli, a young officer in the Roman Revolutionary Party, who held the title of marquis. Margaret and Ossoli communicated only with difficulty: her Italian was still halting, and he had no English, but this was probably no hardship, since they had little to talk about save Mazzini. Ossoli was not in the least literary. In spite of this drawback, and the fact that Margaret was eleven years older than the young Italian, they fell deeply in love.

The language barrier and the discrepancy in their ages were bad enough, but there was another obstacle to their marriage. Margaret was her own mistress, but Ossoli was a younger son in a family of the old-style Roman Catholic aristocracy. None of his relatives even knew of his revolutionary connections, though it is hard to believe his older brothers did not suspect something of the facts. His father was old and ailing, not expected to live much longer. When he died, Ossoli would inherit a share of what the father left, if indeed he left anything, only if he had not estranged the family through political action or some other outrageous behavior, such a marrying a Protestant American woman with no fortune. There was not a chance in the world, as he told Margaret (one wonders with how much difficulty, how many references to the dictionary), that they would sanction the match. When Margaret found that she was pregnant, the lovers' only recourse was to marry in secret.

As was necessary, they did this by civil ceremony. In more peaceful times it would doubtlessly have been discovered no matter how carefully the facts were hidden, but the revolution was boiling up, and nobody paid attention to the strange couple, the middle-aged (by Italian standards) foreign woman and the Roman youth. Ossoli was a member of the Civic Guard, and had to divide his time between his bride and his military duties. Margaret, often alone, wrote letters she dared not send home, or went over and over the situation in her thoughts, facing her problems as clearly as possible. She was pregnant. Everything stood to be gained or lost in the impending revolution. If it failed, her husband would be cast out by his family without a penny, even if they learned nothing about his marriage. If it succeeded, presumably all would be well—but Margaret thought it wisest to expect the worst. Ossoli, she knew, was not equipped to earn a living, certainly not in America; she did not think he could ever learn to speak English. Once again it would be Margaret's task to earn money for her family, as she had done all her adult life—a family now augmented by husband and child. This was assuming that she did not die in childbirth: after all, she was thirty-eight, a late age for one's first lying-in. The future seemed dark.

But Margaret's end was not yet at hand. She moved out to Rieti, a village not far from Rome, where she gave birth to a son, Angelo, and when he was strong enough she left him with a peasant wet nurse and returned to Rome to be near her husband and await developments. It was important that she should witness whatever the imminent revolution might bring, because she knew that Greeley would welcome a series of articles on the situation, and her little family badly needed money.

Ossoli had told her with fair accuracy when the revolution would begin. Hostilities duly commenced, and Margaret, waiting in her lodgings for news of her husband whenever a battle was in progress, swung violently between heights of jubilation and depths of despair as the fortunes of Ossoli's cause seesawed. Often she was in terror for his safety: there were long periods when messages did not arrive from him. While Margaret scribbled articles or simply paced the floor, half mad with anxiety, the revolutionary effort gained so much strength that the Pope and his staff fled from the Vatican into France. In the end, of course, the insurgents failed. The French marched into Rome and reinstated the Holy Father, and everything was over for Mazzini's effort. Ossoli had survived the fighting, but like the other revolutionists he had to go into hiding.

His father had died, but the brothers proved less severe than Ossoli expected, and gave him some small part of his inheritance. With this money and whatever funds Margaret still held, the couple reclaimed the baby and went to Florence, where Ossoli would be safe from arrest. It was close to the end of the year, and they decided to stay on in Tuscany until the winter storms abated before attempting an Atlantic crossing. For a time, then, they were a part of the large foreign community of Florence, and Elizabeth Barrett Browning mentioned them in a letter to a friend. Everyone was much surprised, she said, when the famous American writer turned up with a Roman husband and child of whom nobody had heard before. She said the husband seemed very gentlemanly and treated his marchioness with affection and respect. Nevertheless, in Mrs. Browning's opinion they were an odd, incongruous couple.

Margaret looked on Florence as an oasis between war and the coming struggle for existence that she must wage in America. She dreaded that struggle, but the one bright aspect of Mazzini's failure to unify Italy meant that Ossoli, in Rome under sentence of death, was safe in Florence. And more, it was possible to write freely to her family and friends at home, even—given time—to report to the *Tribune* on the revolution: she had not dared to risk Ossoli's safety before by writing about the political situation. She wrote the whole story of her marriage in a letter to her mother. Mrs. Fuller replied with warm affection, and offered to share everything she had with her daughter's family. They could all live together, she said.

So far so good, but because of general revolutionary fervor, most of Europe had been thrown into turmoil. Shipping between the Continent and the States was disrupted, and was to remain irregular for several years, with the ships that managed to sail westward crowded with refugees. The Ossolis did not get berths until late 1849, and even then their luck was bad, for soon after they sailed they were overtaken by a storm, and the vessel had to put in at Lisbon for repairs. Then little Angelo fell ill and his parents dared not travel until he was better. Finally, in the summer of 1850, the family set out once more from Portugal.

It was July 15 of that year, with only another day's travel before landing at New York, when the ship was suddenly struck by a gale just off Fire Island, in full view of land. Grounded, it began to break up. Most of the passengers and crew jumped overboard and tried to swim to the sandy beaches, but though a few succeeded, more sank and did not resurface. Margaret, with the baby clutched in her arms and Ossoli standing helplessly by, sat on what remained of the deck and resisted all entreaties that she should take a chance and jump into the angry water. From the shore people watched as others still aboard expostulated with her. In vain; she only shook her head and clutched the child tighter, her long hair streaming in the rain. She seemed dazed with terror. At last a sailor snatched Angelo from her grasp, bound him to his own body, and leaped into the boiling sea at the very moment the ship's remaing structure broke up and pitched into the waves, carrying with it Ossoli and Margaret. Next day the sailor, the baby, and Margaret were found dead on the beach, but Ossoli's corpse was never recovered.

CHAPTER 10

Little Woman

"YOU ARE OLD ENOUGH to leave off boyish tricks, and behave better, Josephine. It didn't matter so much when you were a little girl, but now you are so tall, and turn up your hair, you should remember that you are a young lady."

The foregoing, said by Meg to Jo in Louisa May Alcott's *Little Women,* nicely bears out what Andrew Sinclair noted in his *Emancipation of the American Woman*—the emphasis that was placed on being a lady, up to the last years of the nineteenth century. It was understood that females must not behave like males. Apart from everything else, they would not have time: they had their work cut out for them in their own sphere. In the book, "Marmee" summed up the popular feeling about the matter when she told her little women—significant phrase for her daughters, who were all either children or adolescents—what she hoped of them. They were to be beautiful, accomplished and good, and, she went on, "To be loved and chosen by a good man is the best and sweetest thing which can happen to a woman; and I sincerely hope my girls may know this beautiful experience."

The March girls did not slip into their ladylike niches easily. If they had, there would have been no plot, and Miss Alcott, adept storyteller and staunch moralist that she was, knew better than to make such an error. The girls had definite faults to overcome before knowing the beautiful experience of being loved and chosen by some man. Meg thought too much of finery, Amy was selfish, Beth was marked for death anyway so it didn't matter, and tomboy Jo, in her early attempts at writing, could not resist the temptations of the sensational.

"She searched newspapers for accidents, incidents, and crime . . . she studied faces in the street, and characters, good, bad, and indifferent, all about her; she delved in the dust of ancient times for facts or fictions so old that they were as good as new, and introduced herself to folly, sin, and misery, as well as her limited opportunities allowed."

In case we wonder what was wrong with this program, which seems quite reasonable for an aspiring writer, Miss Alcott explains: "Unconsciously, she was beginning to desecrate some of the womanliest attributes of a woman's character."

Everyone knows that Louisa May Alcott used her own sisters and herself as models for *Little Women* and its sequels. She did not copy the family exactly in certain details: for one thing, she rearranged the girls' birthdays to bring them closer together in age, but that is an unimportant difference. The true metamorphosis is found elsewhere, in "Marmee" and "Father"—reasonable, conventional characters in the novels, though Father is shadowy and one is never quite sure what Marmee is up to that takes her away from home all day and sends her back late. It is a lacuna so obvious that I was aware of it even as a young child, but Louisa Alcott could not fill it in without being even more awkward: It would have spoiled her picture of a pure, sweet, wholesome—and, above all, *typical*—American home. To be sure, the absences of the original of Marmee, Abba Alcott, seem innocent enough in our eyes: she worked, that's all. She couldn't manage the household on the money Bronson brought home, and she worked for more. The embarrassing fact, however, was that she actually *preferred* getting jobs to staying at home looking after her daughters. Household tasks and even the children, if the truth were known, bored her. How could Louisa admit that? It is doubtful if she ever faced the reality of Abba; she idealized her mother.

As for Bronson, he was no conventional parson or wage earner. We might think him better than that and a fascinating character as well, but Louisa must have been just a little bit ashamed of him, so she did him over in her book. His Vermont family, poor farmers, had changed their name from Alcock, because of the mildly obscene jokes it inspired. According to Odell Shepherd's biography of him, *Pedlar's Progress,* Bronson had little formal schooling, but his was a good mind with a natural bent toward teaching and philosophy. For a time, after losing his first teaching post, he worked in the South as a peddler, going from one plantation to another. Nothing seems less likely than that the tall, gangling youth should have become a member of Ralph Waldo Emerson's circle, but so it happened, and

Alcott became Emerson's great friend. He had great charm, being good to look at and genuinely unworldly. Thoreau once said of him, "He is the best-natured man I ever met. The cats and mice make their nests in him."

He was good with children, having an unsentimental, patient regard for their intelligence and a turn for fancy, as when he invented a method of teaching them the alphabet by twisting his body to represent the various letters. In 1827 this home-made philosopher married Abigail May of Boston, sister of the Reverend Samuel May who championed the Grimké sisters and, on her mother's side, a descendant of that Judge Samuel Sewall who wrote about his strong-minded daughter and the family friend who stayed in the house belonging to her husband and—as she reminded her spouse—herself. Thus Abba was considered by everyone, including herself, to be Bronson's social superior. She was not pretty. In Shepherd's words: "Her form and her rather large and heavy features suggested strength, persistence, endurance, rather than sprightly grace and charm."

Alcott, teaching in Boston, also wrote and published articles on education which so impressed Reuben Haines, a rich Quaker farmer from Pennsylvania, that he met Alcott and suggested that a school be formed in Germantown with Alcott as head and himself financial guarantor of the project. Haines himself had seven children, and he intended that they should be students there. The Alcotts agreed and moved to Germantown, where their first two daughters, Anna and Louisa, were born, Louisa in 1832. Then Haines died suddenly, the money stopped, and the family perforce moved back to Boston, where Bronson opened the Temple School on Tremont Street.

Louisa's biographer, Katherine Anthony, makes it clear that the education of the Alcott children devolved on Bronson almost exclusively, for, as I have indicated, Abba was not a devoted, home-loving woman, and she didn't like to teach children. She had no patience for the task, whereas Bronson was patient and skillful with infants. Once he wrote a book of practical advice to young mothers, but Emerson dissuaded him from publishing it, fearing it would make the author look ridiculous. He observed his own children and their temperaments, noting that Louisa was "a guileless creature, the child of instinct yet unenlightened by love." For his work at the Temple School he received a good salary—$150 a month, which seemed to him unlimited riches—and he spent much of it making the school elegant and beautiful. Also, as we already know, he employed Elizabeth Peabody and Margaret Fuller as assistants. The third Alcott child,

Betty—Beth in *Little Women*—was named for Miss Peabody. She was the delicate one.

Bronson Alcott's unconventional methods had their opponents, but the Temple School was generally well though of until Miss Martineau wrote derisively of it in her book on America. His champions indignantly pointed out in reply that she had talked with Alcott and watched him at work for only half an hour at most, but her comments planted seeds of doubt in the minds of some of the children's parents, and later criticism of his book, *Conversations with Children on the Gospels,* made matters worse. Then came the row about the mulatto child. In the end of the Temple School closed its doors and the family moved out to Concord, Emerson's town, where the last Alcott child, May, was born.

To earn money, Bronson presided at evening meetings, or "Conversations"—lectures followed by general discussion on philosophical matters. They did not pay well, and the Alcotts were poor. Bronson Alcott had no talent for making or keeping money, and Abba from time to time spoke bitterly to him about his un-American trait of his. "Family straits," he would note resignedly in his journal. Food was scarce, and most of the girls' clothing was supplied by Mrs. Alcott's Boston relatives—old, discarded clothing for grown-up women, which had to be made over. Of course it was Bronson, not Abba, who designed and cut out dresses for his daughters from these garments, taught the children, played with them, wrote letters to them, and often prepared the family meals. Sometimes, too, he actually earned a dollar a day cutting wood.

Emerson kept an eye on his feckless friend and often came to the rescue. In 1842 he did more than that, and sent Bronson to England, ostensibly to broaden his mind, but probably in truth to get him out of the slough of despond. However, though Bronson found in England a group of admirers, pioneers in education who had named their school Alcott House after him, the difficult genius took a dislike to the island empire. He considered it brutal. The English ate too much meat, he said (Alcott was a vegetarian), and killed too many foreigners. He was saddened to see how Englishmen treated their women. His biographer commented, "How could he not have been, coming from a land in which women were regarded as extremely precious creatures and, above all things, 'pure,' into one in which it had long been suspected that they were merely human?"

Alcott was not alone in his opinion on this matter. Other American visitors agreed with him, and claimed that their own compatriots, even the men among them, never indulged in illicit sex at all. Gordon S. Haight cites Emerson, who while visiting London in 1848 asked during the course of an evening with a few eminent English literary gentlemen if prostitution was always as bad in that great city as it appeared to him. He wrote in his journal afterward, "Carlyle and Dickens replied that chastity in the male sex is as good as gone in our times; and in England was so rare that they could name all the exceptions." To which Emerson added, "I assured them that it was not so with us; that, for the most part, young men of good standing and good education, with us, go virgins to their nuptial bed, as truly as their brides." London's prostitutes horrified Bronson too, thronging the city streets as they did, jostling and thrusting each other aside in their greed for clients. As his biographer remarked, the innocent man had no idea that his own Boston possessed at that time more than two hundred brothels. It was not the kind of thing he would have known.

Still, there were those people at Alcott House with whom he could commune, and he saw a good deal of them. They urged him to remain in England and teach; Alcott preferred to go back to Concord, and a compromise was worked out. In September he came home with three new friends: Charles Lane, formerly the editor of a stock-market newspaper, now director of Alcott House; his son William; and a Mr. Henry Wright. The three adults were full of a plan to found a socialist colony to be called "the New Eden." The Alcott females, who were living in Hosmer Cottage, made room somehow for this influx, and the men set to work immediately on various designs, including a complete reorganization of daily life in the cottage, a changeover which did not take place with smoothness.

In fact, it was an extremely troubled winter. Wright did not stay the course and dropped out, but the Lanes remained. One writer has asserted that Charles Lane, whose marriage had gone on the rocks, worked hard to persuade Bronson Alcott to leave Abba and the children, arguing that in socialism family union was out of date. It had given way, he said, to national union, and soon that too would disappear in favor of universal union, in which all lesser relationships would be obliterated. However, he never quite convinced Bronson that this was a correct path to follow, or if he did, his host could not bring himself to do the right thing. Another scholar of the situation believes that Lane fell in love with Abba and she returned his passion, which is why the Alcotts discussed, as they did, the possibility of separation. Or—a third theory—was it a question of love between

Bronson and Lane? Whatever the cause, those months were tense and miserable for the little girls if not for their elders. Everything was different, everything ran on new lines, with Lane teaching the children and Bronson preparing all the meals.

Such an unconventional set-up, with the mother nowhere in running the house and the men all-powerful, may not have distressed Abba, but it was bound to worry Louisa. There she was, familiar with the home lives of her school friends; it must have been agony for her as well as the older girl to feel so out of things, so different. It is no wonder that when she wrote *Little Women* she portrayed a sort of dream house in which everything was conventional and natural. It also explains why in the courtships and engagements of her later books the men respected the girls, the girls begged the men not to drink, and everybody married and lived happily ever after—unless some dear little woman with more feeling than common sense should pay too much for a length of dress material. Dear little woman: all she needed was the gentle moral persuasion of her husband to show her the right way to behave. Nothing less like Abba's relations with Bronson can be imagined, for what is the use of being a writer if you can't build your own heaven on earth?

In the Alcotts' genuine cottage, reality was much more harsh. In the morning every member of the household rose early and sponged himself with cold water, often having to break the ice. The diet was ascetic, without meat or molasses, milk or butter, the last two foodstuffs being prohibited because they were purloined from cows. Even on the chilliest New England morning, breakfast consisted of bread, apples, potatoes, and cold water, eaten by the fire, without plates. Lane wrote proudly to a friend, "The discipline we are now under is that of abstinence in the tongue and hands. We are learning to hold our peace, and to keep our hands from each other's bodies—the ill effects of which we see upon the little baby"—a somewhat garbled passage which seems to mean that talking was frowned on, and that Baby May had been spoiled with too many caresses. The rule of silence was imposed throughout daylight. To give her household an exhaust during these hours, Mrs. Alcott instituted a "post office" through which people could communicate in writing. Perhaps this is how Louisa at ten years old became so fluent with her pen.

With winter at an end at last, the utopians bought a farm not far from Concord, and in June 1843 they moved into the farmhouse. One of their principles was to free domestic animals from bondage—no hauling, no milking, nothing unnatural—so they tried to do the plowing by hand, but it was no use, and they hired a horse for the work. Later they bought a cow and ox and worked them as a team. Even then Fruitlands, as they called their new Eden, did not prosper, possibly because they had started so late in the summer. By December the men admitted that they must abandon the project. Abba and Charles Lane quarreled. The Lanes left, moving to a Quaker colony. Bronson took to his bed and stayed there for weeks, refusing to eat, drink, or talk, until everyone thought he was going to die. But he didn't; in time he got up and resumed living in the world. What was it all about? Nobody seems to know for certain, and the rest of the Lane-Alcott story is equally mysterious. In 1845, when the Alcotts after one of their frequent shifts in residence were settled in a Concord house called Hillside, Abba invited Charles Lane back. He came quite readily, but at the same time Bronson went to New York and stayed there for the duration of the guest's visit—a duration marked by another quarrel between Abba and Lane. This time Lane's exit was permanent. Vague as it all seems, there can be no doubt that his departure was a great relief to the children at least.

It was Hillside that furnished the background to *Little Women*. The Alcotts stayed there for three years, which was a record for them. During this time Louisa grew into a tall, leggy girl of sixteen with no patience for pretty clothes or missish manners. She saw Anna start her own life as a teacher away from home; she herself taught a small class in the barn adjoining the house. She did not care for teaching—like Abba, she lacked patience—but she wrote for one of her pupils, Emerson's daughter, a series of little stories that eventually appeared in her first published book *Flower Fables*. Longing for adventure, she dreamed of becoming successful and rich enough to take care of the family.

Abba too was restless; it was some time since she had gone out to work. Through her Boston relations she became a paid charity worker in that city, and the remaining Alcotts followed. Louisa embarked on wage earning as governess, seamstress, even housemaid. Bronson toured the West, holding "Conversations" and building up a public, and word came from various frontier towns that he was actually making a certain amount of money at last. Despite all these changes, as long as Betty kept house for the Alcotts they had an anchor, and stayed together. But she died of tuberculosis, and Louisa at twenty-five struck out for herself.

The others moved back to Concord, but Louisa lived on in Boston alone in a furnished room. Again she took odd jobs and tried to write, but Elizabeth's death had saddened and made her introspective. She could not get started. Secretly she worried about being a spinster all her life, as seemed likely, until one day at church she heard Theodore Parker preach on the working girls of Boston. The sermon came as a revelation that there were many others like herself, and made her willing to accept facts. She *was* an old maid. Why not?

Then, unexpectedly, her father achieved something that would have been impossible in the old days when the public's memory of Temple School was still fresh: he was made superintendent of schools in Concord, which meant a regular salary and congenial work. He was free to move about from school to school, taking over a class when he felt like it. He was honored instead of jeered at, and when he introduced gymnastics into the curriculum, instead of protesting such a crazy idea the public thought it a fine thing. With the family fortunes so much improved, Louisa allowed herself to go home and take things easier. At Orchard House, where the Alcotts now lived, she had her own writing room in the attic. Like Jo, she wore a special costume when she was there, her "writing suit," a red and green wrapper with cap to match. She began to sell signed stories to the *Atlantic Monthly,* which put her into the front rank of respectable authors.

The Civil War did not at first affect Concord's life very much. Louisa hardly noticed it, because she was hard at work on a novel, but when the end of the book was reached she grew eager to help the cause. There were outlets for ladies who felt like that. She could teach and roll bandages and so on, and for a while she tried to assuage her longing for action in these pursuits, but it was no use: Louisa wanted to go to war personally. In March 1862 she volunteered as a nurse, and was immediately accepted and sent to Georgetown Hospital in Washington. "Bronson Alcott's remark to all and sundry was that he was sending his only son to the war," according to Katherine Anthony.

Louisa was completely untrained as a nurse. To be sure, so were most of her female colleagues, because until then most nurses had been men. It must have been a nightmare to find herself, as she did the minute she arrived, in the thick of things in the casualty ward, just after the battle of Fredericksburg. The wounded were pouring in, and almost as soon as Louisa went on duty a patient died under her hands. Appalled and shocked, she did her best nevertheless, toiling on for four weeks, until she came down with typhoid and Bronson had to come and fetch her home. For a long time her life hung in the balance. Her health never completely recovered, and her once beautiful hair did not grow back properly after it was shaved off, as was the custom for fever patients, but the experience did give her material for a number of articles called *Hospital Sketches,* and they were well received.

She was earning more. It was good to be able to help the Boston aunts pay for May's art lessons at the new School of Design, especially as May showed considerable promise, teaching art and occasionally selling a drawing. Then, before Louisa knew it, it was 1865, the war was over, and everyone was talking of travel. Bronson felt the urge, and quit his post to hit the trail again as a lecturer. At sixty-six, he had an enthusiastic following in the Western states. The wanderlust was catching, and when Louisa was asked by a Boston gentleman to accompany his invalid daughter on a European tour, she eagerly accepted. At Vevey she made friends with a young Pole, romantically thin, tall, good-looking, and delicate, named Ladislas Wisniewski. He was an émigré pianist, thirteen years younger than Louisa, who gave music lessons. Their friendship might reasonably be called love, but if before parting they discussed marriage, which seems probable, the dedicated Louisa refused to consider it. Nevertheless, she never forgot Laddie.

"At twenty-five, girls begin to talk about being old maids, but secretly resolve that they never will; at thirty they say nothing about it, but quietly accept the fact; and, if sensible, console themselves by remembering that they have twenty more useful, happy years in which they may learn to grow old gracefully." (From *Good Wives.*)

It was 1867, and Louisa was earning $500 a year as editor of a children's magazine, when Thomas Niles of the Roberts Brothers publishing house asked her to write a girls' story for them. Miss Alcott was not attracted by the idea and forgot about it for nearly a year, then Niles jogged her elbow again, and she finally got started on *Little Women.* She finished the first part in six weeks and did not think much of it, but showed it to Niles anyway. As the story goes, he was disappoïnted in the manuscript and was in no hurry to bring it out. At last he gave it to a little niece to read, and her rapturous response made him think again. *Little Women* was published several weeks later, during which time Louisa scribbled the second half, or sequel, now known as *Good Wives.* Publication brought immediate success; people went mad for *Little Women.* Mrs. Anthony observed that Louisa Alcott at one bound outstripped every other Concord writer of the period; the fame of Emerson and Thoreau was pale by comparison. What these gentlemen thought of being overshadowed by a female writer of girls' stories is not on record, but Emerson, always the Alcotts' good angel, must have been pleased for Bronson's sake.

A popular indoor recreation was to guess at the source of Miss Alcott's characters in *Little Women.* It was easy to recognize the March family, but Concord people were mystified by Laurie. Where on earth had Louisa found him? When asked, she replied readily: he was Laddie, the Pole of Vevey, whom she had simply transplanted.

She could not believe her prosperity would last, and before she went to Europe for a second time, taking May with her, she considered ways and means carefully, even fearfully. But the journey took place, and May remained in Europe to study when Louisa returned.

At home the woman question and women's rights were being discussed everywhere, and Louisa, as a good New England intellectual, was heartily in favor of them. She visited Vassar, the first college for women in the United States, and amiably signed dozens of autograph albums for the students. She attended the suffrage convention in Syracuse and was mobbed by adoring girls. In New York for the winter of 1875–76, she became immersed in the cause of suffrage and once actually made an impromptu speech about it at a cousin's party. She enjoyed New York and her friends there, Mary Mapes Dodge of *St. Nicholas,* the popular children's magazine, and Jane Cunningham Croly. Mrs. Croly introduced her to Sorosis, America's first women's club, and on New Year's Day, 1876, she persuaded Louisa to help her "receive" at home. On New Year's Day gentlemen always made the rounds, dropping in at each reception for a glass of punch or wine. Only the gentlemen called in this manner; ladies were supposed to stay at home, receiving. In her reminiscences Mrs. Croly's daughter spoke of that day when she was eight years old and Miss Alcott took her on her lap: "The ladies wore full evening dress, the shades were drawn, lights and candles were on, and the rooms crowded most of the time." A most peculiar custom.

Life was not always so frivolous for Louisa: she was drawn more and more into the battle for woman suffrage. In spite of being abnormally shy, she was prevailed on to lead a procession in favor of the cause through the streets of Concord. At a public meeting she demanded that the chairman give seats to the woman-suffrage delegates, which he did. She paid a poll tax expressly to take advantage of a rule that said she could then vote, and she did. She even persuaded the conservative Thomas Niles to publish a history of the suffrage movement.

Her beloved Abba, who had been failing for a long time, died in 1877, just as Bronson was entering into a late blooming and becoming a Grand Old Man. He wrote poetry, he still traveled and lectured, and when he turned eighty his friends opened a summer School of Philosophy in his honor, over which he presided.

Oddly enough May Alcott, who as Amy was the least likable of the sisters in Louisa's books (girl readers simply *hated* Amy because she was a spoiled brat who never got her comeuppance for burning Jo's manuscript), had a fascinating career, not at all on the Alcott pattern. For sheer color she outshone Louisa, and in her sphere was equally successful. May went on living in Paris and made of herself a genuine artist. At least two of her paintings were exhibited in the Paris Salon, and she sold a lot of her work. She was interested in the moderns and became a good friend of Mary Cassatt. At thirty-eight she surprised everyone by marrying a German businessman, Ernst Neiriker, who was twenty-two years old, and explained her action merely by saying that he was beautiful. She added that she intended to prove that one could combine painting and family, and for a season she did so. It was then that her second painting was accepted by the Salon. She wrote a book. She sold more pictures. But she also became pregnant, and childbirth killed her.

Which girl would today's young readers prefer to be—Betty, the self-sacrificing angel who lighted up her small corner and only that corner, only to die quietly in the midst of toiling for her family? Or the dashing, talented May who broke away from New England and made beautiful pictures in Paris, and had her hour of glory? No wonder Louisa Alcott played down May's career and played up Betty's. May did not at all fit into her scheme of what was right for a little woman.

Bronson Alcott lived on and on and on, until March 4, 1888, when the ancient philosopher died. Louisa, the only remaining daughter, hung on just long enough to survive him, submitting to death two days later. She was a woman who knew her duty and did it.

CHAPTER 11

Utopia

ECCENTRIC AS BRONSON ALCOTT AND CHARLES LANE may appear today, we have no right to laugh at them, considering that we too live in an age of communes, of attempts to live the good life all together. Our forefathers didn't use the word "commune" in the same context that our children do, but they had the root of the matter in them. Frances Wright with her Nashoba, Alcott with his Fruitlands—what's the difference? They were not the only examples. Here and there at far-flung points of the country, many others were seeing visions and dreaming dreams of building Jerusalem in America's green and pleasant land.

The only trouble with the picture—the only glaring discrepancy—is that it takes two sexes to make an earthly paradise, and in most utopias of the nineteenth century the enthusiasm of the women who participated seems strangely muted; no woman's voice is heard uplifted in praise. Few complained, either. It is just that they were silent, possibly because they had no time to talk, since being a female in utopia was an all-day, full-time job. Inside or outside, the ladies prepared the food, and in most cases—with a few honorable exceptions—they tended the children. While the men worked in the fields and all that, the women ran the houses or cabins or tents, raised and cooked vegetables, wove cloth and made clothes out of it, and did the little odd jobs that could be done without machinery, such as pounding nuts—if the group was vegetarian—for the main meal. Camping out is fun for men. Is it quite as amusing for the ladies? They did not say, and we shall never know, but their silence is suggestive.

Outside utopia, in the world of ordinary affairs, some of the women were making themselves heard in the only manner open to them, by petition. In the nineteenth century the petition had a peculiar importance hard for us to appreciate. Not only did it serve enfranchised minorities as a means of protest; it was also the only possible way for women, who could not vote at all, to get in touch with the government. Petitions carried no legal weight, but, in theory at least, they had some effect in that elected representatives were thus kept informed of the public temper. The Anti-Slavery Association, which provided the first genuine political organization in which women could participate, also gave them the information, opportunity, and encouragement to employ petitioning on a grand scale, and as a result the activity reached heights never before known in the country. As the papers flowed into Washington, Southern congressmen feared they might be snowed under, and in 1845 they persuaded the House of Representatives to pass the so-called Pinckney Gag Rule forbidding any presentation of petitions in the House.

This outright denial of traditional rights stimulated the Representative for Plymouth, John Quincy Adams—son of Abigail Adams—to take up the cause of the petitioners. He got his chance to be heard when Congressman Benjamin Chew Howard of Maryland made a speech on the subject, a textbook oration full of antifeminist clichés. Howard confessed that he always felt regret when these petitions relating to political matters and signed by women were presented in the House. Surely women had sufficient field for the exercise of influence in the discharge of their duties to their fathers, husbands, and children, without rushing into the fierce struggle of political life? He could not help feeling sorrow at this departure from woman's proper sphere, in which there was abundant room for the practice of the most extensive benevolence and philanthropy.

Adams' rejoinder was sharp and angry. "Why does it follow that women are fitted for nothing but the cares of domestic life, for bearing children and cooking the food of a family, devoting all their time to the domestic circle—to promoting the immediate personal comfort of their husbands, brothers and son?" he demanded. The mere departure of a woman from her home duties, if done in good cause, was a virtue rather than a reproach to her, and he questioned an assertion made by Howard that women had no right to petition because they had no vote. Adams might have been right on this, but so might Howard. It was not a clear point in law.

Meantime, hundreds of women collected thousands of petitions and sent them to Washington in an unending stream of sheets of paper, all filled in. These women came from all classes, but they had at least one thing in common, a desire to make their wishes felt in the only way they could. Perhaps the most remarkable thing about their gigantic effort is that many of them could ill afford the time or energy to do it, because they belonged to a world ignored, never mentioned by, Congressman Howard: they were women who, whatever their proper sphere might be, had to work outside it for their livings. The fact is that in the first half of the century females in America worked at more than a hundred different occupations, usually, as Sarah Grimké noted in a study, for much less money than men earned at the same jobs. In tailoring, for instance, a man was paid two or three times as much for making a waistcoat or pantaloons as a woman who did the same task just as well. In 1855 female houseworkers earned $1.25 a week at the most: childless women might get on the average $58.50 a year, but a woman with young children, because she could not concentrate so well on the job, got only $36.40. Comparisons with the wages of men for similar jobs are impossible, since men never did such work, but it was undeniably low pay. Only necessity could persuade a woman to go out on domestic work.

Not all women accepted these conditions in silent stoicism. Factory employees, at least, tried to improve their lot. In the 1830s groups such as the United Tailoresses Society of New York and the Lady Shoe Binders of Lynn, Massachusetts, tried to organize female workers, but they didn't have much idea of how to go about it, and the men who worked alongside them feared competition and discouraged them at every opportunity. Mill workers were slightly better off, but not much. A typical mill factory was kept at work from sun-up to lighting-up time, as much as sixteen hours a day. In Paterson, New Jersey, women and children had to report for work at 4:30 A.M. and go on as long as they could see, with time off only for breakfast and dinner, until in 1835 they struck for shorter hours; after that their day was limited to a mere twelve hours. Women's wages at the mills, as at other factories, were always less than those of the men by as much as one to three dollars a week, and the women also had to pay their board in the company-owned or -leased houses where they lived. During a trade depression in the 1830s their wages were cut, while at the same time work was speeded up.

The earliest women's strike on record took place in 1824 at a factory in Pawtucket, Rhode Island. All the employees of both sexes struck to get pay cuts restored and working hours reduced, but the women held their meetings apart from the men. It was not a successful action. A more professional walkout was staged at Lowell, Massachusetts, in 1834, when one of the girls was fired. By prearrangement, all the others, sitting at their looms, watched her as she went out into the yard, and when she tossed her bonnet into the air, they left their places and joined her in a protest meeting outside. After that such outbreaks became fairly common in mill towns, but were seldom effective. The women had not yet grasped the principle of organization, and sooner or later they were forced by privation to go back to work without having won any advantages. In December 1844 five Lowell mill girls, meeting at night to discuss methods by which they might gain a ten-hour day, organized the Female Labor Reform Association. Within six months the association had six-hundred members, headed by a president named Sarah Bagley, a determined, able woman. She organized sister associations in neighboring mill towns and taught the girls to fight for their rights, until in 1846 three of her lieutenants became directors, in company with five men, of the New England Labor Reform League. The eight officers trained mill girls how to apply their combined strength, so that when the manager of a large mill in Lowell tried to increase the work load and cut pay at the same time, almost every woman worker in the mill signed a pledge not to accept the increased load without a corresponding increase in pay. And they quietly stuck to the pledge, working just so much and no more—working to rule, as it were—until the speed-up was canceled.

Again in Massachusetts, a petition campaign to reduce working hours in the mills to ten a day was so well supported that the state legislature appointed a committee to investigate general working conditions in the mills. The owners and their friends in government were confident that witnesses from the ranks would never dare to testify for fear of losing their jobs. They were mistaken, for plenty of women gave damaging testimony against the owners, but in the end the girls did not get their ten-hour day in spite of all: the committee was prejudiced in the owners' favor, and decided against the petitioners. The committee chairman, a newspaper publisher, was especially angered with Sarah Bagley and her association because they had helped defeat his bid for election to the state government, and his paper smeared Miss Bagley, discrediting her until she was forced to retire. (Nothing more was heard of her for years, until she turned up again as the first woman telegraphist.) Sarah Bagley was exceptional. Most female factory workers had no energy left after work to do more than take care of their families and houses.

Mill and factory girls, as wage earners, were naturally more aware of the feminist cause than were middle-class stay-at-home women. There is nothing like security to keep the mind inactive. The non-working women were trained to occupy themselves with romance, marriage, and motherhood. But now and then when romance went sour, or when marriage and motherhood were threatened by a husband's drinking, open infidelity, gambling, or some other form of improvidence, women who depended completely upon men began to think about their position and wonder if independence might not be better. Thinking was as far as most of them got, but there were exceptions to the average in both middle-class and working-class life. I have noted some of the individuals who broke away; there were others too who sought change and improvement in communal living.

The list of such communal experiments is a long one, but probably the first in America was the Shaker sect, which originated in England. The Shakers' habits, especially their adherence to celibacy, made them objects of general curiosity and also, of course, condemned them to disappearance within a generation or two, but they were followed by a large number of less esoteric groups of utopians. The most famous annalist of these communities, John Humphrey Noyes, dubbed them "socialisms," and included his own in the list. I have mentioned the Raritan Bay Union in New Jersey, Brook Farm near Boston, and Alcott's Fruitlands. There was also an earlier community than any of these, founded by Robert Owen, a British manufacturer who made a fortune in England and introduced a system of reformed industrial relations, then came to America to put certain idealistic theories into practice. Owen's colony at New Harmony, Indiana, where for a time Frances Wright lived and worked, has been mentioned. In his inaugural address on July 4, 1826, he spoke of "the three villainous powers that plague mankind," and named them as private property, irrational religion—and marriage.

The communities, or "communisms," or "associations" that followed his were almost all short-lived. One, of course, was Frances Wright's subsidiary experiment at Nashoba. Owen's children were more lasting monuments to him than was New Harmony. His son Robert Dale Owen, he who worked with Frances Wright on the *Free Enquirer,* also interested himself in birth control and wrote of it in a book entitled *Moral Philosophy.* He was responsible for a new law in Indiana that assured married women control of their property, and through other legislation he helped to ease the divorce laws in that state. The members of most utopias were preoccupied with marriage affairs as well as those having to do with property. Even Brook Farm—though it is hard to think of Transcendentalists spending so much time on the subject of sexual relations—did so.

Of the more influential utopian colonies, New Harmony was one of the longer-lived, but in time it broke up in disharmony. Josiah Warren, an observer of its last days, came to dislike Owen's theories but believed that some kind of utopia was very desirable. For some years he moved about and lectured, until in 1851 he landed in the village of Hard Times, Long Island, and gathered about him enough adherents to found a settlement based on what he called Individual Sovereignty. Two people there, who believed firmly in Individual Sovereignty, were Dr. Thomas Low Nichols and his wife, Mary. They extended Warren's sovereignty to include free choice of sexual partners, recommending what was called for the first time Free Love. Both Nicholses were quite serious people. In the eyes of the public they were scientists, being hydrotherapists, spiritualists, as well as—it goes almost without saying—vegetarians. Like Robert Owen, they were opposed to legal marriage and thought that sexual partnerships ought not to be permanent even though they were themselves legally married. They were also Fourierists, or followers of Charles Fourier, a French socialist who urged the reorganization of society through groups called phalanxes. Fourier's ideas were much in vogue in America just then, and had been taken up by such prominent men as Albert Brisbane and Horace Greeley. The Nicholses believed that the sexual act should be the source of the most exquisite enjoyment and that such natural passions should not be repressed. In a book published in 1853, *Esoteric Anthropology,* the doctor furnished a list of people he called "affinity-seekers," complete with names and addresses. One does not expect to find this sort of thing in the Victorian era, but there it is.

Josiah Warren may not have agreed with all the Nichols' theories, but in accord with his philosophy he allowed them to go their own way, and people outside naturally took a lively interest in the *outré* goings-on in the colony. A newspaper reporter visited Hard Times and chatted with some of the inhabitants, one of whom told him that they did not believe in association and in fact were not Fourierites at all. They believed in the sovereignty of the individual, which was quite another thing. Yes, he answered to another question, they had schools, in a manner of speaking, a sort of primary affair for small children. The next inevitable question was about the women of the community. "Well, in regard to the ladies, we let them do about as they please, and they generally please to do about right,'' said the inhabitant. ''Yes, they *like* the idea of individual sovereignty.'' He added that the ladies had plenty of amusement—social parties, music, dancing, sports. They were not all ''Bloomers,'' he said, referring to the baggy trouser outfits that had been adopted by some of the modern females; they wore whatever they liked.

''And the breeches sometimes, I suppose?'' asked the reporter.

''Certainly they can wear the breeches if they choose,'' was the reply.

Questioned about marriage, the inhabitant gave a full answer: ''Oh, marriage! Well, folks ask no questions in regard to *that* among us. We, or at least some of us, do not believe in life-partnerships, when the parties cannot live happily.'' Everyone was supposed to know what was best for him or her individually, and others did not interfere. There was no curiosity, no nosing about.

Hard Times was not unique in its loyalty to the conception of free love. The Skaneateles Community of Massachusetts, founded in 1843, though devoted chiefly to abolition, approved also of a certain amount of sexual freedom—only a certain amount, however, the members deprecating ''concubinage, licentiousness, adultery, bigamy, and polygamy.'' What was left consisted of a form of easy divorce, the colonists believing that since marriage was designed for happiness and to promote love and virtue, when people had outlived their affections and could no longer contribute to their partner's happiness, the sooner separation took place the better; nor was there any reason why separated people should not marry again.

It seems to have been a firm rule that diet reform went hand in hand with sex reform. It will be remembered that Bronson Alcott's socialist friends, especially Charles Lane, held to both kinds of idealism, making up in the fervor of extreme vegetarianism what they might have lacked in other directions. The diet principles of Skaneateles were specific. A vegetable and fruit diet was essential to the health of the body, purity of the mind, and general happiness of society; ''therefore, the killing and eating of animals is essentially wrong, and should be renounced as soon as possible, together with the use of all narcotics and stimulants.'' This last provision was put in because narcotics and stimulants were considered sexually exciting, and in spite of all their talk about wedded happiness, the utopians obviously felt that sexual proclivities needed no encouragement. For the rest, various visitors to the colony reported that the inhabitants had their own individual ideas about what was right or wrong in eating. Some ate only boiled wheat and lived apart from the others in a shanty in the woods, where they could feel nearer to nature. One observer from outside, who had been fed bread, butter, and tea for his supper, at breakfast witnessed people eating only bread and milk, or bread and molasses. But there were others who did not stick to this regimen. At a later meal a plate of meat stood on the table, and the visitor overheard a conversation about it between two of the faithful, who evidently did not approve. One of the men said he guessed that the meat eaters had been to some graveyard, to which the other replied that he did not eat dead creatures.

"The No-God, No-Government, No-Marriage, No-Money, No-Meat, No-Salt, No-Pepper system" was the unflattering name bestowed on Skaneateles by a couple of visiting Fourierites. But if they had wished, they could have found plenty of communities where the members were equally self-denying, such as the Prairie Home Community near West Liberty, Ohio, where according to another visitor the idea of a good dinner was coarse brown bread, large unpeeled potatoes, potato soup, and melons for afters. At table on that occasion the stranger salted his potatoes, and one of the regular inmates remarked that if he would refrain from using salt, he would find his sense of taste much improved. The visitor then realized that little salt had been put on the table, and nobody else used it. He saw no "animal food" whatever except milk, which only one or two people touched. Several members followed Sylvester Graham's diet of whole wheat flour, and so on. A second meal at Prairie Home was composed of the same victuals with the addition of apples and apple butter. One rebel, however, kept three pigs, because, as he said frankly, he liked a bit of meat. Nobody objected to this, but few of the others were of his mind.

Ultimately, vegetarianism and the use of Graham flour spread even into Fourierist colonies, or, as they were called, phalanxes. A letter from a member of the Wisconsin Phalanx, dated August 1847, states with pride that thanks to some excellent and interesting articles on cannibalism, the prevailing tendency there was to abandon the use of animal food altogether.

The utopian preoccupation with diet is explained by Stephen Nissenbaum, a sociologist at the University of Wisconsin, as a precaution against what was considered the wrong kind of sexual satisfaction, which the community believed had no connection with the spiritual love of which they approved. They became obsessed with dreadful visions of bodies out of control, of "unbridled lust, drunkenness, rage," and they relentlessly condemned all stimulants that were thought to induce such conditions—not only liquor, tobacco, tea and coffee, spices and drugs, but even meat, custard, and other so-called rich foods. It was thought that the digestive and nervous systems were closely connected with the easily aroused sexual apparatus. Naturally, of all these proscribed stimulants, liquor was considered the worst, and the most powerful image temperance reformers presented to the public was that of the drunken husband taking unspeakable sexual advantage of his hapless wife.

Which makes it hard to understand that in spite of all the anxiety expressed by members of this and that idealistic community on behalf of such defenseless females, the position of women inside the settlement was not far distant from that of their more conservative sisters outside. Those huge if vegetarian meals at the Prairie Home, for example, were prepared by women and girls. The same eyewitness described how he found the ladies, having already prepared the meal and set the table, hard at work sorting wool. At least one other observer noticed that the status of women had been unchanged at the North American Phalanx, in Red Bank, New Jersey. The most successful of Fourierist communities and the favorite of Brisbane and Greeley, it lasted for a record eleven years, then at last split up in 1853. Looking back, the anonymous writer of an article published in the New York *Tribune* of November 3, 1866, "Post Mortem and Requiem by a Fourierist," said: "There was a public table where all meals were eaten. At first there was a lack of convenience, and there was much hard work. Afterwards there were proper conveniences; but they did not prevent the purchase of hair-dye [i.e., the women went white with worry]. The idea that woman in Association was to be relieved of many cares was not realized."

Alas no, this idea has not even yet been realized. Nineteenth-century Christian missionaries who spread the gospel in the Far East had what they considered a solution to this problem and its ramifications: woman's position would never be secure, let alone improved, they said, until monogamy was the firm rule everywhere, in all nations all over the world. They failed to show, unfortunately, how this change might be accomplished. In the meantime, the utopian assertion, that the only answer to the woman question was freedom from marriage, persisted in spite of stubborn facts.

We would expect Charles Lane to have much to say on marriage, and he has not disappointed us. In the *Dial* for January 1844 he published an article expressing the philosophy—which had so nearly destroyed the Alcott marriage—that socialism's great problem was whether the existence of the "marital family" was consistent with that of the "universal family" or community. He enlarged on this statement: the maternal instinct was so strongly in favor of the separate fireside that association, though it appeared beautiful to the young unattached soul, had accomplished little progress in the affections of mothers. A mother will always sacrifice the good of the community to her own immediate family, he asserted, so family life and "associative" life cannot exist together, and, in Lane's opinion, it was family life that should be sacrificed. In support of this thesis he referred to Fourierism. Fourierists, observed Lane, scarcely mentioned marriage, a fact he considered significant. "Fourierists . . . are acute and eloquent in deploring Woman's oppressed and degraded position in past and present times, but are almost silent as to the future," he wrote. Considering women's stubbornly myopic attitude toward their young, Lane implied, their position in the future had better be even less powerful, or goodness knew what would happen to mankind.

In *The Present,* a Brook Farm publication of 1844, Lane further developed his favorite thesis, The Family Must Go, deprecating the American custom according to which a young, newly married couple leave the old folks and set up a new household of two. A wasteful, foolish habit, said Lane. The pressing necessities found in isolated families, the great advantage to be gained in even the smallest union of perhaps two or three families, seemed obvious to him. Yet young people stubbornly refused to unite. Lane asked rhetorically: "Is there some secret leaven in this conjugal mixture, which declares all other union to be out of the possible affinities?" A divided heart, he asserted, is an impossibility: "We must either serve the universal (God), or the individual (Mammon)." Marriage is an individual act, not a universal—an individual act of a depreciated and selfish kind. One's spouse is an expansion and enlargement of one's self, and so are the children.

"The all-absorbent influence of this union is too obvious to be dwelt upon," said Lane. "It is used to justify every glaring and cruel act of selfish acquisition." Indeed, such union was the groundwork of the institution of property, which itself, of course, is the source of many evils, an institution which could not and would not be repealed as long as marital unions were indulged in.

Lane was so convincing and reasonable about the evils of marriage that it is hard to understand why he himself married a few years later. And for the second time, at that.

Lane was not alone in these antiunion ideas; far from it. The century saw the development of a spate of colonies based on similar philosophies. In *The History of American Socialisms,* the nineteenth-century annalist John Humphrey Noyes naturally gave pride of place to his own Oneida Community, which he founded in New York State in 1848. But his view was not distorted by chauvinism. Oneida *was* unique for several reasons. For one thing, it was long-lived: in what is admittedly a different form, it still exists.

Noyes, who was thirty-seven when he laid the foundations of his colony, was a Dartmouth graduate and had read law and theology at Andover and Yale. His background was conventional upper middle class—father a congressman for Vermont, mother a member of the family of Rutherford B. Hayes. Yet, as the author of the book's introduction fairly comments, he was one of the most extreme revolutionaries ever produced by Western civilization, and what he attacked was our accepted sexual morality.

Granted a few rather way-out premises, the system he offered in its place was logically worked out. Noyes argued that the second advent of Christ had already occurred, in 70 A.D.; ergo, the Kingdom of Heaven is here and now, established on earth for all true believers. In the kingdom there is no exclusive possession, in goods or marriage. Every man is married, as it were, to every woman. What Noyes called complex marriage was the rule at Oneida, but that does not mean it was a sexual free-for-all: there were certain rules. According to Noyes's theory, there are two functions in sexual intercourse, separate and distinct—the propagative and the amative. The propagative function, the orgasm, must not be permitted to jeopardize the amative function, which he saw as a purely social affair. Amative sexual intercourse was supposed to last for several hours without orgasm on the part of either partner; to make this possible, once the copulative position had been assumed neither partner should move. Noyes called this practice male continence. It is generally known as *coitus reservatus,* or today, after a more modern sponsor, *karezza.*

Considering these rather onerous regulations, the Oneida Community cannot be said to have approved of *free* love. But in the course of its history through the years it did abolish monogamous marriage, probably through the agency of Noyes himself, and for a particular reason. He had a wife and children, but a time came when he was strongly attracted to another woman in the community, Mary Craigin. Noyes called a meeting of all the persons involved—his wife Harriet, Mary Craigin, and Mary's husband George—to talk it over. After the initial shock, all agreed that he and Mary should marry, and so the rearrangement took place. A similar marital adjustment was promptly adopted by other members of the colony, until in the end it was decided to do without marriage altogether, and mutual attraction led to relationships that were fervent but not necessarily long-lasting. The resulting children were brought up apart from their parents, in the "Children's House," where they were looked upon as everyone's offspring and had as many parents as there were adults in the community. Interestingly, they grew up to be fine specimens of humanity. The collective parents were reasonably fond of them, it seems, but there were no Mrs. Portnoys. The chief witness to these facts is Pierrepont Noyes, a son of John Humphrey who grew up in the Children's House and in retrospect obviously felt no rancor. He wrote: "None of these fathers and mothers . . . had, as I am convinced, any great affection for us individually." This was not a complaint, just a statement of fact.

The elder Noyes was in favor of equal rights for women, and his theories on how to achieve this equality have a modern ring. He said that woman's dress in the ordinary world was immodest because it tended to convert her into a sexual object; she should cut her hair short and dress as much like a man as possible. In this way, he wrote, she "becomes as she ought to be, a female man." And he had firm ideas, as one would expect, about the education of the communal children, who should be brought up without selfish desires for property of any sort. His dictum was obeyed, as Pierrepont reported:

"A review of my early psychology confirms a suspicion I have long entertained, that the desire for exclusive ownership of things is not a primal human instinct. . . . Did primeval man have anything he called his own except food which he devoured as fast as he could?" Musing on the general philosophy of his father's group, he continued: "These Perfectionists adopted communism of property to eliminate material self-seeking; they dressed in simple clothes, tabooed jewelry, and the women cut their hair short to eliminate vanity; they arranged that every member should take his or her turn at the humblest kind of labor to eliminate the selfishness of pride and power; they abolished marriage to do away with the selfishness of love."

Unlike most of the other nineteenth-century socialist communities, Noyes's paradise endured. It never entirely disappeared, but suffered a change that brought it into line with the world he had eschewed. The entering wedge was the outcry brought down on the Oneidists' heads by their renunciation of marriage. Continued criticism on this score forced them eventually to revert to monogamy, and with monogamy—at least, so say the champions of old-style Oneida—came the concept of private property in other walks of life as well. Charles Lane would have said that selfishness in love leads inevitably to hankering after worldly goods, and he might be right in saying so. In any case, the members of the community began making money from the manufacture of fine silverware, and after a time Oneida was transformed into a conventional, hard-working, money-grubbing settlement of nuclear families.

Another utopia was, of course, that of the Mormons. It is doubtful if the church's founder, Joseph Smith, was an idealist on the order of John Humphrey Noyes, though he too renounced monogamy because of personal reasons. Smith's wife was unable to produce healthy, living infants, and he wanted lots of children. Ready to hand was the Bible with its accounts of ancient Jewish patriarchs and their polygamous customs, and Smith decided that the Latter-Day Saints must emulate those worthies in marriage customs as in other matters. Fortunately, he soon had a message from God to this effect, in 1843, and promptly took to himself—though in secret—many wives. Plural marriage, as the Mormons called polygamy, was then practiced by many of the other Saints—also secretly, however. It is an interesting sidelight on their history that Mrs. Smith was one of the last to know about the innovation, and when she did find out she raised hell. She made Joseph send all but two of the ladies back where they came from, but having been allowed those two exceptions, Smith later was able to rebuild his collection to its former size. By the time he met his violent death in 1844 he had twenty-five wives. His argument was that plural marriage was better for women than monogamy because it exalted them all equally; all women could now marry and have children, and those two banes of their existence, prostitution and spinsterhood, would vanish.

It was Smith's successor, Brigham Young, who introduced open plural marriage to the Mormons, in 1852. They seem to have liked it; at any rate, they held on to the custom until they were forced to give it up in 1882, when a national law was passed making polygamy illegal anywhere in the country. The most noteworthy fact about the whole business, it seems to me, is that nearly all the women concerned seem to have accepted plural marriage with equanimity if not enthusiasm. I say "seem to have" because we have incomplete records on what went on in polygamous households back before 1882. It stands to reason that there must have been the occasional fight, but as far as written records show, with the exception of the first Mrs. Smith, Mormon women did not object to polygamy. I have noticed a similar attitude in polygamous countries I have visited where Islam is the state religion; I have often wondered if jealousy is not to a large extent a question of face, as the Chinese put it. If everybody does it, the women may feel that they have nothing to be ashamed of or to resent. Then, too, there is the fact that it's fun to have company around the house—and many hands make light work.

CHAPTER 12

To Be in Silence

REFORMERS IN THE NINETEENTH CENTURY concerned themselves with a number of what sometimes seem to us widely different causes: slavery, women's rights, sexual morals, diet, and dress. Yet if we pause to think about it, they are all related. The women saw many parallels between their position and that of slaves, and their connection with sexual morals is obvious. Dress is connected with both morals and health. What diet has to do with women's rights is less apparent, but religious people are often preoccupied with what they eat, and women, who prepare the food and watch over their men's health, are closely concerned with diet and, especially, drink. In fact, in the nineteenth century they were so interested—usually in a negative sense—in alcohol that it is almost impossible to disentangle the cause of temperance from that of women's rights. Some unregenerate drinkers declared that temperance was embraced by females because so many of these came from New England and were temperamentally averse to convivial jollity.

It was not so simple as that. Drunkenness was a very real threat, especially to the wives of workingmen, but practically all classes of Americans did a good deal of drinking. A surprising note comes from Lyman Beecher, father of Harriet Beecher Stowe and Henry Ward Beecher, who remembered his mild astonishment when, at the age of thirty-five, he went to Litchfield, Connecticut, to serve as Congregational minister. At the first two ordinations he attended, the reverend members drank heavily and the ministerial society actually furnished the drinks. "The side-board with the spillings of water and sugar and liquor looked and smelled like the bar of a very active grog-shop," he later commented. None of the ministers was really drunk, he added, but they were considerably exhilarated. Beecher did not approve.

Liquor was cheap. Account books kept early in the century in Woodbridge, Connecticut, provide some interesting comparisons in prices. In 1804 half a barrel of flour was about the same price as three gallons of brandy, and half a barrel of cider was cheaper. Other entries indicate sales to an innkeeper in New Haven, who seemed to buy enormous quantities of rum, which was also cheaper than brandy; it came from Jamaica. As for whiskey, a lot of people made that at home without benefit of license. A biographer of Amelia Bloomer has pointed out that in the towns especially, workmen insisted on being paid in part with hard liquor, and when the men left their work places on payday many of them went straight to the always handy neighborhood saloon to spend their money on more drink. Some also squandered the wages earned by their wives. The women and children went cold and hungry and were often victims of drunken brutality when the men at last came home. Of course, even some rich women had husbands who drank too much, but for the rich there was at least the remedy of legal separation or divorce, measures beyond the means of the poor. All in all, temperance workers could not exaggerate the evils of drink. Where they made their mistake was in supposing that simple legislation could rid a nation of alcohol.

Then there was the reform of women's dress. Noyes, as we have seen, was interested in the subject, but he was not the only one to think of it; to anybody with an eye to health, women's fashions were taking a turn decidedly for the worse. Skirts were long, full, and as a consequence heavy. Waists were supposed to be tiny, so would-be stylish women pulled themselves in as far as they could bear. Trussed up until she was unable to breathe, yet carrying a unwieldy load of fabric that picked up dirt wherever she might walk, the fashion plate of the midcentury was a model of self-imposed torture, and reformers decided that something must be done for the poor fool.

As one might expect, the Oneidists were in the forefront of the movement to make women wear sensible clothing, and neither should it surprise anyone that the Grimké sisters should be among the first to try out the new reform style of bloomers. Bloomers were an admission that women too are bifurcated, but in this writer's opinion it was not this implication that attracted the attention of the public: it was that they were something new in clothing, and any change in female fashions always gets a lot of attention in the press. Perhaps the press is not as frivolous in this as it seems. Perhaps changes in fashion do represent deep alterations in a country's philosophy. Women, after all, *are* bifurcated, and it may have been a good idea to remind people of the fact. In our generation female agitators wear jeans almost as a uniform, and the idea has grown until other women, while reluctant to sacrifice the appearance of expensive chic, have adopted it so far as to wear pants suits that obviously cost more, yet afford just as much freedom. Then there was the jettisoning of the bra, symbol of constriction and all the rest of it . . . But we are jumping ahead of ourselves.

A new excitement in women's fight to escape the smothering atmosphere of their times started in 1840 in London, where two remarkable American females, Lucretia Mott and Elizabeth Cady Stanton, were victims of crass discrimination when they attended the World Anti-Slavery Convention and were not permitted to sit with the other delegates because of their sex. Mrs. Mott, it will be remembered, was that lady whose superior status among the Philadelphia Quakers was such a bitter pill for Sarah Grimké to swallow. Unlike poor Sarah, Lucretia Coffin was born a Quaker, in Nantucket, in 1793. As a schoolteacher she was not long in learning that she was automatically paid much less than a man would have been in the same post, and she resented the injustice of the situation. She married James Mott, settled in Philadelphia, and at the age of twenty-eight was ordained a minister. She became widely known and respected as a speaker, and gave more and more of her time on the platform to abolition.

Elizabeth Cady, who was a co-worker of Lucretia Mott's in the cause of feminism, was born in Johnstown, New York, in 1815. Her father was a judge there and, for a time, a congressman as well. From early youth the girl was aware of the inequities of marriage, because she sat in the corner of her father's office and heard the complaints of the women who came to him for advice. His library was there for her to read, and the child became indignant when she learned in this way that, as she put it, "marriage makes the husband and wife one person, and that person is the husband." She was referring to the laws that made a woman's property automatically pass to her husband as soon as the couple were married, that prevent a woman bearing witness against her husband in a court of law on the grounds that she would thereby be testifying against herself, and many other anomalies, some of which can still be found, growing out of this concept of a wife's identity.

Obviously a married woman is *not* the same person as her husband, reflected Elizabeth, as she considered the injustices of the law.

For instance, in every state but Ohio a married woman was not allowed to make a will. Wife beating was legal. But to Elizabeth the most shocking fact of all was that a woman, even before she married, even if she was only betrothed, became "virtually the property of the man," to quote the law book, and no gift or deed executed by her between the period of her acceptance of a man's offer of marriage and the marriage itself was held to be valid, "for were she permitted to give away or otherwise settle her property, he might be disappointed in the wealth he looked to in making the offer." Elizabeth's feeling of shock and outrage did not abate with time. Something must be done, she decided, to change all that, and she herself would do it.

Her only brother died, and Judge Cady lamented the fact that she was not a boy, which aroused Elizabeth to do her best and try to emulate the son she ought to have been. She practiced riding until she was an expert horsewoman, and at school studied such unfeminine subjects as higher mathematics and the classics. At first she did not question the religious beliefs in which she was reared; as an adolescent she was leader of the Presbyterian Girls' Club. One of the girls proposed that the club pay for the training of a student at the nearby Auburn Theological Seminary. It was an ordinary sort of thing: many girls' clubs did this, the members arranging concerts, bazaars, and cake sales to raise the money to pay some theological student's tuition. The Johnstown club successfully carried out this program, and when the selected student was to graduate they even scraped up the money to buy him a new suit. Then they invited him to come and preach a sermon at their church. The new young minister came arrayed in the new suit, all trained and prepared through their efforts, and preached his sermon. He did not utter a word of thanks to the girls, but gave as his text a verse from Timothy: "But I suffer not a woman to teach, nor to usurp authority over the man, but to be in silence."

Elizabeth stood up, signaled the other girls to do likewise, and led the club straight out of the building.

In 1840 she married Henry B. Stanton, ten years older than herself, an active abolitionist as well as businessman. The pair went to Europe for their honeymoon, arranging to take in the World Anti-Slavery Convention in London on the way. Among other Americans aboard ship, also aiming for the convention, was Lucretia Mott, traveling with her husband, and by the time the ship weighed anchor on the other side, Elizabeth and Lucretia were firm friends. They disembarked in happy ignorance that in London a storm was blowing up over them. None of the convention's organizers had envisaged the possibility that women would want to attend the sessions, and they were horrified to hear that at least nine women were on the way from America on that ship, all aiming for the hall.

In fact they were merely delegates coming, like the men, to listen to orators speak about slavery and how to abolish it, many of them innocent wives of delegates who wanted to know what was going on. They were *peaceful* women. But the British abolitionists had the idea that any woman interested in such a masculine matter as abolition was bound to be a dangerous revolutionary. Evidently they envisaged a party of maenads who intended to wreck the proceedings. It is difficult nowadays to appreciate or comprehend their fears, but in their English way they were afraid of scenes, and strange shenanigans followed.

To begin with, the secretary of the British and Foreign Anti-Slavery Society came to call on the ladies at their hotel before the opening session to beg them to stay away. The ladies would not consent to stay away, but went to the meeting in company with two Englishwomen, Elizabeth Fry, reformer and Quaker, and Lady Byron, the poet's strong-minded widow, who was an accomplished mathematician. They were witnesses to the violent argument that raged on the subject of their presence. They heard American clergymen shouting, "Turn out the women!" They heard an English clergyman, the Reverend J. Burnet, passionately insist that it would be better to dissolve the convention than allow women to take part. In their hearing, the Reverend Henry Grew of Philadelphia declared that the presence of women would be a violation of the ordinances of Almighty God. Then they heard—and saw—the question put to a vote, when a resounding majority repeated, in effect, the clergymen's demand, "Turn out the women!"

But the women could not be turned out without force, and this measure daunted even the Reverend Henry Grew, so a compromise was reached. The ladies were asked to sit in a curtained recess in the hall, a sort of purdah to contain such dangerous radicals as Mrs. Mott, Elizabeth Fry, and the young bride, Mrs. Stanton. William Lloyd Garrison arrived in England too late to register a personal protest against the insults, but when he heard the story he flatly refused to sit on the platform or take part otherwise in the convention proceedings.

It goes without saying that Mrs. Mott and Mrs. Stanton talked about the matter at length, and by the time the fireworks of the convention were over they had agreed that they must get to work immediately on a program for women's rights. They planned a Women's Rights Convention in America, but for some years nothing definite was done about it, chiefly because Mrs. Stanton was caught up in housekeeping and childbearing, with no time for extramural activity. Henry's interests of course came first. For a time he studied law, then, having been admitted to the bar in 1843, he took his family to live in Boston. Elizabeth managed during their stay in the Massachusetts city at least to keep in touch with the movement. She often visited her father and managed to do a little work agitating for a Married Women's Property Bill in New York, which as a matter of fact became law in 1848. By that time, however, the Stantons had moved. Henry's health suffered in the Boston winters, so in 1847 the family went to live in Seneca Falls, New York, a pretty little town on one of the Finger Lakes, where in time Elizabeth was to bear four or five more children. (Oddly enough, none of her biographers has actually settled the question of how many.)

In Seneca Falls lived Dexter C. Bloomer, Quaker, the editor of the *Seneca County Daily Courier,* who had married about the same time as the Stantons. His wife Amelia was three years younger than Elizabeth. Her education had not been as good as Mrs. Stanton's, which for the time was outstanding, but it sufficed: she had been a Miss Jenks, schoolteacher and governess, before marriage. Now her chief interest was temperance. The cause had been given a boost in 1840 with the founding of the Great Washington Temperance Reformation, an association led by a group of men who called themselves the Seven Reformed Drunkards of Baltimore. (At least six of them actually were reformed; the seventh did not stay the course.) They had taken the pledge together, and now traveled the country lecturing on the wickedness of drink. Two of them came to Seneca Falls on a preaching tour, met Amelia Bloomer, and encouraged her to found the Seneca Falls Temperance Society, which flourished under her enthusiastic sponsorship. She became a regular contributor to the society's publication, *The Water Bucket,* and soon could announce with truth that they had five hundred members—not bad for a village of some two to three thousand inhabitants.

Though the country air of New York was good for Henry Stanton, his wife found it difficult to adjust to this almost rural small-town existence, where servants were hard to get and harder to train. She had always lived in a city, with plenty of help. Now she found herself becoming a household drudge, and she resented it. Inevitably her thoughts returned to the resentments of an earlier date, and she reflected that woman's lot was generally unenviable. How could she make it less so? There seemed no way out.

"My only thought," she later wrote in her memoirs, *Eighty Years and More,* "was a public meeting for protest and discussion."

So it was doubly exciting after a year or two to hear from Lucretia Mott, whom she had not seen since London. Mrs. Mott sent a message that she was visiting friends not far off, in a town called Waterloo, and she asked Mrs. Stanton to come over and spend the day. Elizabeth hastened to do so, and there met not only her old friend but a number of other intelligent Quaker women, who listened sympathetically when she poured out—as she put it—the torrents of her long-accumulating discontent, with vehemence and indignation. They caught her mood, and on the spot it was decided to call that long-postponed Women's Rights Convention that she and Lucretia had once planned.

"We wrote the call that evening," she recalled, "and published it in the *County Courier* the next day, the fourteenth of July, 1848." The "call" was worded crisply, saying only, "The first Women's Rights Convention to discuss the social, civil and religious conditions and rights of women will be held in the Wesleyan chapel at Seneca Falls on Wednesday and Thursday current, commencing at ten a.m. During the first day, the meeting will be exclusively for women, who are earnestly invited to attend. The public generally are invited to be present on the second day when Lucretia Mott will address the Convention."

With only five days to go, the pioneers had to work fast. How did one go about preparing for a convention? There should be some sort of introduction, striking enough to start the thing off with a swing. Mrs. Stanton suggested that they model a statement on the Declaration of Independence, and the others agreed. On The Day, July 19, when the women assembled at the chapel it was found that a joker had bolted the door on the inside, but someone climbed through a window, opened it, and everyone entered, including a few inquisitive men who were not, by the terms of the announcement, invited. The delegates, after conferring a little, decided that the men might stay—which must have reminded at least two of them, Mrs. Mott and Mrs. Stanton, of the London meeting of 1840 when the women were definitely disinvited. Then, since the rule had been broken anyway, they felt free to ask James Mott to take the chair, an odd enough gesture, one might think, from women determined to declare their independence of the rule of men, but indicative of how very unradical these beginners really were. If it comes to that, why was James Mott there in the first place? Perhaps to protect his wife from herself? No, the indications are that he agreed with her aims, and that the request to him to be chairman was the ladies' recognition of that fact. Throughout their struggle, at least in those early days, women were remarkably unchauvinistic about men in the movement.

Lucretia made her opening speech, and Mrs. Stanton read out the "Declaration of Sentiments":

> We hold these truths to be self-evident; that all men and women are created equal; that they are endowed by their Creator with certain inalienable rights; that among these are life, liberty, and the pursuit of happiness; that to secure these rights, governments are instituted, deriving their just powers from the consent of the governed.
>
> The history of mankind is a history of repeated injuries on the part of man towards woman; having in direct object the establishment of an absolute tyranny over her. To prove this, let facts be admitted to a candid world.
>
> He has never permitted her to exercise her inalienable right to the elective franchise.
>
> He has compelled her to submit to laws, in the formation of which she had no voice.
>
> He has withheld from her rights which are given to the most ignorant and degraded men—both natives and foreigners.
>
> Having deprived her of this first right of a citizen, the elective franchise, thereby leaving her without representation in the halls of legislation, he has oppressed her on all sides . . .

Among other points, the declaration accused men of forcing a woman, when she marries, to be civilly dead; of taking from her all property rights; of taking all power into their hands in case of divorce; of monopolizing all profitable employments and underpaying her; of closing all avenues to education (i.e., colleges) to her; and of keeping her in a subordinate position in the Church. It was a heavy indictment. Furthermore, it was true, impressively true—for all it was read out for the first time to a relatively small group gathered in the Wesleyan chapel of a small upstate town.

The group was larger the next day, when according to plan the convention was thrown open to everybody who wanted to come. The session was given to discussion and passage of the resolutions in the declaration. Every resolution was passed until the time came for the last minutes. Then Elizabeth Stanton surprised her audience by proposing one further resolution: "Resolved: that it is the duty of the women of this country to secure for themselves the sacred right to the elective franchise."

This was a startling idea, and many people were shocked. Mrs. Stanton waited for what seemed a long time for someone to second the resolution. At last the silence was broken by Frederick Douglass, the black abolitionist, who stood up to say the necessary words as seconder and in addition made a speech in support of the measure. Finally the vote was put to the assembly, and the motion was passed—but by a smaller majority than had the earlier resolutions. Had Mrs. Stanton gone too far? A number of women thought so, because it was clear that many people were now scandalized or scornful of the whole affair.

"It is easy to be smart, to be droll, to be facetious in opposition to the demands of these Female Reformers," said Greeley in an editorial about the convention, "and in decrying assumptions so novel and opposed to established habit and usages, a little wit will go a long way. But when a sincere republican is asked to say in sober earnest what adequate reason he can give for refusing the demand of women to be in equal participation with men in political rights, he must answer, none at all." This was splendid support for Elizabeth Cady Stanton, as far as it went. Unfortunately, Greeley did not speak for the majority.

But Amelia Bloomer, for one, had been much impressed by the whole affair, and did a good deal of thinking afterward. Undeniably, she reflected, even her own Temperance Society was guilty of placing women in a subordinate role. Women were permitted to attend meetings and listen to men, but nobody dreamed of giving them authority in the workings of the institution. She wondered why this unsatisfactory state of affairs had not offended her before. Soon afterward she broke with the society and helped to found another, the Ladies' Temperance Society, to which she devoted as much time and fervor as she had given to the older body. She wrote no more in *The Water Bucket,* for her society had its own paper, *The Lily,* edited by Amelia Bloomer herself. Its first issue appeared not quite six months after the Seneca Falls convention. *The Lily* was not planned to be a second *Water Bucket,* said Mrs. Bloomer; it would not concentrate on temperance matters, but would be devoted to the general interests of women.

We come at last, by roundabout route, to the baggy pants called bloomers. This is not a good name for the garment, since Mrs. Bloomer had no hand in designing it, but the name is not important. The overwhelming fact is that it was high time somebody did invent bloomers, or at least an equivalent. As I have already indicated, Western fashions for women in the mid-nineteenth century were appallingly unhealthy. Skirts were long and billowing, and picked up dirt. It is said that an expensive floor-cleaning machine specially invented for the Great Exhibition at London's Crystal Palace was never used after all, because it was not needed; the floors were clean-swept daily by the skirts of lady visitors. And the length of her skirts was only one drawback to a woman's costume; she wore an unbelievable amount of stuff underneath the surface—tight-laced stays, corset covers for the stays, and petticoat upon petticoat, limp and stiffened, as many as six at a time. Some women habitually wore twelve pounds of clothing in all. The phenomenon did not go unremarked, of course, because there are always people ready to complain about what women wear, but in that particular era they were quite right. Doctors criticized tight lacing because of its effect on the health of growing girls, and less authoritative voices were raised in praise of ventilating the body. From England came vague rumors that certain women had begun to dress in trousers, but this idea did not at first appeal to American females, who were already somewhat sensitive to the jeers made by their husbands about wearing the breeches in the family. It is an odd thing, but in countries where women have the least legal rights, as in Japan before the war, there are the most jokes about bossy wives. Is this a form of masculine insurance, to shame women before they get uppity?

Dexter Bloomer was appointed postmaster, and gave up the editorship of the *Daily Courier* in consequence. His successor, who had no sympathy with the women's rights movement, one day suggested in an editorial that strong-minded ladies would probably find themselves more comfortable if they wore Turkish pantaloons with a skirt reaching to below the knee. Mrs. Bloomer retorted to these jibes in *The Lily*'s columns by pretending that the suggestion had been made in good faith. She said that the costume suggested by her colleague was a very good idea: in such clothes women would be more comfortable and would enjoy better health too. She thanked the *Courier* editor for thinking it up. It is not certain if either editor realized that just such a costume was actually in existence at that time, but it was. Soon after the exchange, Mrs. Libby Smith Miller, a cousin of Elizabeth Cady Stanton, recently returned from her honeymoon abroad, arrived on a visit to Seneca Falls clad in exactly the outfit described in the *Courier*—long, full Turkish trousers and a tunic to just below the knee. She said she had designed it herself—a remarkable coincidence if true. Mrs. Stanton admired it very much because of the freedom it gave. With all her children and so much housework, she felt she could use a little freedom, and in a short time she had made a copy of Libby's costume. The two ladies walked in their pantaloons through the streets of Seneca Falls, quite unabashed.

Amelia Bloomer promptly followed their example, and was thus the third lady to wear the garment in town, but the newspapers, who gave the story great play, christened the costume "the Bloomer." Perhaps the reporters simply found it a catchy name. Under whatever name, the outfit elicited disapproving comment, especially after Mrs. Stanton, by this time a regular contributor to *The Lily,* published directions on how to make the thing—for the convenience, she explained, of the many women who had written in asking for the pattern. Judge Cady, her father, was much annoyed by the publicity, and wrote that he hoped she would not wear the bloomer when she came to visit him. Henry Stanton approved of it, but the eldest Stanton child, who was away at school, wrote as his grandfather had done to ask his mother not to wear such clothes when she came to see him. Elizabeth replied:

"You do not wish me to visit you in a short dress. Why, my dear child, I have no other. Now suppose you and I were taking a long walk in the fields and I had on three long petticoats. Then suppose a bull should take after us, why you with your arms and legs free, could run like a shot, but I, alas, should fall a victim to my graceful floating drapery. My petticoats would be caught by the stumps and the briars, and what could I do at the fences? . . . Now why do you wish me to wear what is uncomfortable, inconvenient, and in many times dangerous? I'll tell you why. You want me to be like other people. You do not like to have me laughed at. You must learn not to care for what foolish people say."

In spite of such mockery, the bloomer caught on quickly all over the States, and in time was adopted in England too. In the beginning it caused riots in London, but later it was even more popular than in America.

"The costume was a godsend to the theatre, and no fewer than three farces on the theme were produced in London that autumn [1851], with great success," wrote Charles Nielson Gattey in *The*

Bloomer Girls. The shows included "A Figure of Fun, or the Bloomer Girls," and "Bloomerism, or the Follies of the Day," with the "New Adelphi Bloomer Polka" as overture, and so on. Tussaud's waxworks advertised "BLOOMER COSTUME. Five beautiful varieties . . ." and at Webster's annual Christmas pantomime at the Theatre Royal in the Haymarket, the leading lady sang "I want to be a Bloomer."

The public enjoyed their fun, but in America, Miss Flexner has commented in *Century of Struggle,* those women who wore bloomers seriously, as a symbol of revolt against senseless restrictions visited on females, suffered "untold mental torture" in exchange for their physical comfort. They were the butt of unceasing ridicule, until eventually "the persecution became unbearable, and a handicap to the cause." Mrs. Stanton, for one, decided it was not worth it. In 1854 she wrote to her friend Susan Anthony that she was giving up the costume, and when Miss Anthony protested she replied, "We put on the dress for greater freedom, but what is physical freedom compared with mental bondage? . . . It is not wise, Susan, to use up so much energy and feeling that way." After which she resumed petticoats, skirts, and all the rest of the paraphernalia.

CHAPTER 13

Purity and Ladyhood

"WHAT IS PHYSICAL FREEDOM compared with mental bondage?"

Mrs. Stanton asked a good question, but she should have elaborated on it. For instance, she might have pointed out that the women of America were mentally as well as physically handicapped by the assumption that they must above all be ladies. What constituted ladyhood? Many things, varied according to the upbringing of the lady, from white gloves to never telling lies, but the chief idea underlying all codes was that a lady is respectable and *must be seen to be so*. There were dozens of subrules attached to this notion, as anyone who has ever looked into an etiquette book of the period can testify: the very existence of these books is suggestive of the pervasive uneasiness about appearances. A woman who is constantly worrying about how her behavior and clothing might appear to a censorious world is a hobbled woman: she might as well stay at home. To use the modern expression, she should have stood in bed, for in essence, it means the same thing. Stay at home, said the men; stay out of trouble; above all, stay out of my way. Feminists, especially their archetype Fanny Wright, had to break the rules of etiquette or they would have got nowhere, yet most women had a deep fear of being accused of Fanny Wrightism. That fear was bred in their bones. Even Susan Anthony, grim as she was, watched her manners. The highest compliment a woman could receive, especially a woman who tried to help the movement for liberation, was that she was "quite a lady in spite of everything."

Miss Wright didn't feel like that, but then Miss Wright was extraordinary. Her life story, and the life stories of other educated women like Elizabeth Stanton and Lucretia Mott, should not lead us to forget the vast majority of American females who were not, to use their own expression, cultivated. They have left no records, and we can only judge them by what they enjoyed reading, much of which was of poor quality.

The success of Mrs. Lydia Sigourney's verse, for instance, somewhat puzzles us—how *could* it have struck any answering chords?—unless we remember how very limited were the emotions nice women were expected to feel. Nobody was supposed to peer beneath the surface: even the proper reactions like, for instance, religious fervor were kept within bounds. It was not ladylike to go beyond prescribed limits. The right sentiments were maternal love, family affection (which included wifely love), gratitude, loyalty to flag and country, certain responses to certain approved forms of natural beauty such as trees, brooks, and fields of grain, and even the shy, chaste love of the maiden for her swain. There was also, of course, grief. Grief was always all right, as long as you didn't carry it to excess, and therein might lie the secret of Mrs. Sigourney's appeal: few people could write more fluently about gently sorrowful subjects.

There is a clue as to how and why she developed such a peculiarly lugubrious style. It came about because her father, a hired man in Norwich, Connecticut, worked for an elderly widow, Mrs. Daniel Lathrop, and Madame Lathrop, as everyone called her, took a friendly interest in his fourteen-year-old, motherless daughter. In the evening the widow would read *Night Thoughts*, by Edward Young, to the girl. It was a very popular book: almost everyone enjoyed the poet's discussion of death and immortality, and young Lydia Huntley was ineradicably impressed.

According to her biographer, Gordon S. Haight, when Madame Lathrop died, Lydia's excessive grief was the admiration of all beholders. The funeral was scarcely over before she was writing out her emotion in a poem entitled "Gratitude: Lines written on planting slips of geranium and constancy near the grave of a venerable friend," and this outpouring too was much admired, especially by the late lady's friends who from that time on kept a kindly eye on Lydia. "Gratitude" was the first of Miss Huntley's effusions, and she never forgot it. In later life she never forgot any of her works, but wrote them over and over with slight changes, and sold them afresh.

Grown to womanhood, Miss Huntley became a schoolteacher. One of the interested friends of Madame Lathrop made himself her patron, helping her in 1815 to publish a collection of her poems in a book, *Moral Pieces*. The first of fifty such volumes that appeared in her lifetime, it was made up of mostly bad, sometimes worse verse. It seemed always to take her far longer than it need have done to say things, even allowing for poetic license; her elegantly roundabout style maddens modern readers but obviously it suited the general taste of the times (with the exception, one hopes, of Mrs. Stanton and her circle). The poetess had not yet made much headway with her career, however, when at the age of twenty-eight she married Mr. Sigourney. Much older than she, a widower with children, he was nevertheless thought by her friends to be a splendid match for an old maid of humble origin: he had a fine house in Hartford, a thriving hardware business, and a position in the bank. There were drawbacks, to be sure. His children did not accept Lydia gracefully, but she had little cause for complaint. She too had children, two of them, but her household duties did not interfere with the Muse.

In keeping with her higher social position, Lydia now published anonymously. Far from interfering with her hobby, Mr. Sigourney helped her on occasion by adding learned notes to what she wrote, as in her epic on the American Indian, *Traits of the Aborigines*. In this Mrs. Sigourney conscientiously listed Indian foodstuffs, including:

> . . . that tub'rous root
> Which in their clay-built cells, the hardy ones
> Of emerald Erin bless.

Surely it takes only a little thought on the part of the reader to know that she was talking about the potato. Mr. Sigourney might have made it easier, perhaps, with this footnote: "America presented Europe with the *Solanum tuberosum,*" but one cannot help feeling that he broke the flow. Still, he meant well.

Mrs. Sigourney's fame grew so great that even such a learned lady as Mrs. Emma Willard, who founded Troy Female Seminary, was flattered at being compared to her. This seems odd. It is true that Mrs. Willard too wrote poems—"Rocked in the Cradle of the Deep," for one—but they were nothing like so awful as Mrs. Sigourney's. In her turn, Mrs. Sigourney was flattered at being called the American Hemans, and this is a more apt comparison because Mrs. Felicia Hemans' style was genuinely similar to hers. On one occasion a poem by Mrs. Sigourney was accidentally included in a collection of Hemans, and the mistake was not noticed until Mrs. Sigourney herself came upon it quite some time later and recognized her own brainchild.

All this, however, happened after her anonymity had been discarded. This development was the result of Mr. Sigourney's affairs having taken a turn for the worse and continuing thereafter to go downhill. His wife was forced to practice economies, which she described in her customary flossy style: instead of saying that she had to make her family's clothes over, she arranged, she said, to "prolong the existence of all garments, by repair or transmigration." But such a program, merely making do, was not good enough for a woman who, after all, had supported herself before marriage. Mrs. Sigourney went through her desk, collected all her writings, and sent them off in a bundle to a magazine editor. He bought them. She wrote more poems and sold them. She continued to write. She was industrious and persistent; if one editor turned down a poem, she promptly sent it off to another. As she was no longer a lady of leisure who merely amused herself with her pen, she proceeded to sign her outpourings because it paid better. And she sold more and more, growing better and better known, until her name became an asset and editors would sometimes pay merely to use it on the masthead, as if she were an editor of this or that women's periodical. For three years running, Godey gave her five hundred dollars for this privilege for his *Lady's Book*—a significant title for this popular magazine, and one that was bound to help Mrs. Sigourney's reputation as well as its own, because it reassured the women who read it that they were doing the right thing.

Mrs. Sigourney's verse was as easy to swallow as boiled fish—bland, full of highfalutin words, gently sentimental without ever being sexy, and *sweet*. All the virtuous sentiments were there but nothing frightening, and women who had little time to read except for such easy fare were able at once to enjoy it and to feel virtuous. The prolific Mrs. Sigourney made more and more money. As a right-thinking male, Mr. Sigourney did not care for all this unrefined publicity, but what could he do? She was receiving much more income than he was. So he kept quiet, and Hartford saw less of him while the world heard more of his wife.

It was as an established poet that in 1840, carrying a sheaf of introductions to well-known literary people in London and Paris, Mrs. Sigourney crossed the Atlantic to visit the Old World. We have a vitriolic report from the redoubtable Jane Carlyle on her appearance and personality. Mrs. Carlyle resented the fact that her husband had been weak enough to invite "the American Poetess Mrs. Sigourney" to the house for tea, spoiling a pleasant party that included the Wedgwoods and Darwin. She wrote indignantly to a friend, "We had all set in to be talkative and confidential—when this figure of an over-the-water Poetess—beplastered with rouge and pomatum—bare-necked at an age which had left *certainty* [i.e., "a certain age"] far behind—with long ringlets that never grew where they hung—smelling marvellously of camphor or hartshorn and oil—glistening in black satin as if she were an apothecary's *puff* for black *sticking-plaster*—and staring her eyes out, to give them animation—stalked in and by the very barber-block-ish look of her reduced us all to silence."

A cruel description, but one must admit that Mrs. Sigourney was a silly woman.

To be quite fair to the American public, they did not always prefer such trashy writers. Another woman who met with their approval and whose work was slightly better was "Fanny Fern"—Mrs. Sara Payson Willis Porter, whose specialty was the pithy paragraph, the short essay, but who could turn her pen to almost anything as long as it was moral. At least her style was simpler than Mrs. Sigourney's. One of her collections, *Fern Leaves from Fanny's Portfolio,* sold seventy thousand copies in 1853, at the same time Hawthorne's *Mosses from an Old Manse* was bringing him a mere $144.09. Hawthorne was infuriated by this discrepancy.

"America is now wholly given over to a d——d mob of scribbling women," he wrote, "and I should have no chance of success while the public taste is occupied with their trash—and should be ashamed of myself if I did succeed." He was not, in fact, thinking so much of Fanny Fern's trash as of a smash-hit, innocuous novel called *The Lamplighter,* written by Maria Susanna Cummings. "What is the mystery of these innumerable editions of the Lamplighter and other books neither better nor worse?" he demanded. ". . . worse they could not be, and better they need not be, when they sell by the 100,000."

No mystery really, as James Hart pointed out in *The Popular Book,* to anyone but Hawthorne. Those books were what the public liked, and that was that. They liked them because "the main characters were women—women who overcome all sorts of dilemmas through Christian fortitude and faith that eventually establishes them securely in prosperous middle-class homes, tangible symbols of an eventual call to heavenly mansions." Fanny Fern did this sort of thing very well, as can be seen in *How Woman Loves,* a short novel included in a memorial volume of her work. The story opens with Walter and Marion Clay at breakfast. Marion is worried because

Walter has not touched his coffee, and she worries more when he says it is merely because yesterday was a hard day at the bank. After he had gone to work she muses, womanlike, "If Walter would only leave that odious bank! Such a tread-mill life for him to lead . . ."

All day as she does her household chores her busy little head devises pathetic appeals to the board of directors for mitigation of her beloved's sufferings. Dinner time arrives, but Walter does not. Unperturbed, Marion plays with their little son Nettie. "Tell me, Nettie, which do you love best, papa or me?"

"Papa said I must love you best, because he does."

"Bless your baby lips for that answer! Where can that dear papa be, I wonder?"

She discovers all too soon, when her father arrives to tell her that Walter has disgraced them by embezzling from the bank, and is in custody. He says that Marion and the boy must come home with him and forget Walter.

"Never, never, never," cries Marion. " 'Tis false! . . . There is a conspiracy. . . . I will never leave him, though all the world forsake him. Let me go to him, father!"

Father refuses, saying that Walter is sure to be found guilty, and that when he is in his felon's cell the law will free her. If she does not come home with him, she will be no child of his. But Marion stands by Walter, and when we see her next she is in her husband's cell, in his arms. The old jailer, stony-hearted though he is, must wipe his eyes as he leaves them alone together. Walter admits that he is guilty; he too reminds Marion that she can get rid of him with no trouble, but she says through her tears, "Yours till death."

He is convicted, and to comfort him Marion bathes his temples before they part. Then days, weeks, months pass. Whence comes that quiet dignity with which Walter Clay exacts respect even from his jailers? From the knowledge that a true heart throbs for him outside the prison walls, that nightly he is remembered in her prayers, that she daily teaches the boy to "lisp" his father's name. Then at last he is free, free to hasten to the little room where his heroic wife has toiled and suffered. Once more Marion clasps her husband to her breast. The joyful father says, "And Nettie, where is he?"

"On the Saviour's bosom!" says Marion, with a choking voice.

Walter says, "Dead? And you have buried this sad secret in your breast, and borne this great grief unshared, lest you should add to my sorrow!" He kneels at her feet reverently.

It was a very pleasant thought for female readers that a man should kneel reverently at a woman's feet. Many must have sighed longingly at the vision. So different from one's own home life! Perhaps if one managed to be truly womanly, like Marion, doing one's duty as a wife and mother . . .

In spite of the preoccupation of the era with purity and ladyhood, equal-rights women struggled and grew busier. Among the conventions that followed the first at Seneca Falls was a national meeting in Worcester, Massachusetts, in 1850, the announcement of which was signed by men as well as women, Bronson Alcott, Wendell Phillips, and William Lloyd Garrison among others. There were a national convention and a lot of smaller meetings every year, and on the list of speakers, beside the now familiar names of Mrs. Stanton and Mrs. Mott, appeared those of other crusaders, Lucy Stone, Abby Kelley Foster, Antoinette Brown, and Susan B. Anthony. The public learned to recognize them all.

Lucy Stone and Antoinette Brown were both graduates of Oberlin College, which had been founded in 1834 as a spin-off of the troubles at Lane Seminary. It will be remembered that when Lyman Beecher, as president of Lane, rebuked certain overzealous students for helping settle slaves who had escaped to Cincinnati from the nearby South, Theodore Weld and some forty other activist undergraduates walked out of the seminary in protest. One of the things they did in the wilderness was to set up Oberlin, decreeing that it should be open to students of any color and either sex. Its founding was made possible by a contribution from two brothers in the East named Tappan, who were energetic reformers. The first truly coeducational college in the country, Oberlin became a magnet for ambitious girls. It was a place vital for the feminist movement. As Andrew Sinclair observed in *The Emancipation of the American Woman:* "Even if the college professors intended to fit women students 'for intellectual womanhood and a properly subservient wifehood,' the student body itself was rabid with abolitionists and feminists. Radical women there learned to identify their wrongs with the wrongs of slaves."

Even at Oberlin there was some discrimination at the beginning. The first girl students were held down to a special short course, owing to an idea prevalent at the time that women's brains were incapable of grasping the mental work done by male students. But this rule did not last long; after a woman graduated from the full course in 1842 with her brain apparently unscathed, the way lay open for others. Lucy Stone, probably the most famous of Oberlin's female graduates, took her degree in 1847 at the advanced age of twenty-nine—a triumphant achievement for a farm girl from a poverty-stricken family. She was one of nine children, born on a farm in Massachusetts, where throughout her childhood she could see how overworked and tired her mother was, and note that though the women carried half the burden of running the farm, her father's was the only word of authority in the house. At the age of twelve Lucy decided that she could best help her mother by getting an education instead of working all her life at home. To earn money for the project, she went out at sixteen and taught school. It took nine years to save up the money for Oberlin. Her degree won, she determined to speak in public on behalf of women's rights and antislavery, and within a year she had become a professional lecturer for the Anti-Slavery Society.

Small, without beauty, she was impressive on the platform because of her clear, powerful voice, courage, and fervent personality. She did not speak only for abolition; temperance was another of her causes, and so was family planning. Few people had any idea of how to limit the size of their families, apart from abstaining altogether from sexual intercourse, and Lucy, who had seen her mother broken down and prematurely aged by too much childbearing, recommended abstinence as the only answer. "Moral reform within marriage" was her phrase. She had great admiration for Angelina and Theodore Weld, who spaced out their children through abstinence, though her brothers scoffed.

"This waiting three years, Sis, as you intimate is all nonsense," wrote one of them. "Have them as fast as you can if you can, take care of them, and if you can't, trust Providence and obey the command given to our first parents to multiply and replenish the earth and subdue it. Were all to follow the example of Mrs. Weld and the advice of yourself, when think you would the wilderness and the solitary place in the natural world, bud and blossom as the rose?" Another brother, while admitting that many men were not healthy or sane enough to have a lot of children, nevertheless could not agree with her: "Lucy, I think It As Great A Sin To not Suffer These Organs to Be Used At All As To Use Them Too Much."

But Lucy followed her own star. All in all, she thought marriage a poor arrangement, and when Henry Blackwell, an abolitionist and businessman, proposed to her, she would not hear of it. She advanced good reasons for refusing him: Henry was seven years her junior, she was prematurely old, and anyway women were naturally older than men of the same age. Besides, the status of married women simply revolted her. Unconvinced, Henry continued at intervals to propose.

In Lucy's graduating class at Oberlin was Antoinette Brown, whose ambition was to become a religious preacher. Antoinette too came from a farm, though this one was in New York State near Rochester and her people were better off than the Stones and more progressive. In her memoirs she wrote that several of the young men and women of the class of 1847 believed in equal rights for women— "probably one of the most eccentric [classes] that Oberlin has ever seen," she said drily. A passionate admirer of Lucy Stone, she was in agreement with most of the older girl's beliefs, and the two friends kept in close touch after graduation, Lucy barnstorming and Antoinette studying theology. Ordained at last by a liberal minister, Miss Brown became pastor of a small-town Congregational church, but she stayed there only a year, having decided that Congregationalism did not suit her. She wanted as wide a horizon as Lucy's. Declaring that she was finished with preaching unless it might be for the Universalist Church, she went to New York, hoping for a career like her model.

Antoinette did some lecturing, but failed to measure up to Lucy on the platform. However, she felt no envy or spite, and continued to adore Lucy loyally. Fervent friendships between women in the feminist movement were common in those innocent pre-Freud days, when nobody knew enough to hang ugly labels on the relationships. This particular attachment was made permanent in the neatest possible fashion when Lucy at last gave in to Henry and married him, and Antoinette married his brother Samuel.

All the members of the Blackwell family, two brothers and five sisters, were reformers. At the time Henry married, his sister Elizabeth was involved in a grim struggle to become a doctor. The odds against this project would have overwhelmed a less determined woman: it took her years to gain admittance into the necessary medical courses, and when she had done her training she had to start all over again to break through the prejudice that kept her from practicing. In spite of these hardships (or because of them) her younger sister Emily followed in her footsteps. She too became a doctor, and aided Elizabeth.

Henry was thoroughly in sympathy with the cause of equal rights, and promised Lucy when they became engaged that he would never take advantage of his position as a husband. He wrote an agreement that was used in the marriage ceremony, forswearing legal superiority in all ways, promising that his wife need never give up her maiden name, and renouncing all moral and economic power over her. So Lucy Stone remained Lucy Stone after marriage, and to this day women who do the same are often called "Lucy Stoners." They had one child, a daughter.

When she married, Antoinette Brown ceased imitating Lucy Stone. She had no objection to becoming "Mrs. Blackwell," and in the course of time she bore six children. The Blackwell sisters were made of sterner stuff than their sisters-in-law. All refrained from marrying, each adopting a daughter to carry on in the cause. Few women, even dedicated feminists, were capable of such self-sacrifice, though many understood and approved of Lucy Stone's attitude toward marriage. The writer Lydia Maria Child, who had been married twenty-eight years, wrote to a friend on February 24, 1856:

"David [her husband] has signed my will and I have sealed it up and put it away. It excited my towering indignation to think it was necessary for him to sign it, and if you had been by, you would have made the matter worse by repeating your old manly 'fling and twit' about married women being dead in the law. I was not indignant on my own account, for David respects the freedom of all women upon principle, but mine in particular by reason of affection superadded. But I was indignant for womankind made chattels from the beginning of time, perpetually insulted by literature, law, and custom. The very phrases used with regard to us are abominable. 'Dead in the law,' 'Femme couverte.' How I detest such language!"

Susan Brownell Anthony would have said a fervent "Amen" to that. Susan, like many of her co-workers, came of Quaker stock, but her parents differed with the Friends and left them to join the Universalist Church. Susan, born in 1820 in Adams, Massachusetts, went to school until her father lost his money and the Anthonys moved to a farm near Rochester. From there Susan, like Lucy Stone, went out to teach school, and in this work, like Lucretia Mott, she quickly learned that in comparison with her male colleagues she was underpaid. This state of affairs held true even when she reached the high rank of headmistress, and she resented it, though she enjoyed her work and there were compensations in the fact that she was much esteemed. At a town Temperance Fair she made a speech against drinking, and it was well received, partly, as her biographer, Katharine

Susan Anthony, points out, because the place, Canajoharie, was too remote to have caught the idea that there was something wrong in a woman speaking in public. It came naturally to Susan: her father often lectured for temperance and abolition. However, there came a time when she decided to leave and go home. The death of a favorite cousin she had tended and the sudden influx of gold fever—it was 1849—made her restless. Twenty young men of the town had gone to California. "Oh, if I were but a man so I could go!" she wrote to her family. Instead, she joined them in Rochester.

The Fugitive Slave Law was passed in 1850. Susan's people were strongly abolitionist, and her father entertained many people of that persuasion, important leaders of the movement like Wendell Phillips, William Lloyd Garrison, and Frederick Douglass. Susan, cooking the dinner and serving it, heard much of their talk and took part in it at times, as befitted a Quaker woman. Sometimes, to help with the family finances, she went out to work as a substitute teacher. But her first public work came about when she joined the local Daughters of Temperance. Practiced as she was in organizing her pupils, she proved an excellent executive, teaching the ladies how to raise money through fairs and sales. Impressed and grateful, they elected her as a delegate and sent her to temperance conventions around the state.

It was in 1851, coming back from one of these meetings, that she met Elizabeth Cady Stanton, a woman she had long admired intensely from afar. Susan had stopped off in Seneca Falls to hear abolitionist speeches given by Garrison and the English George Thompson, and lodged with Mrs. Bloomer. At that time Amelia Bloomer and Elizabeth Stanton were not close friends—Elizabeth considered Amelia too conservative, and Amelia thought Elizabeth far too radical. However, Elizabeth a few days later invited Susan, along with Lucy Stone, to her house to meet Horace Greeley, and so the long friendship began.

Susan went on with her temperance work until, in January 1852, she came up against a glaring instance of discrimination against women in her own field. At a mass meeting of the Sons of Temperance in Albany, Susan tried to speak and was told that women delegates were not invited to speak there, but to listen and learn. With a few other women who felt as indignant as she did, she left the meeting, and that very evening, having gathered together a few friends, they organized the Women's State Temperance Society, and called a meeting in Rochester in the spring. Mrs. Stanton promised to make the principal address, and Susan hired the hall. It all turned out very well, and the men's temperance society tried to make up with the ladies. But they could not bring themselves to accept the horrible idea that ladies should speak in public, and the two movements remained estranged.

Susan had not accompanied her mother and sister when they attended a women's rights convention, their first. But when what was called the Third National Woman's Rights Convention was held at Syracuse in 1852, she was there and, in fact, was elected secretary. (It was at this meeting that bloomers were worn, so it became known as the Bloomer Convention. Later, as we have seen, the women's rights workers gave up the costume.)

Little by little Susan had moved into the women's rights camp by way of her temperance work, as it became increasingly clear to her that the temperance organizations had no separate existence, since their members had to depend financially on men. Few women had the means to support clubs of any sort, and men generally were not fond of temperance, so the societies, one after another, had to close down for lack of funds. It was the same story everywhere, Susan reflected: without the goodwill of their masters, women could do nothing.

"Woman must have a purse of her own," she wrote, "and how can this be as long as the law denies to the wife all right to both individual and joint earnings?" She would have to start at the roots, she decided, elevating women's legal status—but even there she was hindered, since the only means of legislative reform open to her was by petition. Fortunately, a few men agreed with her and were willing to help. Two of them, William Channing and the Reverend Samuel May, assisted her in drafting a petition in 1854, summing up what was needed to improve the situation. Three changes were fundamental: women should control their own earnings; they should have custody of the children in case of separation or divorce; and they should have the vote.

Then Susan set out to collect signatures in an efficient way that was a great improvement on the old hit-and-miss system. Earlier workers had simply canvassed their own neighborhoods, using up their acquaintances first and then knocking on doors at random. Susan Anthony selected a woman from each of the sixty counties of New York State and put her in charge of the county team. The leader then divided her county into areas and turned each one over to a team member, who canvassed it whatever way she found practical. The end aim, of course, was to interview and explain the petition to every woman in the state. It was a difficult assignment because women seldom traveled alone. Roads were bad and hotels were worse. Each woman had to make her own arrangements, to find respectable lodgings and adequate meals without telephones or telegrams, a good postal service, or money to make up for these deficiencies. Few of us could have coped with such problems—we are spoiled nowadays. Then, after a woman had conquered these difficulties, she had to arrange the meeting herself, hire the hall, get her broadsides printed, advertise in the local paper . . . it is amazing that it was done at all, and even more amazing that it was done well, but it was. Susan Anthony wrote in pride and praise of the women who did the work, tramping the streets and country roads like tin peddlers or book agents, arguing with housewives who might slam the door in their faces or retort angrily that they had perfectly good husbands to take care of them, thank you; they didn't *want* equal rights.

Yet in ten weeks these volunteers collected six thousand signatures. Encouraged, Susan Anthony conceived the idea of having a women's rights convention in Albany, New York's capital, during the legislative session, where the petition could be presented to support a request made by the convention leaders for a hearing of certain women's rights bills. Susan, Elizabeth Cady Stanton, and several associates went into action and arranged the convention. The strategy succeeded in part: Mrs. Stanton was actually permitted to appear before a joint judiciary committee and address the gentlemen on legal disabilities suffered by women. Though the bill failed to pass, the women felt that they had made a step forward.

The rugged Miss Anthony then set out alone to collect more signatures, on Christmas Day, 1854. Wendell Phillips lent her fifty dollars for the project. She traveled through fifty-four of New York's sixty counties holding meetings, lecturing, explaining, exhorting, and, of course, collecting signatures to her petition. She hired halls, printed pamphlets, and put up posters to announce meetings. On her return to Rochester, on May 1, 1855, she had more money than she had started with—expenses $2,291, collections $2,367. Was all this worth the effort? She thought so, and so did Mrs. Stanton, though the outlook was grim. Nothing, it seemed, could shake male complacency. The judiciary committee's report on Elizabeth Stanton's appearance before that body and the petition she presented was finally published, and showed that the gentlemen found it easiest to take refuge from these problems in jocularity. Here it is:

"The Committee is composed of married and single gentlemen. The bachelors on the Committee, with becoming diffidence, have left the subject pretty much up to the married gentlemen. They have considered it with the aid of the light they have before them and the experience married life has given them. Thus aided, they are enabled to state that the ladies always have the best place and choicest tidbit at the table. They always have the best seat in the cars, carriages and sleighs; the warmest place in the winter and the coolest place in the summer. They have their choice on which side of the bed they will lie, front or back. A lady's dress costs three times as much as that of a gentleman; and, at the present time, with the prevailing fashion, one lady occupies three times as much space in the world as a gentleman. It has thus appeared to the married gentlemen of your Committee, being a majority (the bachelors being silent for the reason mentioned and also probably for the further reason that they are still suitors for the favors of the gentler sex), that, if there is any inequity or oppression in the case, the gentlemen are the sufferers. They, however, have presented no petitions for redress; having, doubtless, made up their minds to yield to an inevitable destiny.

"On the whole, the Committee have concluded to recommend no measure, except as they have observed several instances in which husband and wife have signed the same petition. In such cases, they would recommend the parties to apply for a law authorizing them to change dresses, that the husband may wear petticoats and the wife the breeches, and thus indicate to their neighbors and the public the true relation in which they stand to each other."

CHAPTER 14

Ladies in the Civil War

It is a truism that war hastens the liberation of women into public life, because all of a sudden they are needed more than they are when everything is peaceful. The Civil War is always cited as a case in point, since it occurred just when women were becoming adept at proclaiming their grievances, and making headway, and gaining confidence. Of course the war helped—but there is a question that is worth asking: Would the North have won without the help of its women? Because, no doubt how many folk tales we have heard about the gallant Southern ladies and their quick-wittedness and how they always saved the silver from the Yankees, they could not, on the average, have been very much of a help in the conduct of the war. It was the North, where the women's rights movement was born and waxed strong, that produced such nurses as Dorothea Lynde Dix, Clarissa Harlowe Barton, and, for that matter, Louisa May Alcott, though she was not particularly effective because she quickly fell ill. Neither Miss Barton nor Miss Dix was a fighter on the order of Elizabeth Cady Stanton and Susan Anthony, but they were quite tough in their own way, as was Jane Swisshelm, also a fighter, though not in the front lines. Then for contrast we have a lady of the old school, a Southern lady, a figment of the imagination it is true, but, I think you will agree, a fair portrait of a familiar type, the protected, beloved household pet.

Whatever women feel about war, it does give them one advantage: they get the chance to fill the shoes of absent men, a novel taste of power. The girl making guns, the farmer's wife managing the fields and livestock, the city woman who suddenly becomes the chief buyer in a department store—even though they feel distress and loss, they experience a new pride as well.

"Look at me," says such a woman in her private thoughts. "I'm alone, but I'm making a good job of it."

Those few who serve at the front, however, feel even prouder. In the War Between the States certain women handled military-connected careers that they would never have dreamed of in times of peace, though according to a contemporary account, *Woman's Work in the Civil War,* their contributions were no more valuable than those of really *womanly* women who stayed at home. "Men did not take to the musket more commonly than women took to the needle," the authors, Dr. Linus Pierpont Brockett and Mrs. Mary C. Vaughan, declared, but even they admitted that when it came to the war effort some women did much more than needlework, and they included in their book an honor roll of more than four hundred women who did outstanding work during the war. The writers seemed astonished by the abilities of the women who managed the United States Sanitary Commission:

"Nothing that men commonly think peculiar to their own methods was wanting in the plans of the women. They acknowledged and answered, endorsed and filed their letters; they sorted their stores, and kept an accurate account of stock; they had their books and reports kept in the most approved forms; they balanced their cash accounts with the most pains-taking precision," the authors marveled, as if these feats were beyond the capabilities of the ordinary housewife. Even more, the commission was led by systematic, persistent, and faithful females, who evinced talents "which, in other spheres and in the other sex, would have made them merchant-princes, or great administrators of public affairs." Not only did the ladies write letters and answer questions capably, but, *mirabile dictu,* "they became instructors of whole townships in the methods of government business, the constitution of the Commissary and Quartermaster's Departments, and the forms of the Medical Bureau . . . In the ten thousand Soldiers' Aid Societies which at one time or another probably existed in the country, there was in each some master-spirit, whose consecrated purpose was the staple in the wall, from which the chain of service hung and on whose strength and firmness it steadily drew."

Maintained by volunteer labor and at first amorphous, the Sanitary Commission quickly took shape as women from all over the North and West came forward to help. Eleanor Flexner describes it as the right arm of the Union hospital and medical services: "Behind the famous greeting, 'hello, Sanitary,' which echoed down the rows of cots to the women bringing jelly, fruit, clean clothing, soap, and other essentials to the ragged men, lay the work of a complex organization which, by the end of the war, numbered some 7,000 local societies throughout the North and West, and which raised—and spent—the huge sum of $50,000,000." Decorum demanded that men should head the commission, but women did most of the work from the highest echelons down to outposts in obscure communities where they organized bazaars to raise money, food, and other comforts.

Closely associated with "Sanitary" was Dorothea Lynde Dix, who had already had a distinguished career and was now fifty-nine. She was born in Maine in 1802, and started—of course—as a schoolteacher, but at thirty-six she had to stop work because of stubborn "lung trouble." After a rest cure she went to Boston, which is where she first became interested in her lifework, the treatment of the insane. In the whole country there were only eight lunatic asylums, and these were run with ignorance and extreme cruelty. Miss Dix forgot her health and set out on a two-year tour of Massachusetts, investigating the situation of the insane in jails, almshouses, and houses of correction. What she learned horrified her. She incorporated her findings in a memorial, and persuaded a male friend to present it to the state legislature—for a woman could not do such a thing. The memorial aroused angry reaction, but it was effective: a bill was passed providing improvement in the treatment of the mentally disturbed. Miss Dix continued investigating, extending her efforts throughout the nation, and in the early 1840s she presented—still by proxy—another memorial to the state government.

Dorothea Dix was a good example of a ladylike woman. In spite of her fervent belief in the necessity of her work, she was careful never to appear in public on her own, much less speak in public on even her favorite subject—there was no Fanny Wrightism about her. That kind of thing, she felt, was for men. She once wrote to a friend, "I am naturally timid and diffident, like all my sex," and she must have believed it in spite of much proof that others of her sex were not timid or diffident at all.

She happened to pass through Baltimore on April 19, 1861, three hours after the Sixth Massachusetts Regiment had been driven from the city, on her way to offer her services to the army Surgeon-General in Washington. Arriving safely, she was immediately appointed superintendent of women nurses, with orders to select and assign nurses to field or permanent military hospitals. She had such wide powers that the military took steps to curb them, and thereafter she had to function under the orders of the medical officer in charge, who was of the right sex. However, she did not complain. It was as if she had expected something of the sort. She was the ladylike, diffident Miss Dix; of course she did not complain. Nevertheless, her name is on the honor roll.

Clarissa Harlowe Barton was of a different temperament. She was born in 1821 in Oxford, Massachusetts; much younger than her brothers and sisters, Clara was petted and spoiled as if she were an only child. Her father, who had served in the Indian wars, told her stories of adventure, of battles and military maneuvers, until her mind was filled with those "unwomanly" matters. When one of her brothers fell ill, Clara was his devoted, skillful nurse, and he too talked to her at length of manly preoccupations, amusing himself during his long convalescence by teaching the child how to use tools and tie knots as if she might one day have to survive in the wilderness.

In adolescence Clara was at once practical and oversensitive, so painfully shy that her worried parents consulted the famous phrenologist Lorenzo B. Fowler and asked what they could do about her. Fowler said that the girl needed responsibility; perhaps she ought to teach school for a while. Accordingly, at the age of fifteen she became a teacher, and she proved a good one, interested and enterprising. After a few years she herself organized a school in North Oxford. Then she persuaded the authorities of Bordentown, New Jersey, to found a much-needed free school, promising to donate her services unpaid for the first three months. The school grew so fast that the townsfolk provided a new building for it, complete with a male principal—at which point Clara resigned, because she was no longer boss. She never cared for a subordinate position.

After this disagreement she went to Washington and worked in the Patent Office. Still there at the beginning of the war, she witnessed the disorderly arrival, on April 19, 1861, of the Sixth Massachusetts Regiment, which had been driven out of nearby Baltimore. Many of the men had lost their baggage in pell-mell flight, and Clara began to help them. She showed great aptitude for relief work. On her own initiative she advertised in the papers for contributions of food, clothing, blankets, and money for the troops, and when material began to pour in, she made herself head of a clearinghouse, or depot, to distribute it. She became so well known for these activities that in July 1862 the Surgeon-General gave her permission to go anywhere at the front or behind the lines that she might wish to, "upon the sick transports" to hand out comforts to the sick and wounded and to nurse them. Clara always played a role invented for herself: she was not associated with the Sanitary Commission or any other organization, because she felt that she functioned best on her own.

When the war ended, Miss Barton traveled about the country lecturing on her experiences, and helped to organize a search for missing men, until in September 1869 she went abroad for a holiday and found herself embroiled in more hostilities—the Franco-Prussian War. Then at last she joined an institution, the International Red Cross of Geneva. Clara had not heard of the Red Cross before, for the United States had adhered to its isolationist policy and refused to sign the Geneva Convention when that body was formed. Miss Barton admired the effectiveness of the Red Cross, and grew determined to bring America into contact with it. After returning home she toiled incessantly to achieve her end, lecturing and writing steadily on the subject. She was a small woman—five feet tall and of slight build—and, like so many American ladies, she had frequent bouts of ill health, but she continued campaigning in this one-woman struggle until at last, in 1882, she won. The American Red Cross came into being, with Clara Barton as its president.

Honesty compels me to admit that the story does not have a happy ending. Miss Barton, still determined to be boss, insisted on managing everything in the organization. It grew rapidly and she lost control. Details went wrong, things were neglected, and accounts were muddled. Unhappy underlings, who found it impossible to keep order, complained publicly in louder and louder tones, declaring that no one woman, not even Clara Barton, could handle the job properly. In spite of her fierce self-defensive tactics, the others got their way at last, and the Red Cross was investigated by a special commission. Sure enough, they uncovered much that was irregular, which could not have surprised them inordinately, for it was 1904 and the president was eighty-three. Miss Barton was forced to resign, and she departed still fully convinced that she was in the right and everyone else was wrong. During the seven years that followed, her friends found difficulty in persuading her not to cross the border into Mexico, to set up another Red Cross there. But the problem evaporated when she died.

Certainly Miss Barton was awkward during her latter years, but let anti-feminists take note: she *did* invent the American Red Cross.

Perhaps because she alienated so many people in Washington, Mrs. Swisshelm's name does not appear on that roll of honor in

Woman's Work. Yet she did her part in the war, in her highly individual style. Born Jane Grey Cannon in Pittsburgh, Pennsylvania, in 1816, she grew up to be one of those redoubtable little women that America produced in considerable numbers, being, in the words of Arthur J. Larsen, who edited her letters, "of slight figure, of less than medium height, with pleasant face, eyes beaming with kindliness, soft of voice, and winning manners." As one who had to earn a living for herself and her child, she had more reason than either Miss Barton or Miss Dix to resent the place of the female in the American scheme of things. Her parents were Scotch Covenanters, and her upbringing was strict. Jane's father died of tuberculosis when she was seven, and all the children had to work for whatever pennies they might bring in. Before Jane reached maturity, four of the siblings also had died of tuberculosis. She herself made lace for the market until it was discovered that she had a talent for painting, after which she made pictures for sale.

Pennsylvania had no public schools, though there were several colleges for boys. Jane attended a "subscription" school sporadically, until she had learned enough to qualify as a teacher at the age of fifteen. An intelligent girl, she thought for herself even at an early age. She met James Swisshelm at a church social, and admired him—a young man "over six feet tall, well formed and strongly built, with black hair and eyes, a long face, and heavy black whiskers," as she described him in her autobiography. He was the son of an old Revolutionary soldier who lived in the country near Pittsburgh. It is not clear what he was doing at a Scotch Covenanter chapel party, since the Swisshelms were the leading Methodists of the neighborhood. Probably he was after Jane: certainly he soon made his intentions known. Mrs. Cannon, mistrusting Methodists, tried to dissuade her daughter from accepting his attentions, but the whiskers were irresistible. Besides, James promised that Jane need not fear mother-in-law trouble because they would leave Pittsburgh as soon as they were married, and go to the Allegheny River to set up a sawmill. The wedding was celebrated when she was twenty-one.

Immediately afterward the bridegroom broke all his promises. Saying that there was plenty of room in the Swisshelm house, he told Jane that she might as well move in, even though she did not get on with her mother-in-law. And since Jane was a bright girl, he said, she should change over to Methodism and become a deaconess . . .

Years later, in retrospect, Jane wryly commented that her husband was not to blame in all this: he was only behaving like the Englishman of old who held that marriage annuls all previous contracts between the parties concerned. At the time, she admitted, she was not so philosophical: "I thought not of general laws, but only felt a private grievance." She told James she would not consider either becoming a Methodist or living with old Mrs. Swisshelm. Then she went home to her mother, continued to teach, and remained on reasonably good terms with her husband. After all, she wrote, never in twenty years of marriage did he strike her, and was always ready to take care of her when she was ill. But he could never understand how so frail a thing could be so obstinate.

In the end she had her way: two years after the wedding James yielded and took his wife away to Louisville, to join his brother in the lumber business. They sailed down the Mississippi, Jane wide-eyed at her first glimpse of the outside world. She was puzzled, however, by Louisville. Why were so many men off work in the middle of the morning? They were great dandies in their shining black broadcloth and stovepipe hats, with gold chains and diamond studs, but why did they stand around idle on corners and doorsteps by the hundreds, looking like crows on a cornfield fence?

A closer acquaintance with the town taught her that they were what she bitterly called the advance guard of woman whippers—that is, slave owners who lived on the proceeds of their female slaves' toil and progeny. They were a vast army that stretched back to the Atlantic and around the shores of the Gulf of Mexico. Jane resented their "lascivious stares" which insulted every unaccompanied woman, but most of all she was horrified to learn that they all lived, more or less, on the proceeds of selling their own mulatto children and on the work of the mothers which was often "extorted by the lash." One white-headed veteran existed entirely on the natural increase and wages of his nineteen women: a girl of eighteen lived with him in a fashionable boardinghouse, waited on him at table, and slept in his room, while her yearly wages of $175 were credited on his board bill. Slave-whipping and general exploitation were the rule in Louisville. Jane tried to swallow her indignation and never thrust her opinions on people, but when Southerners asked for them—and everyone did, she said—she told the truth. As a result, she was not popular. When she tried to run a school for black children, the endeavor was immediately stopped. Whether or not because of her, James's lumber business did not flourish, and to earn money Jane made corsets and dresses.

Two years after the Swisshelms arrived in Louisville, Mrs. Cannon wrote to say that she was very ill and would like to see Jane before dying. Her only other surviving daughter, Elizabeth, had married and gone to Minnesota. Jane wanted to leave immediately, James objected, and the couple quarreled. For a wife to disobey her husband was a serious matter, and Jane could not quite do it until she had prayed and thought at length. In the end she made up her mind and departed, after telling James that, come what might, she would never again live in a slave state. She nursed her mother until the lady died. When James came back to Pittsburgh there was a kind of reconciliation, made easier by the fact that each of them was somewhat better off than formerly. James had inherited his father's house and Jane came into one half of her mother's property, the other half going to Elizabeth. But a grievance against James remained in his wife's mind, never to be wholly forgotten: he had billed her mother's estate for her own services in nursing. There was an obvious similarity between her position and that of the slave girls of Louisville, and Jane felt humiliated, all the more so because her husband was within his legal rights in making the claim.

The thought rankled so much that she was grateful when she was asked to go to Butler, near Pittsburgh, and teach in a seminary. At least she would be away from James. She stayed in Butler for two years, teaching and writing. Poems and articles signed with a pen name were published in the town paper and in Philadelphia periodicals, but she signed her own name to a poem in which she attacked Methodist ministers for discriminating against blacks in their churches.

Relations between the Swisshelms worsened, if that was possible, over the sale of a piece of land Jane had inherited from her mother. Her signature to the deed was no good in law without her husband's, and James refused to sign unless the money was handed over to him. Jane wrote in her autobiography, "Mother's will was sacred to me. The money he proposed to put in improvements on the Swisshelm site. These, in case of his death before his mother, would go to his brothers. I had not even a dower right to the estate, and already the proceeds of my labor and income from my separate estate were upon it." She refused to give him the money. On her way home to Butler from a stormy interview she reflected that all humanity's advances had been made because of the pressures of injustice. Providence had given her a sign, a hint, of her duty. "The screws had been turned on me that I might do something to right the great wrong that forbade a married woman to own property," she decided.

She sought out law books and studied the question, then wrote a series of articles about it in the fashionable journalistic form of letters, which were published in the Pittsburgh *Commercial Journal*. As so often happens in these matters, hers was only one voice among many lifted in protest just then against the laws pertaining to married women's property, though they were as old as the country itself. In Philadelphia, Mrs. Mott too agitated for reform, until in 1847 and 1848 the Pennsylvania state legislature passed two bills allowing married women to hold property in their own right. Jane may not have exaggerated her influence in feeling that she had contributed to the victory. Stimulated, she conceived the daring idea of publishing a newspaper of her own, and approached the *Journal* editor, Robert M. Riddle, with a proposition. She would put up the money and edit her paper, she said, and Mr. Riddle was to print the paper on his press.

"What do you mean?" asked Riddle in alarm. "Are you insane? What does your husband say?"

Jane assured him that as long as she used her own money her husband would not care at all. Still Riddle demurred: had she considered all the expense involved? Did she realize that she would have to buy a desk, for instance? He pointed out that she could not do her work at home; she would have to spend a lot of time in the office. Jane was startled. She had not thought of this particular difficulty, and the prospect was daunting. She had heard of only one woman who actually worked in an office—Mary Kingston, whose father employed her as a clerk. And *his* office was at home, in the Kingston house. Modesty assailed Jane: she became suddenly conscious of her sex and her temerity.

"Here was I, looking not more than twenty, proposing to come into the office of the handsome stranger who sat bending over his desk that he might not see me blush for the unwomanly intent."

However, after a few minutes' thought Jane recovered her aplomb. Had she not been writing all along that women had the right to earn their livings as bookkeepers, saleswomen, and clerks? Why not publishers too? It should make no difference that Mr. Riddle was an elegant and polished gentleman, a man of the world with a reputation for gallantry. She told him that she would buy a desk and try not to get in his way, and so it was arranged. On the days when she and Mr. Riddle both worked in the office, each at his own desk, he was careful to open all the shutters so that the world could look at them.

Jane's paper, the *Pittsburgh Saturday Visiter,* made its first appearance on January 20, 1848. Riddle had questioned her spelling of "visitor," but Jane had Dr. Johnson's dictionary to back her up, and so it remained. The paper was strongly antislavery in sentiment, but if the owner expected abolitionists to welcome her support she was soon disillusioned. Most antislavery leaders were also antifeminist, and they made it plain that they did not want female help, to which Jane immediately retorted that she belonged to no party and needed no allies. An even stronger reaction came from the many editors who were stirred up by the fact that a woman was publishing a paper. Jane wrote:

> A woman has started a political paper! A woman! Could he believe his eyes? A woman! Instantly he sprang to his feet and clutched his pantaloons, shouted to the assistant editor when he, too, read and grasped frantically at his cassimeres [pants], called to the reporters and pressmen and types and devils who all rushed in, heard the news, seized their nether garments and joined the general chorus, "My breeches! oh, my breeches!" Here was a woman resolved to steal their pantaloons, their trousers, and when these were gone they might cry, "Ye have taken away my gods, and what have I more?" The insistence of the peril called for prompt action, and with one accord they shouted, "On to the breach, in defense of our breeches!" . . .
>
> "That woman shall not have *my* pantaloons," cried the editor of the big city daily; "nor my pantaloons," said the editor of the dignified weekly; "nor my pantaloons," said he who issued manifestoes but once a month; "nor mine," "nor mine," "nor mine," chimed in the small fry of the country towns.

But Horace Greeley gave the *Visiter* a respectful welcome, and so did a number of other editors of standing.

It was enjoyable to run the paper, dividing her time between antislavery agitation, arguments for the rights of women, and, presumably, wifely duties—for in 1851, at the age of thirty-five, Jane bore her first and only baby, a girl. But her health and vitality suffered, and when the child was a year old the mother reluctantly admitted to herself that she could no longer shoulder the responsibility of the *Visiter*, and it was merged with the *Journal*, leaving her free. This meant more friction with James at home, until in 1857, after one last demeaning quarrel with him over money, she picked up the child and moved out to her sister Elizabeth's house in St. Cloud, Minnesota. Elizabeth's family made her welcome, but were scandalized when she said she meant to move into the forest with her little girl and live there. Minnesota was still the frontier, they warned, and the Sioux could not be trusted; she must stay with them for at least a while.

Though Jane did not relish being dependent on her sister, she had to consent. Fortunately, she was strong again, and when a new chance of work came along she was glad to take it. The owner of a recently defunct newspaper in St. Cloud, having heard of her reputation, asked her to revive the periodical and edit it. Jane brought out the first issue of the *St. Cloud Visiter* in December 1857. But the publication faced one considerable difficulty: St. Cloud could not support an independent newspaper; it had to have powerful political backing to survive financially, which meant that Jane must decide to which party she owed her loyalty. If anything, she was a Republican, but the only backer on the horizon was a rich man named Lowry, a Democrat, who thought Jane might perfectly well become a Democrat too if he helped her paper. She was insulted by the suggestion. To put him in his place, I regret to say, she wrote and published an unflattering portrait of a lady who, though Jane did not name her, was all too obviously the wife of Lowry's good friend and attorney, James C. Shepley. Lowry's group was infuriated and vowed vengeance. One evening Lowry, Shepley, and Mrs. Shepley's brother broke into the office of the *Visiter* and wrecked it. They threw most of the type into the Mississippi and left an insulting note on Jane's desk. Such an outrage was too much for the town's solider citizens: they immediately called a meeting and voted to replace the type, repair the press, and subsidize the paper.

Naturally, everyone was waiting for the next issue of the *Visiter,* in May 1858, and they were not disappointed. In the first editorial Jane crowed over her enemies: "Dying is not difficult, yielding is impossible," she wrote. Shepley promptly brought suit for libel against her and against the new backers too, which worried Jane because it implicated others. She insisted that her champions stay out of the affair, leaving the whole matter to her. Then, in a personal interview with Shepley, she promised to print an apology for the offending article if he would withdraw the action. She gave a further promise that never again, in that case, would she refer to either matter in the *Visiter*'s columns. Shepley was mollified and agreed, whereupon Jane duly printed the apology and exoneration, on July 29. All was quiet, until the time came around for the *Visiter*'s next issue, on August 5. The *Visiter,* however, did not appear. In its stead, readers were offered a paper with a brand-new name, "*The St. Cloud Democrat:* Editor and Proprietor, Jane G. Swisshelm." Why "Democrat" instead of "Republican" she did not explain, but the *Democrat* carried the full story of the Lowry affair, exoneration and all.

"If these fellows destroy our office again, as they now threaten to do, we will go down to Hennepin County, and publish the St. Cloud *Democrat* there,'' threatened the editor.

At first merely to make money for the *Democrat,* then because she developed a taste for it, Jane lectured at abolitionist meetings on women's rights and slavery. ''Woman and Politics'' was one of her favorite lectures, but after the Civil War started she spoke also on ''Women in the War of the Rebellion.'' Editorially, she had begun to incline toward the Republican Party all over again until a crisis deflected public attention in St. Cloud from politics; in 1862 the Sioux Indians of Minnesota went on the warpath and massacred hundreds of whites in the Minnesota River Valley. They then moved on toward St. Cloud, drawing dangerously close when they attacked Sauk Center and Maine Prairie, only twelve miles off. In an editorial, Jane turned violently against ''these red-jawed tigers whose fangs are dripping with the blood of the innocents!'' She became convinced that their revolt was part of a Southern plot, and vigorously opposed missionaries who begged that the Indians be treated with mercy. She felt so strongly that in January 1863 she set out on a speaking tour of the East, appearing in Chicago, Philadelphia, Brooklyn, and Washington to say that the Sioux should be drastically punished. In Washington, thanks to Secretary Edwin M. Stanton, she was offered a job as clerk in the War Department, and took it so that she could remain there at the center of things. She sold the *Democrat* at long distance, a nephew taking over the paper.

For some reason Jane was not put to work immediately on her new job, and she abhorred a vacuum. Looking around, she found that nurses were badly needed for the wounded soldiers pouring into the capital. She volunteered for service in the Campbell Hospital near the city and toiled there for months. There too, according to the autobiography, she witnessed great stupidity, mismanagement, and downright heartlessness in the way officials treated wounded men. On one occasion the wife of a wounded man begged for her help. The husband, in the last stages of camp fever, had no straw to lie on—bedding of any sort was short—and the wife had begged in vain either for straw or for permission to take him home and let him die in comfort. Both requests were turned down. Jane Swisshelm took up the matter with the great Miss Dix, who, as she said scathingly, was neither shocked nor surprised. ''I had never seen her before,'' she wrote, ''but her tall, angular person, very red face, and totally unsympathetic manner, chilled me.'' Jane had expected Miss Dix to offer her an ambulance, ''the best in the service,'' exclusively devoted to her own use, to bring a bed that same morning for the man, but Miss Dix made no such suggestion. She said that she had engagements all day and so could do nothing then or the next day, because that would be Sunday, and she never worked on Sunday. On Monday she did rebuke the surgeon in charge about the matter, which made Mrs. Swisshelm unpopular around the hospital; in the meantime the man died, still lying on the bare ground.

Such incidents drove Jane to work like a fury, until she had a breakdown. Recovered, she at last took up her duties at the War Department. After the end of the war she started another paper in Washington, the *Reconstructionist,* but it had a short life because the editor disapproved of Andrew Johnson's methods and said so, frankly, in her editorials. Johnson got her fired from the War Department. Without a salary she couldn't carry on with the paper, so that was that. What on earth was she to do next? James had died, not that she would have appealed to him, but before there was time to despair, she found that she had a valid claim, after all, on the old Swisshelm estate. Stanton encouraged her to fight the case in court, and she won it. Thereafter Jane Swisshelm lived in Swissville, as the place was called, in reasonable comfort, until she died at the age of sixty-eight.

Jane Swisshelm was courageous, tenacious, sometimes vain, often irrational or at least unjust, but for the most part admirable and even lovable. She was real: one feels that one has known her. And of course she *was* real, whereas our next specimen of American womanhood was not.

In 1867, when the war was still a vivid memory to Americans, there appeared a new kind of novel which can fairly be called realistic. It was not tailored to fit the popular taste like the happy-ever-after stories of Louisa Alcott or the moralistic milk-and-water of Fanny Fern. Not because it was very popular—it was not, though it was not a failure either—but because it affords a credible picture of ladies of the period, we should scrutinize the heroine of John William De Forest's *Miss Ravenel's Conversion from Secession to Loyalty.* It was a topical story of the war, with vivid and truthful scenes of battle: De Forest himself served with the Union Army and knew what he was talking about. But his realism extended further. It was hard to care as much for Lillie Ravenel as her creator did, but we recognize her as we recognize her aunt, wicked Mrs. Larue. They are three-dimensional women, not cardboard figures. The novel is one of those works that mark a transition in American literature. As far as this reader is concerned, its only serious drawback is that the qualities in his heroine that De Forest seems to admire do not seem at all admirable today—and he can hardly be blamed for that discrepancy. We must accept that where to us she appears ignorant, illogical, and tiresome, to him she was ignorant, illogical, and delightful.

On the eve of the Civil War, in New Boston (New Haven), a young lawyer of the town, Colburne, meets Ravenel, a doctor and amateur geologist from New Orleans, who has brought his motherless daughter to the North because he has strong abolitionist feelings and is no longer comfortable in Louisiana. Colburne's first sight of the girl is in the doorway, good-humoredly scolding her father for wearing spectacles, which, she says, make him look as old as Ararat. Catching sight of Colburne then, she rustles away in confusion. Any strange man, evidently, is enough to confuse Miss Ravenel. In their sitting room she asks her father what has kept him so long, adding, "I have been as lonely as a mouse in a trap." Lillie Ravenel cannot bear to be alone. She wants to talk, and we cannot blame her, for after all, she has nothing to do.

On the differences between North and South, particularly on slavery, she does not see eye to eye with her father. "Like all young people and almost all women she was strictly local, narrowly geographical in her feelings and opinions."

Colburne, a typical New Englander, slightly priggish and thoroughly abolitionist, nevertheless falls in love with the pretty Southerner. "Miss Ravenel . . . was very fair, with lively blue eyes and exceedingly handsome hair, very luxuriant, very wavy and of a flossy blonde color lighted up by flashes of amber." She has the fascinating habit, too, of blushing and fluttering when she meets a man.

As the war proceeds, Lillie is unregenerate enough to dance for joy at the news of Bull Run, but then she meets the darkly good-looking, virile Colonel Carter of the Union Army and begins to change her mind. Dr. Ravenel correctly suspects that Carter is a heavy drinker and a wencher, but Lillie is too innocent to share his impression. The fortunes of war take all our leading characters, Colburne (now a captain), Carter, and the Ravenels, to New Orleans, where the Ravenels live next door to Lillie's aunt, Mrs. Larue. Lillie likes Carter more and more as their acquaintance ripens, but when he is not there she is idle and bored. "Where are you going?" she demands at sight of her father leaving the house—"eagerly and almost pettishly, in a semi-aggrieved tone. . . . If he would go, it was 'When will you come back?' and when he returned it was 'Where have you been?' and 'Who did you see?' and 'What did he say?' "

When Southern ruffians attack Dr. Ravenel, his daughter's loyalty moves toward the North. As the novelist muses, "Women, especially warm-hearted women offended in the persons of those whom they love, are so terribly illogical!" Then Colonel Carter proposes to Lillie—"Such a moment as this is one of the supreme moments of a woman's life"—and her conversion is complete. She agonizes when her lover is at the front: "Is there no list of killed and wounded? Has our loss been heavy? What do you think? . . . Oh, Papa, don't, please, go to the hospital today. I can't bear to stay alone."

After the marriage Colburne, as one of Colonel Carter's officers, observes him being flagrantly unfaithful: at Fort Hudson he witnesses a scene of debauchery—"a sloppy table, with bottles and glasses and the laughing faces of two bold-browed, slatternly girls." The colonel, in an old dressing gown and dirty slippers, face flushed, eyes bloodshot, is winking, leering, and slightly unsteady. Soon, however, Carter is made quartermaster and stays at home with his bride, indulging in crooked methods to make money. Lillie gets pregnant and becomes—for the modern reader—unbearably coy about it:

"She had repeatedly hinted to her husband that she had a secret to tell him. When he asked what it was she blushed, laughed at him for the question, and declared that he should never know it, that she had no secret at all, that she had been joking. Then she declared that he should not guess it; thought it the strangest thing in the world that he should not know it. At last she made her confession: made it to him alone, with closed doors and in darkness; she could no more have told him in the light of day than in the presence of a circle."

We are wholly in accord with Carter when, in reply to his wife's protests because he is being sent back to war, he says indignantly, "My darling, you want to make a woman of me." A harsh fate indeed, if it were possible.

After he has gone Lillie finds that he has been carrying on an affair with Mrs. Larue, and the discovery nearly deprives her of her reason. She does not see Carter again or forgive him, and he is killed in action. Months later she is taken by Dr. Ravenel, with her infant son, back to New Boston, and eventually marries Colburne. We are left to reflect that never once in the long story has our heroine done anything but love, pester her father, wait, watch, weep, and, at one high point in her life, give birth. Yet, as I have said, she is a real person. That is why her portrait, and the author's manifest approval of the original, are so shocking.

CHAPTER 15

Any Male Inhabitant . . .

WHEN ONE LOOKS BACK at the beginning of feminine protest and the first tentative attempts of American women to be objective about their condition, one is impressed by the modesty of their demands. However shocking these may have been to the men of their day, it seems to us that none of the women could with justice be called extremist or even unduly ambitious. With the exception of "Mary Astell," the seventeenth-century English rebel who wrote about the subjection of women, nobody seems to have questioned the underlying assumptions that defined woman's status in the general scheme. In Judeo-Christianity and especially the Pauline ethic, woman's place was clearly defined and limited; in nineteenth-century politics it still was. Woman was the great Mother, but at the same time she was intrinsically inferior to man. She was man's inspiration, also his slave; above him and beneath him but never on a level with him. Man was master. Everything depended on him. Yet the Family, which was all-important, depended more directly on woman, and she must never forget her responsibility for it.

Evidently no one was aware that this tight conception of family did not necessarily derive from the earliest civilization of the West. People thought of the modern family structure as permanent, a direct inheritance from our earliest fathers, a manifestation of one of our fundamental instincts. If all social customs did not have divine origin, at least they were assumed to be "natural" and therefore right. Family life was assumed to be the same as it had always been—a pattern of monogamous pairing for life, yet contradictions of this "natural" life style were visible to anyone who read the Bible. With the exception of a few radicals like John Humphrey Noyes and Joseph Smith, people ignored the evidence of the Book of Genesis, for example, in which it is told how Sarah, wife of Abraham, did not have chilren for ten years, so she handed over her handmaiden Hagar to her husband to be his wife—"And he went in unto Hagar, and she conceived . . ." And what of Jacob, who was fooled into taking Leah for a wife but later got the sister he wanted, Rachel, and kept them both? Then Rachel, because she thought she was barren, made him sleep with her maid Bilpah, and Leah, after having change of life, handed over *her* maid Zilpah to the ever-ready Jacob, and Rachel's womb was opened by the Lord—it goes on and on, a most unedifying tale that was simply ignored by people in the nineteenth century. To them, one man with his one wife and their children, living in a cozy group, represented the norm.

Women who complained that they were not treated justly were presumed to be flying in the face of nature, and the nuclear family was a concept so generally accepted that even the most extreme feminist did not question its durability. The family was firmly believed to be the armature of society, its very bones, and Mrs. Stanton herself would not have tried to change it very radically. What she and her colleagues hoped for was merely reform of a superficial kind—explicitly, change through the polls. Everything would be made right, they thought, if only women had the vote.

Saying this is not to downgrade their accomplishment in raising women's status. They were not the only people to invest heavily in the doctrine of democracy as a panacea, or to believe in it as a force that can alter the universe. It is not the suffragist faith that is surprising; it is that such women moved as far as they did beyond the position allotted to them. When we look at pictures of nineteenth-century women, those smothered, swaddled bodies and hobbled feet, and when we read the pap on which their minds fed, we realize the gigantic scale of their achievement. After all, they were opposed not by a foreign enemy it was easy to hate, but by their own husbands, sons, and lovers. In this war, love itself had to give way.

> Man's love is of man's life a thing apart:
> 'Tis woman's whole existence.

Byron's lines were the essence of fashionable philosophy, yet many married women, if they had told the truth, would have testified that for them existence was often nearer hatred than love, and that marriage however happy is a mixture of both. Still, in spite of such reality, ladies eagerly read romantic slush, *Lady Audley's Secret* or

The Fatal Marriage, and allowed themselves to indulge in a kind of half-belief. They were not averse, either, to being told by everyone that they were angels of the domestic hearth, that there is something sacred about motherhood, and that the price of a good woman is above rubies. They were willing to agree that they were too fine and delicate to worry their pretty little heads over mundane matters: it was flattering, and made up for many indignities.

Nevertheless, here and there, a few exceptional women were beginning to demand a better education for their sex, though they found it hard going. As men quickly argued, to ward off the extra expense, the interference with accustomed routine, and all the mysterious danger inherent in women's beginning to think for themselves, why should it be necessary? Weren't they themselves responsible for the family, and couldn't they do all the thinking necessary?

Even today arguments in favor of educating girls tend to be few and repetitive, so it is not surprising that one of the basic excuses for this supposedly heinous exercise was used back in the 1820s by Catherine Beecher when she conducted her seminary for females in Hartford, Connecticut. Miss Beecher felt it necessary to excuse herself, even though her motives were pure—she was trying to keep girls out of the factories. Let them teach instead, she said, or better, let them be properly trained for their rightful job of housekeeping, and she emphasized those subjects that would today come under the heading Home Economics: cooking, sewing, and so on. As we have seen, she attacked Angelina Grimké for advocating women's rights and appearing on lecture platforms. Her attitude seems illogical in an educational innovator, but within her limits Miss Beecher was consistent. In the kind of world she wanted, right-thinking women stayed at home, and with her seminary she was merely trying to temper the wind for those who could not. Yet there is something puzzling about her ambition to train teachers, since according to her their only object was to train more teachers to train teachers—and so *ad infinitum.* If girls were not to engage in more diverse careers . . .

However, Miss Beecher did provide another justification for what she proposed to do in schooling females. Women ought to be educated, she explained, so that they might be worthy mothers of men, the achievers. Of course they should not themselves enter the arena of life—that was an offensive thought. But it would be as well if they were able to give good counsel in the nursery.

Admittedly, the argument sounds far-fetched. Yet even now it is common currency and crops up in every discussion of female education; inevitably the moment arrives when someone says, "What's the use of spending a lot of effort and money on a girl when she'll only get married as soon as she's out of school?" In Catherine Beecher's time, just as today, advanced women were infuriated by such reasoning, but a few pragmatists among them were willing to go along with it because, as they said, education is education, even when it is bestowed for the wrong reasons. Once a girl has learned the trick of thinking, she can safely be left to go on by herself.

Oberlin having led the way by introducing coeducation at its founding in 1833, in due course and at deliberate speed other institutions followed its example. For some time, however, these advances toward higher education for women were rather markedly confined to the Western states that today are called the Middle West, probably because their women were of the type, found at the frontier, of unusually assertive character. Since they were also comparatively few in number, they usually got their own way more easily than women in the East. Antioch, the second college after Oberlin, opened classes to girls in 1852. Next to take the giant step was Iowa State University, in 1858, and five years later came the turn of Wisconsin State. Here, however, the authorities cautiously limited their permission and allowed coeds only in the normal training courses, so that the girls had to fight their way, year by year and course by course, into other departments. In 1858 and 1859 a dozen girls vainly besieged Michigan, but were fought off each time by the board of regents.

Of course the Civil War put a halt to all such activities for the duration. Afterward, however, the girls' struggle for education at Michigan was resumed, but the regents held out until 1870, by which time the barricades around a large number of other universities had been stormed, and other colleges had been founded, as Oberlin had been, as coeducational institutions from the beginning. By the time Michigan gave in and became coeducational, girls were attending classes with men in such far-flung places as New York, California, Massachusetts, Illinois, and Ohio.

In the meantime, the development of schools exclusively for women continued. Among the first to follow in Miss Beecher's footsteps was Prudence Crandall, a Quaker girl from Hopkinton, Rhode Island. Miss Crandall's efforts, however, were directed mainly toward educating black girls, rather than women in general: she was an abolitionist and, not merely incidentally, a deft propagandist. In 1834 in the little town of Canterbury, Connecticut, she opened a school for black girls and in consequence was subjected by the town's worthies to bitter persecution. They started out with simple verbal protest, but feeling mounted until the school building was attacked and set on fire, after which Miss Crandall's classes came to an end. The development was no surprise to her; her fundamental intention had been to dramatize the evils of race prejudice, and in this she indubitably succeeded, for the case had widespread repercussions.

The early girls' schools, like their prototype in Hartford, trained pupils only to a point roughly the equivalent of today's junior-high-school level. For example, Mount Holyoke, of South Hadley, Massachusetts, started out this way.

Mary Lyon, the founder of Mount Holyoke, was born in 1797 on a Massachusetts farm. Having had a struggle to achieve her own education, she wanted fervently to help other underprivileged girls surmount similar difficulties. Her approach was practical. Realizing that nobody could succeed in building a school without a firm financial base, Miss Lyon in 1834, the year that saw the destruction of Prudence Crandall's school, set the figure of twenty-seven thousand dollars as the minimum capital on which she could manage to run the establishment. She also decided that her school would be a new kind, with higher sights than the others. Pupils would be selected by entrance examination and would be expected to complete a three-year course instead of the customary one that lasted two years. But convention decreed that a woman could not personally solicit funds for even such a worthy reason as this: like Dorothea Dix, Mary Lyon had to find gentlemen to act as her representatives and even to claim credit for her ideas. She found men willing to act in this way and sponsor the projected school, but when it became obvious that they were making a hash of the campaign to collect funds, Miss Lyon ruthlessly sacrificed good form and took over—and after all, the heavens did not fall. On the contrary, her temerity was rewarded and she got the necessary money from various sources, mainly parents who cared about the welfare of their daughters, but also girls who raised funds from bazaars, dances, and the like. In November 1837, Mount Holyoke opened. Though it did not attain the status of college until near the end of the century, by that time it was highly regarded and able to take its place in the forefront of women's educational institutions, along with Vassar, Wellesley, Smith, and Bryn Mawr, which had been founded in the meantime.

The enforced pause in the development of education during the Civil War gave people the chance to think again about girls and what was due to them. The idea of endowing colleges instead of mere schools for women caught on among a few moneyed people in the North, especially those of New England, once they were relieved of the necessity of worrying about abolition. All of a sudden there was a spurt in the building of women's colleges. Matthew Vassar, a businessman of Poughkeepsie, was the first to start by making a generous endowment for Vassar College, which opened in 1865. Then Wellesley and Smith, both in Massachusetts, opened their doors in 1875 in a neck-and-neck race, twenty-four hours apart. Like Vassar, Wellesley was endowed by a man, a rich Bostonian named Henry Durant, but Smith's money was provided by a spinster named Sophia Smith. She at least had not been caught up in any recent fad: the college had been a hope of hers for much of her life.

The three colleges all had entrance requirements pitched as high as the authorities dared place them, so that they equaled those of the best men's colleges, which sounded a good thing, but there were disadvantages too in this approach. Few girls had been trained to meet such exacting specifications, and most applicants failed the first examinations. There would have been almost no students in the opening classes at Vassar and Wellesley if their governors had not met the problem by creating preparatory departments—cram courses—where candidates could make themselves ready, then take the examinations again. (The nation has had to turn to similar expedients recently, in preparing underprivileged black students for college with cram courses.) It was a few years before the various girls' preparatory schools were able to do what was required of them, but the situation was remedied at last and the colleges were able to discard their cram courses, Wellesley in 1881 and Vassar in 1888. Smith, on the other hand, took the Spartan road and simply turned away all applicants who did not qualify. Such heroic measures took their toll—the first class at Smith was composed of only fourteen students.

Naturally all this development pulled up the female education system forcibly, by its boot straps, but alert observers must have realized that there was danger in such aristocratic institutions: private, expensive colleges would never produce widespread improvements but only an intellectual elite. There is nothing wrong with such an elite, of course, but it was not what the college founders meant to create; they wanted to improve the standards of education for all American women. Sophia Smith especially envisioned her college as a force that would change the world for women. She wrote in her will: "It is my belief that by the higher and more thorough Christian education of women, what are called their 'wrongs' will be redressed, their wages adjusted, their weight of influence in reforming the evils of society will be greatly increased . . . their power for good will be incalculably enlarged." Miss Smith could hardly have expected such a wealth of benefits to come all at once, but she obviously believed that her graduates would spread light throughout the multitude of their sisters, rich and poor. What she never realized was that for the great mass of women, daughters of poor immigrants and freed slaves, and even to most white middle-class females, these blessings would be very slow in arriving.

Fortunately the public school system improved rapidly during the same years that saw the birth of women's colleges. It might have been swamped or at least dislocated just after the war if liberated slave children had swarmed into the regular schools, but here the abolitionists saw to it that Southern authorities opened special colored schools, to tide them over the first rush. Of course faults developed, even then. Though these schools were designed for both sexes, little girls were usually kept at home to help with housework while their privileged brothers attended class. Black girls were victimized much as white girls had been in colonial times, perhaps in part because African tradition decreed such treatment for females. While little black girls had to struggle for their right to go to school, the bigger ones who aspired to higher education had an even harder time. And the situation did not improve with the years: three decades after the end of the war, things were much the same. In 1892 a Latin teacher in Washington, a black woman, complained of it: "I fear that the majority of colored men do not yet think it worthwhile that women aspire to higher education." There was also the fact that higher education must have cost more than many black families could afford, but whatever the cause, Eleanor Flexner has observed that many places in schools and colleges for black girls went unfilled: "There was a growing Negro population, in the North and West, with access to better schools than in the South, yet the number of Negro graduates from the major women's colleges was still infinitesimal at the time of a study made . . . in 1900, and not much better when a second one was made ten years later."

Everything considered, it is remarkable that any black girls managed to win degrees and enter professions, but some did. The first black female lawyer in America, Charlotte Ray, took her degree at Howard University Law School in 1872 and practiced for years. Some few girls became doctors, but most black women, even those who won degrees, occupied humbler niches, as nurses or teachers. Of course, one could say the same of white girls holding degrees; the difference is in numbers. In proportion, more white women than black made their way to the top. For the blacks there were many more hurdles to cross, and many more were forced out of the race.

Through the war Elizabeth Cady Stanton, Susan Anthony, and their colleagues had agreed to hold their tongues and cease to agitate for women's rights, reasoning that no one would listen to them anyway and that their position would be better afterward, since women were proving themselves capable of adequate, intelligent action in a man's world. It did not take long, however, to prove that the gains made by their sex vanished after the war like the morning dew. When Johnny came marching home again, his first action was to snatch back his job from whatever female had held it down while he was away. There was nothing she could do about it; amid all the excitement and jubilation her protest would have seemed abhorrent. Soon dispossessed females were a glut on the labor market. It was hard enough for any of them, but hardest for those who now had to take care of maimed husbands or fatherless children.

Mrs. Stanton's group reasoned that now was the time to make women listen and persuade them to demand the vote as a means of improving their lot. Now was the time, as well, because of the war's main outcome, the liberation of the slaves. It was a foregone conclusion that the Reconstructionists would give blacks the franchise as soon as the necessary constitutional amendment could be drafted, and it seemed reasonable to hope that women too would be enfranchised; their cause had run in harness with that of the blacks since early in the abolitionist campaign. But the suffragists underestimated male resistance to this proposal. They were too sanguine. Women's work in the war had not wrought a miracle: nothing had altered the antifeminist reaction of the average man to the idea of woman suffrage. He was against women's rights, he had always been against them, and his recent experience had not made any difference to the case. So what if women *had* run the Sanitary Commission well enough? It was merely a projection of housekeeping, which women knew innately how to do. So what if his wife *had* managed the farm without catastrophe while he was away? No use encouraging her to get a swelled head over it. A woman was still a woman as God had made her, and her place was at home with the children, not traipsing around the polls among a lot of riffraff.

The feminists must have been aware of this sentiment, but they did not realize its full strength. They still expected the support of the triumphant Republican Party on the votes issue, and they were really shocked and surprised when it was not forthcoming. The Reconstructionists were preoccupied with the mechanics of enfranchising freedmen, and they had no time for the old story of women's rights. In spite of all that had been said on lecture platforms and at conventions, these rights seemed to the politicians a problem that had nothing to do with having won the war. The worst betrayal, in the opinion of Mrs. Stanton's colleagues, was dealt to them by their old allies the abolitionists, who now turned their backs on the cause and refused to listen. For they too were deeply involved with Reconstruction and the many problems concerning blacks—resettlement, education, work for homeless drifters. They were anxious to avoid embarrassing and clouding the issue, and they thought that women's rights, however deserving a cause, would imperil the Negro's chances of getting the vote. The ghost of the old Grimké-Weld controversy had come back to haunt the feminists. For a while victory had seemed close. In 1866, sorely disappointed, the women's leaders felt that they were worse off than ever.

And when the suggested draft for the Fourteenth Amendment was published, the worst fears of the embattled women were realized, for in the text the right to vote was said to belong to "any *male* inhabitant" of the United States. This was the first time such a qualification had ever been set out in the federal instrument, even tentatively, though in state constitutions it was commonplace, and its significance was not lost on the woman suffragists. As an important part of their strategy, they had planned to get women's right to the franchise stated clearly in the federal Constitution, since this inclusion would automatically make it law in every state in the Union. Contrariwise, if the draft amendment should pass just as it stood, the women would have no chance of victory for years to come. All the work would start again: they would have to fight wearisomely for suffrage, state by state, across the country. Instead of advancing during the war, the cause of women's rights had been pushed back by the amendment—if, as seemed likely, it passed into law.

Elizabeth Stanton was so offended by the word "male" in the draft that she threw to the winds her work for abolition and the North's recent victory over the South. If women could not have the vote, she declared, the Negroes should not get it either. Her stand estranged a number of her former associates, who were shocked and angry. One of them, her old friend Frederick Douglass, retorted in public that the Negro had suffered far more than the white women of America: there was no possible comparison. It was the black man's turn to share in whatever good had come out of the Civil War, he said; the urgent problem was to relieve the freed slaves. If anyone had to wait, let it be the women—and a fairly large number of whites thought Douglass right. Julia Ward Howe even argued that if too much fuss of this sort was made over the amendment, the whole thing might stall: the blacks would lose out, and the women would be no better off than they already were. In the heat of argument it remained for the female black abolitionist Sojourner Truth, who had often appeared on the lecture platform as an associate of Mrs. Stanton, to remind the world that there were black women as well as black men, and that they too should have the vote. "If colored men get their rights, and not colored women theirs," she warned, "you will see the colored men will be masters over the women, and it will be as bad as it was before." This eminently commonsensical remark may not have made the impression it deserved on everyone who heard it, but Elizabeth Stanton did calm down after a while and accepted the inevitable—a state-by-state campaign.

First step in this program, as Mrs. Stanton and her friends saw it, was Kansas, where in 1867, recasting their state constitution, the people were holding a referendum on woman suffrage and the black vote. It would be a test case, and the woman suffragists made up their minds to concentrate on Kansas. But none of them had as yet started on the journey when they got the bad news that the recently formed American Women's Equal Rights Association had come out in favor of the Fourteenth Amendment draft in its entirety, without requesting that the offending word "male" be deleted. Never mind: Kansas remained to be convinced, and Lucy Stone with her husband Henry Blackwell spearheaded the attack, traveling to their goal well ahead of the referendum date and campaigning all the way. After them came Elizabeth Stanton and her faithful ally Miss Anthony. It was an uncomfortable trip for everyone, in primitive conditions, and in the end it proved futile, for in spite of meetings, posters, lectures, and debates, the men of Kansas voted down both the women's and the blacks' franchise. This did not in the end matter to the Negroes, since in 1868 the Fourteenth Amendment (unreformed) became part of the Constitution and they got their vote, but for the feminists the battle of the states had still to be fought.

Much would depend on changing the attitude of ordinary American women, for whom everything they had been taught heretofore was the direct opposite of what Mrs. Stanton's group believed and expounded. Ladies did not resent things as they were. Ladies did not take militant action, or demand their "rights," and of course every woman wanted to behave like a lady. The rules of genteel behavior sentenced ladies to a private existence: there was still, in the 1870s and later, a widespread fear among women of being accused of "Fanny Wrightism." And it was almost as bad, they thought, to be accused of enjoying rude health; it was far more aristocratic and ladylike to be delicate. At any rate, one did not talk too specifically about health, because bodily functions were not mentioned in good society. Strictly speaking, ladies did not have bodies at all. As tough a warrior as Angelina Grimké, whose husband was sympathetic and understanding, underwent years of discomfort, even agony, rather than let the world know that she had "female trouble"—a prolapsed uterus. Such matters were shrouded in mystery, whispered about, terrifying. Like priestesses, ladies partook of this mystery: to think of them in connection with such a mundane thing as the vote was incongruous.

Such were the attitudes the woman suffragists set out to alter. It was all the more difficult to do because they themselves were not free of the Victorian blight. Most of them, therefore, spoke to their female audiences only of proper, unsexy subjects, of legal and political reforms. In her private life Mrs. Stanton had many problems. She had a difficult, demanding marriage, but she never allowed it to impinge on her public work. Fortunately, as she wrote to Susan Anthony, her childbearing days were now over; her faith was in the franchise, not in private felicity. For many women, indeed, the cause of feminism offered compensation for personal disappointments. In espousing it they found in themselves new talents and learned, like women workers in the war, that they could actually organize, plan strategy, and effect events as well as men did. Acting together, they could at least shake the earth a little, even if they failed to move mountains. It was an exhilarating discovery.

But they were for the most part of the middle class, and for the success of feminism working-class women were probably more important, since they were in closer contact with the inequities that harassed their sex. Working women knew from harsh experience that they were always paid less than men for doing the same jobs. Yet where men did not engage in the work at all, as in the seamstress's trade, pay was ludicrously small. Called up to sew uniforms during the war, many seamstresses were now unnecessary, and could not make a living.

Susan Anthony set out to organize the women who did manual labor, and teach them how to form unions. She found help among a number of workingmen who approved of unions and had some of their own. Two groups, the cigar makers and the printers, welcomed the women who worked with them and invited them to join their unions. But Susan Anthony aimed further than this: she advised women to form unions without men, so that they might be independent. Out of her efforts came two organizations, the Working Women's Association and the Protective Association for Women, the latter concentrating on getting legal aid for its members when necessary, and finding jobs. All in all there was a good deal of industrial organization among women early in the 1870s, when female typesetters, laundry workers, collar makers, textile workers, and shoe workers formed their own unions. Unfortunately every one of them, along with men's unions, disappeared in the depression that afflicted American trade in 1873–74, and after the economy had recovered, the women's organizations did not get a new start. Unlike men, women were always being interrupted by what society accepted as prior claims on their time—leaving their jobs to get married, to have children, or to look after relatives. In any case, most of their work was unskilled, and the pay was not enough to induce them to stay on at one job rather than another.

To marry and bear children was still the most important thing. In spite of the most spirited, talented feminist exhortations, improved education, and native intelligence, as long as women were subjected—or, rather, subjected themselves—to uncontrolled breeding, this situation would not change. As antifeminists so truly said, there was no flying in the face of nature.

One good thing came out of the Kansas failure, an incident guaranteed to cheer Elizabeth Stanton and Susan Anthony—a munificent, surprising gift from a comparative stranger named George Francis Train, often referred to as "The Eccentric Millionaire." Train, a tall, skinny man, had made his money in various ways and in many countries. He had owned ship's companies, introduced trams into England, been in the retail business in Australia, and in America helped to organize the Union Pacific Railway before turning his attention to philosophical causes. At the time the ladies encountered him in Kansas he was enthusiastic about women's suffrage. Seemingly out of the blue, all of a sudden there he was, making speeches. One day he asked Susan Anthony why there was no newspaper representing women's rights, and she replied that they had no money for it. A few days later Train announced that he was founding a feminist weekly to be called *The Revolution,* to be run by Susan Anthony and Mrs. Stanton. The women had scarcely caught their breath when they found themselves on a subsidized journey back to the East, and in all the principal cities on the way Train organized meetings for them to address.

The Revolution first appeared January 8, 1868. Then, having found for it a second backer, Train rushed off in pursuit of another cause, Fenianism, or the liberation of Ireland, for which he was shortly put into jail in England, but thanks to the other angel the paper was able to carry on for a considerable time, proving a valuable forum for women's suffrage and such peripheral matters as divorce, property rights, and employment.

In spite of this shot in the arm for the cause, however, the split in the women's movement, first visible when its leaders disagreed over the Fourteenth Amendment, widened during 1869. After lengthy discussions Mrs. Stanton and Miss Anthony came to the conclusion that the Women's Equal Rights Association could no longer be considered representative of women's interests, because many men in the membership favored working for the black male franchise in advance of claiming votes for women. What was needed, the friends thought, was an exclusively female organization. Therefore, just after the Equal Rights Association's annual meeting in January 1870, they formed the National Woman Suffrage Association, with Mrs. Stanton as President, which was open to any woman who agreed with their aims.

The formation of NWSA angered a number of people, including Lucy Stone and Julia Ward Howe, and as a retort they formed their own body, the American Woman Suffrage Association. AWSA women were more conservative than those of the NWSA; some were not even sure they wanted votes for women, and all favored a more cautious approach to campaigning than Mrs. Stanton's. They too had a paper, the *Woman's Journal,* which was not dependent on fly-by-night eccentrics but was solidly endowed. The *Journal*'s competition, in fact, pushed *The Revolution,* sore beset by money troubles as it was, off the stands and killed it. The AWSA considered the NWSA not quite respectable because some of the latter's members had radical notions, such as that divorce and women's unions were good things. The members felt themselves amply justified, therefore, when a lady named Victoria Woodhull came along and brought notoriety and embarrassment to her friends in the NWSA, merely by association.

CHAPTER 16

Victoria

THE BEAUTIFUL VICTORIA WOODHULL, *née* Claflin, was born in Ohio in 1838. Several books have been written about her, and no wonder: she was a fascinating character, not simply an opportunist, not altogether a phony or the complete blackmailer, but something of all these. She was not exactly a tart either, and certainly she was no fool. Perhaps it is safest to say that she was an oddity, and that it was bad luck for Elizabeth Cady Stanton when Mrs. Woodhull declared herself a champion of women's rights.

She did many other things first, however. As a young girl she earned money as a clairvoyant. Married at fifteen to a drunkard, Canning Woodhull, she bore him two children. In 1866 she left him for Colonel James Harvey Blood, a St. Louis man with a keen interest in spiritualism. It was from Blood that Victoria picked up her education and many of her ideas, such as women's rights and "free love." After the lovers had managed—each of them—to get divorced, they married each other, and Blood moved into the Claflin family. For a while they all lived on money earned by Victoria and her favorite younger sister, Tennessee, through selling spiritual advice.

Mrs. Woodhull, as she continued to call herself, was not completely cynical about this work, though Tennessee seems to have been willing to fake any amount of spiritual advice. Several times Victoria made important decisions because of visions she had while in trance, as for instance in 1868, when she was told by no less a ghostly authority than Demosthenes that a new life awaited her and hers in New York at a particular address. Victoria lost no time in taking the household straight there. Who was living in the house when they arrived, and how they were persuaded to move out, is not explained by the lady in her memoirs. But it was a fortunate location, since the recently widowed Commodore Cornelius Vanderbilt, a seventy-six-year-old millionaire, lived nearby, and he had great faith in spiritualism.

Vanderbilt was delighted with the pretty sisters. Tennessee, who claimed to be a magnetic healer, relieved his various aches and pains, while Victoria, as a medium, put him in touch with dead-and-gone friends. It seems to have been Tennessee alone, however, who was his sleeping partner. Vanderbilt, a financial wizard, encouraged his new protégée to play the stock market, and soon, thanks to his advice, they were making more money than they had ever seen before. Then he suggested that they go into business for themselves as brokers, and in 1870 they duly opened an office, the first American women ever to invade Wall Street in a professional capacity. The venture stimulated a great amount of comment in the newspapers, which were full of stories about "the Bewitching Brokers," and clients thronged the offices on Broad Street. The commodore, though he married again, visited them every day, which increased public confidence in the sisters' financial acumen.

Soon Victoria began entertaining an even more startling ambition, to be President of the United States. The first step in her campaign, she decided—or her friends decided for her—was to own a newspaper. She had plenty of talent to draw on. For a long time the Claflin house had been open to the Bloods' friends of the radical intellectual sort, and their leading light was a sixty-year-old eccentric named Stephen Pearl Andrews, whose mind seethed with ideas.

Andrews had been an abolitionist, had invented a universal language, and believed in world government and what he called the "social revolution." More practically, he had introduced shorthand into the United States. Andrews agreed with Blood's ideas on reforming marriage customs and advocating free love. He was altogether a compatible friend. The two men encouraged Victoria in her Presidential ambitions, and on April 2, 1870, she announced to the public her intention of joining the electoral race as a nominee in 1872. This, in a country where women did not even have the vote, was startling, but Blood, Andrews, and the Woodhull, as she was sometimes called by reporters, treated it as more than a stunt: they were in earnest.

A month after the "Pronunciamento" in which Victoria made her announcement, three friends brought out the first issue of *Woodhull & Claflin's Weekly,* a good, respectable-looking paper, even if some of Andrews' articles seemed rather impractical. Apart from plenty of discussion of Mrs. Woodhull's candidacy there was space for a piece advocating a single standard in sexual morality and several that treated of women's rights generally. The New York *Herald* was one of many contemporary journals that made the *Weekly* welcome and had kind words for it. As the *Herald*'s editorial put it, "While the two hostile divisions of women's righters are passing their time in refusing to coalesce with each other and in flooding the country with resolutions and chatter, there are at least two advocates of the woman movement that endeavor to show by example and precept that their sex, with ordinary fair play and industry, can take care of itself." A sour note was introduced by the *Tribune*, which accused the new paper of being soft on prostitution because of an article that deplored police shakedowns of brothels. But on the whole the *Weekly* fared much better than *The Revolution* or the *Woman's Journal* had done.

Naturally, Mrs. Woodhull's pronunciamento and the pro-women's-rights tone of the *Weekly* attracted the attention of at least one "hostile division" of feminists. Elizabeth Cady Stanton wrote to Victoria, whom she had not met, to remind her that the NWSA was soon to hold its annual convention in Washington, and she added, in what was no doubt a half-joking attempt to induce Mrs. Woodhull to speak out, "Will you ask Demosthenes if there is any new argument not yet made on the 14th and 15th Amendments that he will bring out through some of us at the coming convention?" The Fourteenth Amendment had not, after all, settled the question of the franchise for Negro males. It was the Fifteenth, which was passed in 1870, that did this—but women were still left out of the bill, and that was Mrs. Stanton's point.

Mrs. Woodhull could do better than that, and did. Because she was a pretty woman with money and influential friends, she actually succeeded in presenting to the Senate a "memorial," or petition, demanding votes for women. Hitherto all such petitions had been joint efforts with many signatures, but Victoria's was signed with hers alone. Supported by a Louisiana senator and a representative from Indiana, it was referred to the House Judiciary Committee and its author was invited to read it to that body on January 11, 1871, which happened to be the date of the NSWA's opening session.

News of Mrs. Woodhull's impending congressional appearance sent the NSWA members into frenzied consultation. All of them had heard of Mrs. Woodhull, and most had been scandalized by certain of the rumors. Could they afford to let such a notorious lady, who advocated free love, meddle with their cause? On the other hand, how was one to stop her if that's what she wanted to do? The Woodhull campaign for women's rights appeared to Susan Anthony in the light of a calamity. "A lady quite déclassée in any society," she said severely of Victoria, and she was joined in her misgivings by Mrs. Isabella Beecher Hooker, one of the many children of Lyman Beecher and a half-sister of the renowned Reverend Henry Ward Beecher of Brooklyn. However, Elizabeth Stanton was all for Mrs. Woodhull or anyone else who supported the cause.

After talking things over, the ladies decided to go and catch Mrs. Woodhull's performance before the Judiciary Committee, even though this meant postponing their opening session a few hours. They were pleasantly surprised. Dressed in excellent, quiet taste, the pretty Victoria read her memorial in what Miss Anthony admitted to be a clear, musical voice, in a manner hesitant at first but soon gaining power and confidence. The petition was well written—though, to be sure, rumor said that General Benjamin F. Butler and not Victoria had written it. At any rate, Mrs. Woodhull was an ornament to women's suffrage, the NWSA ladies told each other, and they were delighted when Victoria and Tennessee turned up at their opening session that afternoon. A reporter who was also there called them "the two New York sensations," and described their appearance approvingly: "both in dark dresses, with blue neckties, short, curly hair, and nobby alpine hats." In response to a request, Victoria read out her memorial again, and the meeting's enthusiasm was tremendous. Eventually it got nowhere, of course: the Judiciary Committee, having had its fun, resolved bluntly that the prayer of the petitioner be not granted, that the memorial be tabled, and that the committee be discharged from any further consideration of the subject. Which was no surprise to anyone.

Nor did it astonish the NWSA that members of the AWSA should be scathing about the new friendship between the NWSA and Mrs. Woodhull. To various hints and criticisms of the lady, Mrs. Stanton retorted: "When the men who make laws for us in Washington can stand forth and declare themselves pure and unspotted from all the sins mentioned in the Decalogue, then we will demand that every woman who makes a constitutional argument on our platform shall be as chaste as Diana. But, if Victoria Woodhull must be crucified, let men drive the spikes and plait the crown of thorns."

Mrs. Woodhull then embarked on a lecture tour and spoke extensively on women's rights. She made many converts, not least among hitherto doubtful suffragist leaders. Isabella Hooker was enthralled by her, and was sure that if only her elder sister Catherine Beecher were to be exposed to the Woodhull charm she would take back the unkind words she was always writing about Victoria and join Isabella in fervent admiration. Mrs. Hooker was mistaken in this. Catherine Beecher was strongly antifeminist, and she had an unshakable sense of propriety; on both counts Mrs. Woodhull was offensive to her. Still, because Mrs. Hooker so much wished it, Miss Catherine Beecher and Mrs. Woodhull met and went out together for a drive. Unfortunately, Catherine Beecher's idea of talking things over was to lecture her companion, and soon sparks were flying, with Victoria saying that all this stuff came ill from any sister of Henry Ward Beecher, considering his well-known sexual misdemeanors among the ladies of his congregation. And, indeed, there had been much talk about Henry Ward Beecher. The women parted in furious silence.

Henry Ward Beecher, a plump, florid, fifty-eight-year-old man with a mellifluous voice and a splendid style of oratory, had been for years the leader of the flock of the Congregational Plymouth Church in Brooklyn—and also, for a while, president of the NWSA, for he was a liberal man in such matters. He was exceedingly popular, and the church was jammed every Sunday, not only with the locals but with people who came by ferry from Manhattan just to hear him. His amorous proclivities were not quite a secret, but his faithful followers never permitted themselves to listen to the stories. Even more successful financially than Harriet Beecher Stowe with her best-selling novel, Henry Ward Beecher added to his income by publishing sermons and writing for periodicals. For a time he contributed a series of articles to a weekly paper, the *Independent,* owned and published by one Henry C. Bowen, and when he left it and moved over to a rival periodical, the *Christian Union,* Bowen was incensed. Bowen already had a grudge against Beecher: on her deathbed some years earlier his wife had admitted to him that she and the preacher had been lovers. As long as Beecher wrote for him, Bowen was willing to forgive it, but now, with his star writer's defection, his wrath was great.

To edit another of his papers Bowen had hired a tall, good-looking man, a thirty-five-year-old with flowing yellow hair, named Theodore Tilton. Here too Beecher's amativeness would cause trouble. By a coincidence, Tilton too, who had once been very friendly with Beecher, now hated him and for the same reason as Bowen: late in 1870 his pretty little wife Lib—short for Elizabeth—had broken down and confessed, in a storm of tears, that she and Beecher had been having an affair. Tilton, like Bowen, hesitated to publicize the story because he feared the effect on his children. But he felt impelled to take steps of some sort, so he made Lib write the whole thing down and sign it, then carried the paper around in his pocket like a bomb he could always explode if he wanted to. He was a strange man, however, with fluctuating emotions: he showed it to best friends here and there.

When Bowen decided that Tilton was an unsatisfactory editor and fired him, Tilton's resentment found a new object. He forgot his grievance against Beecher and made friends with him again. He destroyed his wife's confession, started a new magazine called *The Golden Age,* lost money on it, and threatened to expose Bowen for his slandering ways in falsely accusing Beecher of having sexual relations with Lib. Bowen, alarmed, consented to meet both Tilton and Beecher to talk things over. As a result he gave Tilton seven thousand dollars in support of *The Golden Age,* and promised not to talk any more—if he ever had—about Beecher and Lib. It was too late, however, to close the stable door: Mrs. Tilton in the first remorseful phase had already told everything to her good friends Susan Anthony and Elizabeth Stanton. And Mrs. Stanton in her turn told it to her good friend Victoria Woodhull, possibly as an example of masculine perfidy.

Victoria had never been implicated in blackmail attempts, but she knew the technique. The Beecher-Tilton story fitted in directly with her ideas on liberated sex and the wrongfulness of organized religion: she could now taste the joys of power while at the same time feeling virtuous. She wrote an article setting out the whole story, then summoned Theodore Tilton and showed him a proof of the piece, telling him that she would like to be sure of her facts before publishing it, as she intended, in the next week's paper. Tilton was horrified, and implored her to change her mind. This was their first meeting, and as they talked, Victoria, according to her own account, noticed that he was very attractive. At the same time, even in his distress, Tilton (he too later talked; they were not a reticent pair) began to appreciate her beauty and intelligence. Soon the two editors fell into each other's arms, and the article was forgotten—for the moment.

During the following few months the lovers were inseparable. Tilton was hard at work on an admiring biography of Victoria Woodhull, to be printed in *The Golden Age* and later published as a pamphlet. Colonel Blood made no objection to his wife's extramarital adventure, because he was a sincere man who practiced what he preached. He never objected to his Vicky's affairs: he *believed* in free love. At any rate, after six months or so the lovers cooled off. The *Weekly* continued to hold back the Beecher article—incidentally, it published Marx's *Communist Manifesto* about that time—but Victoria expressed a desire to meet the Reverend, and Tilton invited them both to his house and introduced them. According to Mrs. Woodhull in later days, the encounter was a social success: Mr. Beecher admitted that he too felt love should be free, but said he would not dare to talk this way from the pulpit. The two had several meetings, and more than once they argued the question of Beecher's "hypocrisy," without his becoming convinced of her point of view. However, Victoria had other matters to discuss with Beecher. Two of his sisters, Harriet Beecher Stowe and Catherine, kept writing unpleasant things about her, and she wanted Henry to make them stop it. Unfortunately, he could not persuade Catherine to detest, though Harriet was more amenable.

On November 20, 1871, Mrs. Woodhull was to give a lecture at Steinway Hall, New York, on "Free Love, Marriage, Divorce, and Prostitution," which, she announced, was intended to silence the voices and stop the pens of certain people who "slandered, misrepresented, abused and vilified" her. She wanted Beecher to introduce her that evening, but he flatly refused to do so even when friends advised him that it would be better not to make an enemy of Mrs. Woodhull. And his refusal did make an enemy of her, though for a time her feeling was not apparent. Tilton saved the day and moved in to introduce her himself. The lecture went reasonably smoothly at first, though she said a lot of things that people in the audience thought shocking, such as that marriage should not be maintained by force of law if one of the partners loved someone else. The world did not need laws for love, said the lecturer. Some in the audience hissed at this, but others cheered. Then people grew heated, on the platform and off, until somebody called up to the speaker, "Are *you* a free lover?"

"Yes!" retorted Victoria passionately. "I am a free lover! I have an inalienable, constitutional, and natural right to love whom I may, to love as long or as short a period as I can, to change that love story every day if I please! And neither you nor any law that you can frame have the right to interfere!" She said much more, but this was the heart of the matter, and her hearers, having got what they came for, went home enthralled and scandalized.

The Woodhull household suffered for this courageous statement.

They were put out of their house by the owner, the brokerage business fell off, and the sisters found it hard to keep the *Weekly* going until, while Victoria was absent on a lecture tour, Tennie increased the paper's circulation by a trick. She published a letter purportedly from the madam of a brothel saying that the writer, who was retiring from the business, would be willing, if the sisters liked, to hand over to them two large ledgers containing the names and addresses of her principal clients. A number of New York men sweated blood for some days, until Victoria returned and admitted that the whole thing was a hoax. Harriet Beecher Stowe now had something fresh to write about against the Claflins, and the word "blackmail" was mentioned. Another writer spoke gravely in the *Woman's Journal* of the harm Mrs. Woodhull was doing the suffragists with her talk of free love, but Victoria, unrepentant, wrote in the *Weekly* of how her two husbands (Canning Woodhull had recently come home to die) had lived in the same house in perfect harmony. She said, "These people were not rivals. They were brothers, and in spite of all attempts to make them enemies, they remained friends to the last."

When the NWSA held their annual meeting in January 1872 in Washington, Mrs. Woodhull sat on the platform between Mrs. Stanton and Miss Anthony. She spoke, and her vigor and eloquence, as always, carried conviction even to those who were prejudiced against her. Afterward one delegate wanted to nominate her for president. Susan Anthony, more cautious, defeated the move, but Mrs. Woodhull outplayed her.

At the end of April, *Woodhull & Claflin's Weekly* came out with an announcement that the NWSA was to hold another convention on May 9 and 10, this time to form a new political association called the People's Party, for which they would nominate their own Presidential candidate. Actually a convention *had* been planned, but the People's Party was news to everyone, evidently, but the Claflin sisters, and so was the fact that the announcement was signed by leaders of the NWSA—Elizabeth Cady Stanton, Susan Anthony, Isabella Hooker, and others—since none of these ladies had really signed the notice. They received the tidings with varying amounts of indignation. Mrs. Stanton did not mind at all, but Susan Anthony, who happened to be in Illinois when she read the *Weekly,* nearly exploded with rage, and took the first available train to New York. She was even angrier to discover when she arrived that none of her colleagues was boycotting Victoria Woodhull. The only one who shared her mistrust of the woman was old Lucretia Mott, and even she was somewhat pacified when Mrs. Stanton wrote to her, "I have thought much about Mrs. Woodhull, and of all the gossip about her past, and have come to the conclusion that it is a great impertinence in any of us to pry into her private affairs." Mrs. Stanton refused to listen to Miss Anthony's warning words, and the May convention opened in a tense atmosphere.

Immediately, Mrs. Woodhull asked for the floor and announced that the new People's Party would convene in partnership with the NWSA. Susan Anthony quickly declared that there was to be no such partnership, and requested any People's Party members who might be there to leave the hall forthwith. A rustle sounded from all over the room as people stood up and walked out, led by Victoria Woodhull. Among them, unfortunately for Susan Anthony's feelings, were quite a few NWSA members. At this crucial point Mrs. Stanton, who felt obliged to support Victoria, unhappily tendered her resignation as president of the association, and the meeting elected Susan Anthony in her place.

The evening session was even stormier. Victoria walked in again, and in spite of all the new chairman could do, she took over, orating until Miss Anthony had the lamps turned out, and conveying an invitation to all and sundry to attend *her* meeting next morning at Apollo Hall. Next day brought proof that Mrs. Woodhull had kidnapped the NWSA convention. The majority failed to turn up at Steinway Hall because they were over at the other house, forming the new party—and during the second session Mrs. Victoria Woodhull was nominated candidate for President of the United States, with Frederick Douglass as her running mate. (His reaction to the news is not on record.)

Victoria had beaten Susan Anthony, but soon a torrent of adverse publicity was released, and worse was to come upon the new candidate. One could hardly have expected newspapers not to make the most of this chance to be funny at the expense of militant women; even in more sober moments journalists pointed out how hopeless it was to try to elect a female who was not only female but underage as well. Probably Victoria never really expected to get anywhere in her election attempt. It is hard to be sure what went on in that enigmatic head, but the campaign was hard on her family and she was bound to resent that. They were persecuted in many ways. They were again put out of a rented house and for a time had nowhere to live; landlord after landlord turned them down. The brokerage-office rent was suddenly raised to impossible heights, until the business folded. Vanderbilt was no longer interested in helping them. The *Weekly* ceased publication, for the editors had run out of money.

Perhaps irrationally, Mrs. Woodhull blamed the Beechers for all this misfortune. She was convinced that Harriet and Catherine, at least, were conspiring to destroy her, and it was peculiarly galling to hear that Henry Ward Beecher's church was planning to celebrate his twenty-five years in their pulpit. Brooding on these matters, she went to Boston to attend the annual convention of the National Association of Spiritualists, who had a year earlier, at Troy, New York, done her the honor of electing her their president. This year she wanted to bow out, in order to devote herself completely to the Presidential campaign. It seemed to her that the members were not glad to see her. Many greeted her coldly, then retired to some corner to whisper to each other.

Mrs. Woodhull, sitting on the dais with the other officials, was duly called on in her turn, and stepped up to the lectern to make her report. Suddenly a force seized her, as she said later, and without conscious volition she began to talk of what was on her mind—Lib Tilton and her seduction by Beecher. The furious, indignant phrases poured out: Mrs. Woodhull had never been more eloquent. The spiritualists had no chance to ask what it all had to do with them; they were caught up, shocked, fascinated, and many wept. Victoria followed up her recital of events by assuring them that the affair, *qua* affair, was not sinful; it was the hypocrisy of all concerned that offended morality. Over and over she hammered at this point, that for five years the truth had been concealed. It was her duty to lay bare the whole story, she said. One member of the meeting later reported that the speech made her flesh creep and her blood run cold. But all of them were impressed, so much so that on the spot they reelected Mrs. Woodhull as their president.

The secret was dramatically out—but no newspaper dared to touch it as yet. The libel laws frightened the editors, and each hung back, hoping another would dare break the silence first. To be sure, many already knew the facts, for during his first agonies Tilton, as I have said, had shown his wife's written confession to a lot of people. They were probably sure, too, that Mrs. Tilton was only one of Beecher's many conquests, but libel is libel, and according to the law the truth is no excuse for malicious stories. Who would be the first to break the silence? Mrs. Woodhull, of course: she managed to scrape up enough funds to bring the *Weekly* out of its hibernation and publish a special number dated November 2, 1872, not far from Election Day. In this edition the story was repeated, with the added detail that Mrs. Tilton, pregnant at the time she confessed her sins to her husband, had a miscarriage shortly afterward. That aborted infant, said the *Weekly,* might well have been Beecher's. Throughout the article Victoria maintained her special tone of high-minded reprimand. Look on this titillating story, she seemed to say, and blush for man's perfidy, not for his infidelity but for covering it up. Victoria's duty, she insisted, was to tell all.

"It is the paradox of my position that, believing in the right of privacy and the perfect right of Mr. Beecher socially, morally and divinely to have sought the embraces of Mrs. Tilton, or of any other woman whom he loved and who loved him, I still invade the most secret and sacred affairs of his life, and expose him to the opprobrium and vilification of the public," she wrote. "What I do is for a great purpose. The social world is in the great agony of its new birth. Somebody must be hurled forward into the gap." And to Beecher she awarded the honor of being the sacrifice. Theodore Tilton she declared to be no hero: she accused him of bogus sentimentality over the affair, of putting on airs and agonizing merely because he thought he should. He was no vestal virgin himself, said Mrs. Woodhull—and she of all people should know. Off with all veils, away with hypocrisy! Victoria Woodhull intended to usher in a Universal Washing Day and tell everything about everybody if they wouldn't do it themselves.

Was she sincere in all this? Again, it is impossible to tell. It sounds like a kind of reversion to her childhood and her mother's fondness for revival meetings. At any rate, Tennessee hurried to support her sister's efforts and did her bit to expose the sins of mankind with another "biography" in the same issue of the paper. This concerned a lesser-known figure than Beecher, a stockbroker named Luther B. Challis, who for a time had been Tennie's great and good friend. In the article she alleged that Challis and another man had debauched two young girls fifteen or sixteen years old, and that "Challis, to prove that he had seduced a maiden, carried for days on his finger, exhibiting in triumph, the red trophy of her virginity." This item would not be out of place in a Forty-second Street porn shop today, and it gave other writers on the *Weekly* a moment's pause. However, after that one moment they went ahead and put it into type. Was it not Washing Day?

The public really blew up when the paper went on sale, with the sisters besieged by reporters and the *Weekly*'s first printing, an unusually large one, selling out in a few hours. Some hundreds were bought and burned by Henry Ward Beecher and friends, but many more escaped. At this point Anthony Comstock, a living symbol of end-of-the-century morality, stepped in and got the sisters arrested for sending obscene literature through the mail. He was just in time, as it happened, for another lot of lawmen were on their way to grab both women on a charge of libel, in an action instituted by Challis. In court the U.S. Attorney demanded the enormous bail of ten thousand dollars for each Claflin, arguing that not only had they sent out obscene literature, but they were guilty of "a most abominable and unjust charge against one of the purest and best citizens of this State or in the United States." The paragon was unnamed, however, and the sisters' lawyer got the bail scaled down to eight thousand dollars for both.

During the legal wrangling, Victoria and Tennessee remained calm. Reporters noted that they were dressed alike in the neat, tailored costumes they liked; that pretty Tennie was bright-eyed and apt to dimple at some amusing twist in the proceedings, whereas the beautiful Victoria was grave as always. They were remanded in custody for a week. Train, the "Eccentric Millionaire" who first helped Mrs. Stanton and Miss Anthony after the Kansas election, offered to bail them out, but they were told that as soon as they stepped out they would be nabbed again on the Challis charge, and this would mean going to Jefferson Market Prison, a noisome hole. So they decided to stay where they were, in the comparative comfort of Ludlow Street Jail. Later they were dismissed on a technicality, but were immediately popped back into prison, their society now augmented by Colonel Blood; and there they all remained for a month—not thirty days of unrelieved monotony, since they were permitted to chat with reporters.

During this long incarceration, friends were busy in their behalf. Train of course worked hard, though he was becoming so eccentric that he was not much use. More effective were the ladies of the NWSA, even Susan Anthony. She didn't like Mrs. Woodhull any better, but she could see that the delay in liberating the prisoners was a veiled revenge for her attack on Beecher, and like Mrs. Stanton, with whom she had become reconciled, she knew that the story in the *Weekly* about him was true. If their testimony could help to free the prisoners, she and Mrs. Stanton agreed, they would give it. The Beechers quarreled about the case: when Isabella Hooker heard that

Henry had said that the story was entirely false, her indignation was great. She implored him to tell the truth, and after he refused she turned to another brother, the Reverend Thomas, who was of her mind. He said that Henry had sacrificed integrity to expediency, and added, "Of the two, Woodhull is my hero, and Henry my coward . . . You cannot help Henry. You must be true to Woodhull."

Henry Ward Beecher, meantime, went about his business as usual, preaching to adoring, loyal congregations and pretending that nothing out of the way was going on. Finally the press tired of the law's delay, and several influential papers set up a clamor for action, until on December 5 the three prisoners were freed on bail, rearrested on a slightly different charge, and again freed, all within a few minutes. During their sojourn in jail, of course, the election had been held and Ulysses S. Grant had been elected, with Victoria last in the race with no electoral college votes at all, but at least she had made some sort of a record—no woman had stood for the office before, especially not from a jail cell. Train tried to make a point by printing a paper of his own and daring Comstock to come and get him. Comstock did, and Train went into the Tombs at about the same time that the *Weekly* came out. He was to stay there a long time, too.

The year 1873 gave Mrs. Woodhull just the busy, trouble-threatened time she seemed to like. Comstock continued to dog her, and managed to trick the *Weekly* office into sending him a few copies of the disputed number through the mail, upon which he swore out another warrant for Victoria's arrest. This happened just as she was billed to give a lecture about her recent experiences—"The Naked Truth," she called it—at Cooper Hall, and police were stationed at the hall doors waiting for her as the audience thronged in, but did not see her. Someone was just making an announcement regretting the speaker's unavoidable absence when a little old lady, cloaked and bonneted, wandered onto the platform behind her, threw off the cloak and bonnet, and stood revealed as—Victoria Woodhull, of course. Her lecture proved to be as dramatic as her appearance, and the police, very politely, let her finish it before they arrested her. For some weeks thereafter, the Claflin sisters and Blood were in and out of the courts, until Victoria's old friend General Benjamin Butler, an astute lawyer, published an open letter in the *Sun* arguing that no trial was necessary because the law against obscenity was never intended to apply to newspapers, but to pornographic pictures and books. In the end the grand jury found the accused not guilty.

Despite protests, the Plymouth Church authorities felt bound to investigate all these charges against their beloved pastor. Reluctantly and without fanfare they did so, the more peacefully because Mrs. Woodhull and entourage, by a strange coincidence, departed for Europe at the same time. The Plymouth Church inquiry completely exonerated Henry Ward Beecher—not that outsiders were forced to believe the authorities—and when it was all over Victoria and the others came back, early in 1875. Even then she remained discreet during a follow-up suit that Tilton brought against Beecher for alienation of his wife's affections and criminal libel. When summoned, Victoria refused to take the witness stand, and without her testimony Beecher was again exonerated, but not by an overwhelming majority. Many people remained unconvinced of his innocence, and it does look suspiciously like a whitewash. Afterward Tilton went to live in Paris.

The Claflin sisters' connection with the NWSA dropped off, though Victoria ran for President four times more, with the same lack of success each time. Apart from this strange compulsion she became more and more conventional in her behavior, and actually in later years divorced Blood in order to marry a rich English banker. Tennessee, always a loyal imitator of her elder sister, also married an Englishman, an elderly millionaire who became a baronet, so Tennessee ended her life as Lady Wood. Residing in England most of the time, the sisters gradually lost interest in American affairs—except for the Presidential elections. In 1892, in the United States, Victoria got herself nominated, for the fifth and last time, by a little group of women in Washington, and then announced that she was also the accepted candidate of the NWSA. The NWSA promptly denied it.

We should not hold it against her that in 1927, interviewed by an English newspaper shortly before her death, she claimed that it was she who got the vote for American women. She was nearly ninety, after all, and she had a lot of memories. Small wonder if they got a bit mixed up.

CHAPTER 17

Four Women

TO MANY OF HER ADMIRERS ELIZABETH CADY STANTON *was* the nineteenth century. It is true that her long life nearly spanned it—she was born in 1815 and died in 1902—but they meant far more than that. As the leading spirit of the women's movement, she very nearly brought it to what she would have considered the supreme triumph—getting the vote. As it was, she was responsible for many changes in woman's status, evident in the different attitude of males toward females and, what was even more important, of women toward themselves. Four women in particular, twentieth-century types rather than nineteenth, could never have lived their diverse lives if it had not been for Mrs. Stanton and the battles she fought.

Of course her resignation from the presidency of the NWSA was not final; once the smoke and fury of the Woodhull quarrel had cleared away, Mrs. Stanton was again elected, and was reelected each year after that until 1890. Then the two rival organizations combined as the National American Woman Suffrage Association, and Elizabeth Stanton reigned over that too, as president for the next two years. In 1892, however, she resigned in earnest, because, as she said, she wanted time to herself for various projects, lecturing and writing. She was seventy-seven.

Many of this remarkable woman's sayings and writings are memorable. She was particularly vivid and spirited in her speech whenever she felt called on to defend herself. For example, people wrote to her objecting to what they called her "belligerent attitude" in certain of the columns she wrote. She replied, "Is there an instance in all history of an oppressed class being secured in all their rights without assuming a 'belligerent attitude'?"

At the Congress of Women in New York in 1873, to an audience made up largely of conservatives, she spoke out against what she called indiscriminate births when the mother is diseased or the father intemperate and licentious. As we would put it, she advised birth control. Julia Ward Howe was much distressed, and accused Mrs. Stanton of recommending infanticide. But she was not, said Elizabeth; infanticide (i.e., birth control) was already a fact, and would continue as long as a woman was not the sovereign of her own person. Such plain talk on this subject embarrassed many of her hearers.

As the years passed, she thought more and more about divorce. To think of something was, for her, to write of it, and in the *North American Review* of September 1884 she urged changes in the divorce laws to make them more liberal. This of course brought down on her head the wrath of the clergy, and soon she was busy arguing with many men of the cloth. Even earlier, she had been called upon to state her views about morality and the double standard when some members of the NWSA protested against permitting Mormon women to attend the convention of 1869 because they were polygamists. Mrs. Stanton wrote indignantly to Miss Anthony, "If the Congress of the United States can allow George A. Cannon to sit for Utah in that body without it being supposed to endorse polygamy, we could permit Mormon women the same privilege in our Association without being accused of embracing their principles. If Congress can stand Cannon with four wives, we might stand the women with only the fourth part of a husband!" She felt all the more strongly about this because the Mormon women had come from Utah expressly to attempt to safeguard their right to vote now that Utah, heretofore a territory, was to become a state.

More and more did she devote her thought to the theory that women tended to accept their low status humbly and meekly because they were brainwashed—though that was not her term—from the cradle to the grave by religion. Much to Susan Anthony's disapproval, she worked for a long time on a book she called *The Woman's Bible.* It consisted of a series of commentaries on all mentions of women in the Scriptures, and attempted, as she said, to undo the mischief wrought by faulty earlier interpretations. Miss Anthony, while not quarreling with these ideas, felt that her friend was going at the problem backwards; that once women had the vote, their grievances, together with their acceptance of a low status, would vanish like snow in the sun. The two friends never came to agreement on this point, but on another they were in harmony: both believed that the new surge of militancy shown by the Women's Christian Temperance Union, which had been founded in Cleveland in 1874 but was now extending into a world force under its second president, Frances Willard, must not be permitted to overbalance the work of the NAWSA.

The last decades of Mrs. Stanton's life were full of disputes over her *Bible*. On one occasion a deputation of Jewish women called on her to protest what they called her unfair attack on Judaism. Their religion, they said, *exalted* wives and mothers rather than insulting them.

But did it? Mrs. Stanton asked them how it was, if that were so, that every week in the synagogue men could be heard saying in prayer, "I thank thee, O Lord, that I was not born a woman."

This meant nothing, said the ladies—at least, nothing degrading or humiliating.

"But it does, nevertheless," said Mrs. Stanton. "Suppose the service read, 'I thank thee, O Lord, that I was not born a jackass.' Could that be twisted in any way as a compliment to the jackass? Oh no, ladies, the Jews accord us women no more honor than do the Gentiles."

In spite of such spirited exchanges, the cause lagged. In 1894, when the constitutional convention once more ignored the demands of suffragists, Mrs. Stanton wrote to her friend Mrs. Clara Colby:

"Well, you see, we were defeated in the convention. The point made by our opponents is that a majority of women do not ask for the vote. What step in progress was ever asked for by a majority? If, in 1776, we had waited for a majority to assert our national independence, we should still be under the British yoke. If Luther had waited for the majority to protest against the tyranny of the Church, we should all be subjects of the Pope today. Luther's coadjutors were few indeed. Jesus had fewer still. The grand principles of human brotherhood he annunciated two thousand years ago are not accepted throughout the globe by a majority. Why should the indifference of the majority of women handicap the intelligent minority?"

She must have felt especially disappointed because though four years earlier, in 1890, after a separation of twenty years, the two suffragist associations—NWSA and AWSA—had come together at last, dissension did not vanish. In 1900 she wrote, "Our movement is belated, and like all things too long postponed now gets on everybody's nerves. . . . Something sensational should be done . . ." But not by her. She had long retired from the association's active service, and in 1902, having (at the age of eighty-seven) just written a long letter to President Theodore Roosevelt asking him to immortalize himself by emancipating his countrywomen, Mrs. Stanton died.

If Jennie Jerome had not become a European, one might easily imagine her queening it over some big American city; she was very much a national type of society woman. However, she was early influenced by her mother's predilection for Europe and its culture—insofar as Mrs. Jerome could appreciate culture—and she was transplanted at a young age. A preference for Europe over America was characteristic of rich Americans at that time—Jennie was born in 1854—and with so much travel on the part of millionaires' daughters from the United States, there was a fairly high incidence of alliances between Dollar Princesses and the scions of foreign nobility. Several of Jennie's childhood friends from her native land married English peers, as she herself did. I have in my possession a book published in 1867, *Queens of American Society,* which gives the reader some light on the way such women thought. The writer, who signs herself simply "Mrs. Eliot," speaks again and again with obvious admiration of her subjects' visits to the Old World. There was Mrs. Harrison Gray Otis, Jr., of Boston, for instance, who was widowed at an early age and left with young sons.

"Anxious to secure them the best advantages of education, and to improve her own mind by study and observation, Mrs. Otis took her sons to Europe, remaining abroad seven years," wrote Mrs. Eliot. "During that time she visited many friends of rank and distinction, and was received with marked favor among literary circles and the aristocracy of different countries, being presented at various courts." And there was Mrs. Richard Derby, daughter of a physician in Maine and wife of a wealthy gentleman of Boston: "She spent much time in Paris, and was a favorite with the last king of France." A Miss Harriet Preble of Manchester, near Pittsburgh, was deemed an ornament of society because she was born in England and passed her childhood and youth in Paris.

Quite a number of American women with rich husbands were convinced that their own countrymen and culture were hopelessly crude when compared with the ambience of Europe, and their idea of bliss was to be able to live over there. Some of them actually persuaded their husbands to make the move, but the majority, who found their spouses woefully stubborn in the matter, had to make do with the second best of frequent voyages. If she could not emulate some Henry James matron and buy a palazzo in Venice or a shooting box in Scotland, a mother could still acquire polish for her daughter by sending her to France or Switzerland to a finishing school or, like Mrs. Harrison Gray Otis, Jr., take her children abroad and chaperon them in desirable European spots.

Jennie Jerome's mother, though she came to it late, managed to make a complete break with her native country, because she had the excuse of her husband's misbehavior. Leonard Jerome, a dashing fellow with a talent for making money and a zest for spending it, was so merrily and publicly unfaithful that in 1867 his wife Clara at last decided to get away from it all and take their three daughters to Paris. Jennie, the middle one, was the prettiest, though all were pretty, and she was a talented pianist. She was thirteen years old at the time. The break between her parents never got far enough to grow into divorce, but Leonard Jerome's visits to Paris were infrequent. However, Clara was contented with her lot; she had everything she liked—elegant clothes for herself and the girls, balls, music, and, above all, royalty. She had the happiness of becoming a friend of Empress Eugénie and met all the leading figures of society. Her eldest daughter, Clarita, made her debut at the imperial court. Then all this dazzling gaiety was spoiled by the Franco-Prussian War, and the Jerome women had to flee to England.

For a long time they regretted their lost paradise, but in time they grew to like England in spite of the fickle climate and the dearth of continental beaux. Ultimately, all three girls married Englishmen. Jennie's match was probably the most impressive; on April 15, 1874, she became the wife of Lord Randolph Churchill, a younger son of the Duke of Marlborough. The marriage was opposed by the bridegroom's family on the general principle that she was not English; also, Leonard Jerome's fortune seemed to them to lack solidity. Leonard and Clara were not quite satisfied with Lord Randolph, either. But the young people had their way, and Lord Randolph commenced a brilliant career in politics.

Jennie bore two sons, the eldest, of course, being Winston Churchill, but in spite of a good beginning the marriage could not in honesty be called a success. Lord Randolph's mind failed after a time, possibly because of the so-called tertiary effects of syphilis, and his career came to a halt. His last years were miserable, but Jennie found compensations. Queen Victoria was living in gloomy seclusion, her own respectability as heavy and smothering as history depicts it, but the aristocracy of England permitted itself a wide latitude in morals and took the Prince of Wales as a model. Jennie, with the charm and beauty that were to last all her life, had many admirers and enjoyed life thoroughly: she was her father's daughter. But she had one fault that often rendered existence difficult—she was hopelessly extravagant and scarcely ever out of debt.

On the other hand, she was unusually intelligent and talented. It was impossible for her to live idly. Much of the time she was busy helping her sons by arranging for them to meet influential people, and when even this did not fill her life she turned to publishing, an unusual pastime for women of her class. She edited a magazine, and published the works of some of the outstanding writers of her time. Her friends were amused, and told each other that it was the American in Jennie that led her into such strange paths. During the Boer War, in which both boys were involved, Jennie managed to get a ship from America and, after raising the necessary funds, she outfitted it as a floating hospital and took it to South Africa.

Then she married again, and the world whispered and snickered a little over her choice, for he was only two weeks older than Winston. The critics probably felt justified when after some years the couple were divorced, but Jennie paid no attention, and went even further in her choice of a third husband: at the age of sixty-four she married a man of forty-one—several years *younger* than Winston. After three years of a reasonably happy marriage, she died.

Jane Addams too was a national type, though no one could have been less like Lady Randolph than she. Laura Jane Addams was born in Freeport, Illinois, in 1860, the eighth child of John H. Addams and his first wife. The couple when newly married—John was twenty-two—had come from Pennsylvania and settled on the Cedar River in northern Illinois. John had been schoolteacher and miller's apprentice. Here on the site of what would grow into a town named Cedarville he set up a flour mill and prospered. He became a leading citizen. He owned a bank, battled successfully to bring a new railroad to the town, and helped found the Republican Party of Illinois. He was a friend of Lincoln, and for a time was a senator in the state legislature. His wife Sarah died in 1863 from miscarrying their ninth child, so that Jane was left motherless at the age of three. In his picture John Addams looks stern and forbidding. Once when Jane, puzzled by the fact that he attended different churches on different Sundays, asked what his religion was, he said that he was a Hicksite Quaker. Jane adored him with what in her autobiography she called doglike affection, and trotted after him everywhere at home but desisted out of doors—because, she said, people should not see that such a handsome man was father to such an ugly little girl. However, witnesses said she was not ugly. Small and slight, she carried her head awry because of a curvature of the spine.

As a young child she was precociously anxious about the world. At five or six she first noticed the poverty-stricken area of Cedarville, and according to family legend she said that someday she would have a nice big house like that of the Addamses, but it would not stand among other big houses: it would be surrounded by "horrid little houses like these." Perhaps she really said it. She was a serious child, the kind people call old-fashioned.

When she was eight John Addams married a widow named Ann Haldemann, a forthright, commanding, handsome woman, fond of music and riding. She had two sons, one of whom became a surgeon and married Jane's sister Alice. The other, George, nearer Jane's age, became interested in biological research. For some years George and Jane spent most of their time together, and because of her companion Jane made up her mind to study medicine. She wished to go to Smith College, and easily passed the entrance examinations, but then her father, who was a trustee of Rockford Female Seminary near Cedarville, decided for some reason that she would do better there. She regretted this. Smith College conferred degrees and she wanted one, whereas Rockford, though chartered as a college with permission to confer degrees, had never become one in actuality. However, John Addams' word was always law to his youngest daughter, and without argument she enrolled at Rockford in the fall of 1877.

It was a small place. When Jane was a senior her class, the largest yet, consisted of seventeen students. And though Smith probably offered little in the way of luxury in those early days, the Rockford regime was especially Spartan. Each girl had to supply her own equipment—bedding, books, furniture, even a teaspoon. An hour's exercise every day was the fixed rule, and when the weather was bad the girls walked inside the school grounds, round and round on a wooden walk, for the full hour. The chief interest of the principal, Miss Sill, was to turn out Christian missionaries. She had longed to be one herself, but finally decided that she could do more good by producing others. Jane Addams did not wish to be a missionary. On this point, as on many others, she did not see eye to eye with Miss Sill, but the pressure put on all the young ladies troubled her conscience, and one day she asked her father for advice. He said, "You must always be honest with yourself, whatever happens."

Fortified, she returned to Rockford more than ever determined to resist Miss Sill, but youth is a notoriously worrying time, when intellect and emotion struggle against each other as if never to be reconciled, and Jane often asked herself what she *did* want to do. It must be something good for humanity, that was all she could be sure of. She thought a good deal about religion. Her letters to her best friend, Ellen Gates Starr, were full of these matters, but when she was not brooding, Jane enjoyed her studies and went in zestfully for writing on the seminary magazine and debating. Her senior year was marked by a refreshing struggle over that old grievance about degrees. Interestingly enough, practically all the girls in school were suffragists—an indication of how the spirit of feminism was spreading through the country. As feminists they agreed with Jane and joined her in the argument with Miss Sill, saying that Rockford should be a college and that girls who studied Greek and higher mathematics—Jane did Greek, and with a girl named Catharine Waugh went in for calculus as well—should have the recognition of a B.A., if only to prove that women could be as intellectual as men. In the end Jane and Catharine between them forced the issue and Miss Sill had to consent. Rockford Female Seminary became Rockford College for Women, and Jane got her B.A.—though it came a year late and she had to go back to collect it.

That summer of 1881 was overtaken by tragedy when her father, at fifty-nine, suddenly died of a burst appendix. The shock was severe, but she tried to carry out her plans and actually registered that autumn at the Women's Medical College in Philadelphia. For seven months she worked hard, but her heart was not in it and she broke down. The leading doctor for nervous complaints, S. Weir Mitchell, treated her, probably according to his favorite method of keeping the patient in bed with nothing to do, but as soon as Jane went back to Cedarville she fell ill again. After another six months during which she stayed in bed, her brother-in-law Dr. Harry Haldeman operated on her spine. Though this procedure seems to have improved her back, she was told afterward that she could never have children.

In late 1883, to "relax her nerves," she went to Europe with her stepmother. The two women did the usual things one did on a Grand Tour, but the first experience that really impressed Miss Addams was a trip made in London one evening with a group of other tourists, under the guidance of a city missionary, to see the slums around Mile End Row. It was a Saturday night, when hucksters auctioned off from their carts the decaying foodstuffs left over from the day's trade. Sitting on top of their omnibus the party looked down on the scene, where ragged people clamored around the carts bidding for spoiled vegetables. Jane, appalled, saw one man, who had bought a cabbage, sit down on the curb and then and there devour it, "unwashed and uncooked as it was." In her memoirs she said that she never forgot the "myriads of hands, empty, pathetic, nerveless and workworn . . . clutching forward for food which was already unfit to eat . . . I have never since been able to see a number of hands held upward . . . even when they belong to children who wave them in response to a teacher's query, without a certain revival of that memory . . . of the despair and resentment which seized me then."

The yeast had begun to work, though she still did not know what to do. Restless, undecided, self-questioning, she waited. At twenty-five she joined the Presbyterian Church; later she changed her allegiance to the Congregationalists. She tried sheep farming, but was unsuccessful: the sheep got foot rot. At the end of 1887 she went abroad again, looked at more sights, and by prearrangement met Ellen Starr in Rome. They were in Madrid at Easter. With Ellen and other friends she went to a bullfight. Carried away by the spectacle, she stayed on though the others expressed disgust and left their seats. Miss Addams sat alone, dreaming of childhood games when she and George had pretended to slay dragons, and thinking of the Christian gladiators of ancient Rome who had died like these bulls in the arena. The cruelty of the proceedings did not dawn on her until she came out and met her friends and hear their reproaches. Suddenly she saw the enormity of her enjoyment, and felt that they were also reproaching her for having frittered away so many years doing nothing for humanity.

Next morning she told Ellen Starr of plans that must have been maturing in the back of her mind for a long time, and Ellen eagerly promised to help her put them into action. What Jane Addams thought of was a big house among a lot of horrid little ones—a settlement house in some Chicago slum area. Before going home she went to England to see Toynbee Hall, in Whitechapel, founded not long before by Oxford men who wanted to bring the different social classes together, widen the horizons of the underprivileged, and give educated people something constructive to do. Miss Addams visited the hall and talked to various social reformers. After investigating a few similar experiments in other parts of the country, she at last sailed for America, where she arrived in the summer of 1888. Immediately she began a search in Chicago for the big house. It took her five months to find Hull House, on South Halsted Street. Originally it was built as a suburban manse, but it had long been surrounded by the poor of the expanding city and their decayed little hutches.

Jane did not intend to form merely another charitable organization. At an Ethical Culture summer school in 1892 she explained her aims: ". . . a movement based not only on conviction, but upon genuine emotion, wherever educated young people are seeking an outlet for that sentiment of universal brotherhood, which the best spirit of our times is forcing from an emotion into a motive. These young people . . . feel a fatal want of harmony between their theory and their lives, a lack of co-ordination between thought and action . . ." (There is a parallel to be drawn here between her aspirations and those of the Peace Corps of the 1960s.) After a moving description of the empty existence not of the poor but of the middle classes, she ended: "This young life, so sincere in its emotion and yet so undirected, seems to me as pitiful as the other great mass of destitute lives. One is supplementary to the other, and some method of communication can surely be devised." Just as surely, she was thinking of her own life when she said this.

To gather enough money for the project was a slow business but not impossible: the young women had the help of many. When they moved in and became residents of Halsted Street they were accompanied by their friends Florence Kelley and Julia Lathrop. Another of the founders was Dr. Alice Hamilton, and very soon Mary Rozet Smith, one of Jane's good friends, joined their number.

Chicago, hog butcher of the world, was a roistering amalgam of industry supported by the largest immigrant population in the country: 70 percent of the city's people had been born abroad. Naturally, a big proportion of these were victimized in sweatshops. One of Hull House's investigators described their neighborhood: "the filthy and rotten tenements, the foul stables and dilapidated outhouses, the piles of garbage fairly alive with diseased odors . . ." And the children! The investigator tried to count the inhabitants of the block, "but the effort proved futile when she tried to keep count of little people surging in and out of passageways and up and down outside staircases, like a veritable stream of life."

The founders' method of getting started was direct and simple—they invited twelve young women of the neighborhood to come in for a reading party, asking two of the guests to come early for dinner and help them wash up afterward. They started a kindergarten. They organized children's clubs. They encouraged everyone who wished to do so to drop in uninvited and treat Hull House as a gathering place, a center.

At the time there was no such subject as sociology taught at the universities. This was practical social work, and soon, of course, it turned into efforts at reform. Florence Kelley asked the state Bureau of Labor to back her up, and when they acceded she investigated the sweatshops. Her report was so vivid that the legislative committee pushed through a law against sweatshops in 1893. Alas, the manufacturers fought back until the law was rendered useless, and Jane Addams, inevitably, was tagged as a radical.

The story of Hull House is a long one, and so was the career of Miss Addams. She became a public figure. Her early interest in woman suffrage was revived on Halsted Street, and she worked hard and efficaciously to bring about one particular triumph: in 1913, women in Chicago got the right to vote in municipal elections—that was six years before they could vote in national elections. Theodore Roosevelt asked for and got her help in his Progressive Movement, though later he was disappointed in her for her pacifism. She made many trips abroad, was given any number of honorary degrees, wrote books, and in 1931, when anger against her staunch pacifism had died down after the end of the First World War, she received the Nobel Peace Prize.

It was natural that Charlotte Perkins Gilman, writer and lecturer, should have known Jane Addams. They had much in common besides the fact that both were born in 1860 and died in 1935: their paths crossed more than once. But Charlotte Gilman's life was far stranger than Jane Addams' and probably more painful as well. She was a great-grandchild of that famous and fecund divine Dr. Lyman Beecher; her father, Frederick Perkins, became known among scholars as a librarian in spite of getting himself expelled from Yale for beating up a professor. When Charlotte was still a baby he deserted his family, and though she saw him now and again during her life, she was never quite sure why he left home. What she did know was that her mother was often unhappy and always distressed for money. They were forever packing up and moving away from debts—here and there, to Provincetown, where her mother had been born, to Hartford, where she saw Aunt Harriet Beecher Stowe, and to other parts of New England. They even lived for a time in a community of Swedenborgians with whom Mrs. Perkins was briefly taken. Education for the Perkins children was naturally scrappy until her mother inherited a bit of money from a great-aunt and was able to send Charlotte and her brother to good schools.

At the age of sixteen she wrote to her father asking for advice on what to read, as she wished to help humanity. Any question involving books got a reply from him. He sent her an excellent list and some magazines, and this, she said, was the beginning of her real education. She read thoroughly on biology, anthropology, sociology; she went to a course of lectures on history, and as for religion, after reading a good deal she made up her own. At seventeen she began trying to earn more money to help her mother, painting cards and doing a little "governessing," after the fashion of Louisa Alcott. At this time she became very friendly with the family of William P. Channing, the son of William Ellery Channing. Her best friend through life was his daughter Grace.

It was a time, she wrote, of large beginnings. Strong-minded girls insisted on going to college, though they were ridiculed for it. Women worked in shops and offices, though a man she met in 1880 who owned a store told her that he was severely criticized for employing saleswomen—they were so *unwomanly*. Certain young men were called "fast," and some girls were known to be "pretty gay." This sort of thing was not for her, Charlotte decided; she preferred calisthenics, at which she was very good. She never wore corsets, all her clothing hung from her shoulders, and she made for herself a side-garter suspender to which her skirts buttoned. She loved textiles but not fashion. Every day she ran a mile, and she made up five rules for health: "Good air and plenty of it, good exercise and plenty of it, good food and plenty of it, good sleep and plenty of it, good clothing and as little as possible." At twenty-one she was a self-made young woman and gloried in her splendid health, "and with clothes," she wrote, "would have been beautiful. But one does not call a philosophic steam-engine beautiful. My dress was not designed to allure."

Nevertheless, a painter named Charles Walter Stetson fell in love with her and she with him. They were married in 1884, and were "really very happy together," she wrote in her memoirs, as if puzzled at the memory. She learned to cook and keep house. The idyll ended when she got pregnant, because for the whole period she was sick and depressed. Baby Katharine, born in 1885, was a "heavenly" infant, but Charlotte's depression did not lift. All day she would lie on the sofa and weep: "A constant dragging weariness miles below zero. Absolute incapacity. Absolute misery. To the spirit it was as if one were an armless, legless, eyeless, voiceless cripple.

Prominent among the tumbling suggestions of a suffering brain was the thought 'You did it yourself! You did it yourself! You had health and strength and hope and glorious work before you—and you threw it all away . . . ' " For five months, nursing the baby, tears ran down her cheeks. It was thought that she needed a holiday, so she went to visit the Channings in Pasadena, California. She was cured quickly in that lovely country, and came back to her husband—where she immediately fell ill again.

She consulted S. Weir Mitchell, who told her to rest and never again to touch a paintbrush or pen. Dismissing him as a fool, she left his consulting room and never went back. So it went, until in 1887, "in a moment of clear vision," the unhappy couple agreed to get a divorce. Finally free, even though a wreck, she returned to California in 1890 to make a life for the child and herself. She stayed there for four years. Even in her last days, in happier times, she looked back sadly on the collapse of her "so laboriously built-up character." She was never to be free of onsets of this mysterious illness, when she would forget things she had read and people she had met. She had spells of utter exhaustion when she dreaded having to pack for some trip. Reading her book, one marvels that in spite of all this she went on in the most energetic way, making her living, giving talks for a pittance, traveling all over America and England by the cheapest routes, and producing her books of poetry and short stories.

In California she and Grace collaborated on writing plays, of which nothing of profit came; she wrote other things; she kept a boardinghouse; she sent money now and then to her mother; and she battled with spells of sickness every so often. During her first year of freedom she wrote thirty-three short articles and twenty-three poems, not including ten verses for children. She taught classes occasionally, but never dared take a regular job for fear her nerves would let her down. She found that she was very good at teaching children. One of her stories, "The Yellow Wallpaper," concerned a nervous breakdown and was generally thought to be the best thing she had ever done. Finally, she began lecturing on a peculiar plan—no tickets were sold, but after the talk a collection was made, and Charlotte kept what was left over after the hall had been paid for. Once she made five dollars for talking to the Friday Morning Club of Los Angeles, but usually it was less than that. She discovered a true talent for preaching, thanks no doubt, she said, to her Beecher blood: she preached in church now and then—it did not matter what denomination.

People did not understand her pleasure when her ex-husband married Grace Channing. They asked curious, prying questions, and then, when she sent Katharine to live with the Stetsons, became angry with her, saying that she had given the child away. Charlotte could not understand their attitude, and it hurt and angered her. Katharine had a talent for drawing: Grace and Charles would take her to Rome to develop it. Wasn't it best for Katharine to let her go, even though Charlotte would miss her terribly? Especially as the child loved Grace as much as she herself did. Charlotte never forgave her California critics for their remarks.

Having moved to San Francisco, where she found it possible to live on ten dollars a week, she published her first book, a collection of poems entitled *In This Our World,* which helped her reputation though she made little money out of it.

"Thirty-five years old," she wrote of herself at this time. "A failure, a repeated, cumulative failure. Debt, quite a lot of it. No means of paying, no strength to hold a job . . ."

She decided to go East; on the way she visited Jane Addams at Hull House, and inscribed her name in the guest book "Charlotte Perkins Stetson. At Large." Through all her bouts of sickness, she managed to meet her engagements. Sick or well, in all the years, as she said, preaching was always ready. She talked on many subjects without preparation: all she required was that it be something that interested her. Once Jane Addams asked her to stay in Chicago and take charge of a subsidiary settlement on the North Side, in the district called Little Hell, but Charlotte refused, as she always refused regular jobs. Her health would not permit such a commitment.

She worked for woman suffrage whenever she made the chance, believing it to be "reasonable and necessary," though she never thought it would cure all ills. ". . . by no means as important as some of the protagonists held," she said. Once she attended a suffrage convention in Washington as the California delegate. She spoke for socialism too, for she thought the real basis of that system was right, in spite of Marx's mishandling of it. In the spring of 1896, she said with admirable understatement, her lectures were somewhat scattered: Chicago; Milwaukee; Detroit; Evanston, Illinois; Washington; Philadelphia; Springfield, Illinois; Grand Haven, Michigan; Aurora, Illinois; Providence; Lynn, Massachusettes; Boston; and Kansas City. The tour ended in Topeka, where she first spoke on "How to Be Good and How to Stay So." The next night she addressed another Topeka audience in the same hall on "The Heroes We Need Now."

She was making more money—as much as seventeen dollars for two lectures in one day, though a lecture usually paid less than half that sum. At any rate, she saved up enough to sail for England in July of that year, to attend the International Socialist and Labor Congress as a delegate from California. She thoroughly enjoyed England, where she met George Bernard Shaw and Charlotte Payne Townsend, who later married the dramatist, the Webbs, and William Morris, whom she greatly admired. Yet she often had "dismal" patches, even in the midst of her exciting life in England.

Back in America she spent some time with Mrs. Stanton, reporting, "To have been with her and 'Aunt Susan,' as we called the great Susan B. Anthony, seemed to establish connection with a splendid period of real heroism."

It was in 1896, in New York, that she followed a sudden impulse and went to Wall Street to look up one of her cousins, Houghton Gilman. She had been fond of him when they were children, and wondered if he remembered her. He did, and they continued to see each other. At the same time she began writing a book with the forbidding title—at first—of *The Economic Relations of the Sexes as a Factor in Social Development*. Later, I am glad to say, she changed that to *Women and Economics*. She wrote it at a fast pace: 1,700 words the first day, 2,400 the second, 3,600 the next, and 4,000 the next. At that rate she soon finished the first draft of 35,000 words, which was something less than half the completed work; still, she said, it had the root of the matter in it. *Women and Economics* was a success at home and even more so in England. From that time on she had many requests for articles, and one cannot wonder: here at last was proof of her lively, strong mind.

In *Women and Economics* she states that the relation of the sexes depends on one rule: the man feeds the woman. In no other species of mammal is that rule followed, though here and there a bird supplies his mate with food during the incubation of her eggs. Man, on the contrary, keeps his woman the year round. Look at the great cats, said Charlotte, or many other animals: the mother not only takes care of herself but is exclusively responsible for her children as well. In this unnatural state of ours, woman must make herself attractive, or starve. Man, she continued, is oversexed, or he would not demand this attraction out of season, as it were . . .

Charlotte was to write on other stimulating, controversial theories. She proposed doing away with most of the housework that trammels women by having the cooking and cleaning done by special groups of people whose only job this would be. Cooked food would be provided to workers at other pursuits, their living quarters would be cleaned by specialists, and they would be left free to do creative work.

In 1900, at the age of forty, she married Houghton Gilman. For a time they lived in a New York apartment, and, true to her principles, they ate their meals next-door at a boardinghouse. Much to her joy, she could now take Katharine back, and the girl stayed with her until she herself was married. For twenty-two years the Gilmans remained in New York, then they bought a house in Norwich, Connecticut.

It was the custom in Norwich to put up little plaques wherever someone of note had lived. "Our ancient mansion I found decorated with two, on either side the front door," she wrote, "one a list of ancestors, the other announcing, 'Lydia Huntley Sigourney was born here.' "

The Gilmans spent the rest of their lives peacefully gardening, thinking, and writing. Summing up, Charlotte observed that the most salient change in the world she had once known was the lowering of standards in sex relations. She blamed for this "the sexuopathic philosophy, which solemnly advocates as 'natural' a degree of indulgence utterly without parallel in nature . . . In the widespread attacks upon marriage it is clearly shown that the attackers do not know that monogamy is a 'natural' form of sex relationship, practised widely among both birds and beasts, who are neither 'Puritan' nor 'Mid-Victorian.' "

In January 1932 she discovered that she had inoperable cancer of the breast. For a while she concealed the fact from her husband, but collected a stock of chloroform against the time when the pain should become unbearable. She did tell him at last, but as he died soon afterward she had only herself to consult when the moment of decision arrived. On August 17, 1935, when her malady was well advanced, Charlotte Gilman calmly took her own life.

It would be easy to make fun of Carry Nation, but I don't intend to do it. She is included here not because she was good news copy for a while but because she represented a lot of American women of the period—poorly educated if not ignorant, firmly convinced of her principles, and tough.

She was born Carry Moore in Garrard County, Kentucky. Her father was a sometime farmer, sometime horse dealer, and he owned slaves. Her mother was insane, suffering from the conviction that she was Queen Victoria. Carry was born in 1846 and spent much of her early life with the blacks; she said in her autobiography that she was seven or eight before she ate at the "white folks' table." Nobody in the family had strong objections to drinking; on the contrary.

George Moore liked to move about, looking for somewhere better to live. He took his family to settle in Missouri for a while, close to the Kansas border; a bad choice of territory, because the Moores were caught in the crossfire of some preliminary abolitionist trouble between the states. Carry was very ill at this time, and during her convalescence happened to attend a temperance revival meeting—a popular pastime in that vicinity—where she got religion, had herself baptized, and never looked back: she was a firm teetotaler from that time on. George had lost most of his money, Mrs. Moore was never much help around the house, and Carry was left to do the housekeeping and look after the other children. She was nineteen and quite pretty when she met Dr. Charles Gloyd, who had come to teach in Missouri and boarded at the Moores'. He wanted to marry Carry, but Carry's mother didn't like him and this delayed matters. At last, on November 21, 1867, they did marry—and Gloyd was drunk at the wedding, but Carry was too innocent to realize it.

Gloyd hung out his shingle in Holden, Missouri, and sent for his parents to come and live with them. The bride heard from her mother-in-law for the first time that her husband was a drunkard, and the news terrified her. Now that the secret was out, Gloyd spent more time away from home drinking, and his pregnant wife had to go out looking for him. Never a silently suffering type, when she had run him to earth she would get down on her knees and pray aloud for his soul, inviting bystanders to join her. Then George Moore heard how things were going and came to fetch her home, leaving Gloyd to his own resources, which killed him within six months.

The following years were full of toil and misfortune. Carry's child, a girl she named Charlien, suffered from some strange disease. Moore's affairs were sometimes better, sometimes worse; he did manage to give Carry some land, on which she built a house. She got a teaching certificate and held a job until she quarreled with her boss. It was then that she decided to marry again, someone, she said, who would take care of her and her family, which meant Charlien and her mother-in-law Mrs. Gloyd.

The man she selected was David A. Nation, Civil War veteran, part-time editor, attorney, and self-proclaimed minister of the Christian Church. He was nineteen years older than Carry, but she may have thought this an advantage. They married and went to Texas, where they bought a ranch and tried to grow cotton on it. The venture failed, so Carry took over the local hotel, a sad little shanty, and ran it as a boardinghouse, aided by Charlien and Mrs. Gloyd. At this point her constitution failed her: she became prey to insomnia, hysterical fits, and nightmares that made her scream.

In the hope that David would be able to find work elsewhere, the household moved to another Texas town and Carry took on the responsibility of a bigger hotel. This was a strategical error, for George Moore, after Carry's mother died, came to join them, and Charlien, who had married, brought her husband there too. After all, they probably felt, there was plenty of room. And still David did not find work.

It was after her father's death that Carry started behaving strangely, stopping people in the street to ask if they loved God. In one church after another she annoyed the congregation until they requested her to stay away. Then she organized her own Sunday school—she was very fond of children. She was so fervently sure of herself and her mission that she always had a following, even though she had enemies too. Once when there was a long drought she prayed loud and lustily for rain, and the rain came. People said that you couldn't argue that sort of thing away. Then a fire swept over the town, but nobody could make Mrs. Nation stir out of her wooden hotel. She remained praying on the floor, saying that the building wouldn't burn. Nor did it, for the fire stopped just short of it.

Then David Nation wrote something in the paper that offended certain locals, and they beat him up, so Carry exchanged the Texas property for another place in Medicine Lodge, Kansas, and took her family there. Nation became minister of the Medicine Lodge First Christian Church, and might have been happy enough if his wife had not spoken out during his sermons, telling him to speed it up. She also told him when it was time to stop, then marched him out.

She now turned more and more against drinking, and often berated the town's druggist for peddling whiskey. He was probably doing it, too. Since 1880 Kansas had been officially dry, but people had been getting around the law for a long time. It also worried Carry that so much sex was going on, and she did a lot of interfering in people's private lives. But her real enemy was liquor, and soon she decided on stronger measures against it. A commonplace expedient of those who wanted a drink was to get a prescription for it, since liquor could be sold for "medical, scientific and mechanical purposes," whatever that meant. But it was not really necessary even to have a refillable prescription, as some men did: there were joints, or speak-easies (though that word was not yet in use), openly operating in Kansas towns. Carry listed these places in Medicine Lodge and read them out in church. Then, with a woman who sympathized with the cause, she set out one Saturday afternoon with a hand organ belonging to her friend. The ladies stationed themselves in front of a joint and started singing hymns to the accompaniment of the organ.

There was nothing new in this. For some years WCTU members had been doing something similar outside saloons all over the states. Here in Kansas, however, the illegitimacy of the bar lent a certain piquancy to the proceedings. After the first hymn Carry entered the place. There was a scuffle, and female sympathizers in the crowd picked up Carry's cry, aimed at a policeman, "Do your duty! Do your duty!"

As a result of the fracas the joint was closed, and Carry moved on to bigger efforts. In February 1900 she committed her first smashing. Leading a group of women, she crashed into a drugstore and found a keg. Shouting, "Roll out the broth of hell!" she rolled it into the street. One of the women ran and fetched a maul, and Carry took it and smashed the keg. When men tried to catch the liquid in their caps, Carry set it on fire. At last the authorities actually closed down all the crypto-saloons in Medicine Lodge, and Carry became a heroine to the women.

In June of that year she rode to nearby Kiowa in her buggy, which she had filled with missiles, and made the rounds of three joints, throwing brickbats and empty bottles through the plate-glass windows, smashing the large mirrors hung over the bars, and breaking all liquor bottles in the place. The town officials were not only angry but perplexed. How could they prosecute Carry for damaging places that had no legal right to exist?

At first the regular WCTU centers disapproved of Carry's actions, which they considered unrefined, but as she got results, they became convinced that she was on the right track. Of course she was arrested frequently and sometimes spent as much as a week in jail, but she was never subdued. In Wichita, Carry damaged a painting of Cleopatra in Her Bath because it offended her sense of morality; this exploit sent her to jail for several weeks.

Newspapers all over the country began following Carry's adventures, and William Allen White in the Emporia *Gazette* came out in her favor. At some time during her expeditions she adopted the hatchet that became her symbol and began selling miniature pewter hatchets as souvenirs. She used the money for the cause, for she had to pay out practically all her savings in fines and lawyers' fees. In Topeka she encountered that *rara avis*, an honest police chief, who agreed with her and said that he didn't care if she smashed every joint in town. It was there too that she awed the crowd by picking up a cash register and throwing it, unaided, into the street, though it was of such a weight that no strong man could have done it.

This was America, where publicity was king. Soon an entrepreneur was trying to make money on Carry Nation by sending her on a lecture tour, but it didn't work very well. Carry could not be depended on to stick to the script, and often insisted on speaking on subjects that did not interest the audience. At Coney Island, though, she gave them something of what they wanted when she marched out on the boardwalk and broke up a cigar stand. Carry did not care for smoking, and often snatched an offending weed from some surprised bystander's mouth. Probably she disappointed her public, too, because outside of Kansas she was not justified in smashing up saloons, a fact that moderated her behavior somewhat.

Still, Carry had her moments. In Chicago she insisted that a bar proprietor cover up the nude statue he kept in his window. He did so, but later made the statue even more alluring by displacing the drapery at strategic points. A Yale undergraduate wrote begging her to come to New Haven and save him and his companions from sin; they were often served such dishes as ham with champagne sauce, he said, which made him too dizzy to do his work. The earnest Carry never realized when she was the subject of a joke, and she had a splendid time at Yale. The Yale Club still cherishes a photograph of her surrounded by youths who had carefully set the scene, with everyone in the party holding up glasses of water—but the water glasses have been retouched, and are now beer steins.

Even while she was away from Kansas the place seethed, for she had started a political upheaval. There were fights, mob scenes, and one accidental death from a bullet during a battle over cases of liquor. All of this, of course, helped the temperance movement beyond the boundaries of the state. Mrs. Nation divorced her husband in 1901 and went on with her travels. She moved all over America and visited Canada and the British Isles. She appeared on a music-hall stage in London, where people threw vegetables at her—this was in 1909—and lectured in Ireland. After that trip, however, she slowed down and retired to Arkansas, only coming out now and again for some special meeting. It was at one of these, in Eureka Springs, Missouri, that Mrs. Nation suffered a stroke. About to address the meeting, she found herself unable to utter a word. This was in January 1911, and she lingered for six months more, in a listless state that was almost a coma, until release came on June 2.

It is good to know that she had money, about 10,000 dollars to leave Charlien—money she had saved up for years from lectures and even her ventures in hotelkeeping.

Carry Nation's was not a sympathetic character. Her dying removed from the scene a picturesque crusader who, though she would probably have scorned much of the feminist philosophy even if she had understood it, nevertheless acted it out. Carry Nation was a power in the land. She dramatized the cause of temperance where less direct methods had failed, and taught the women of America how to go about achieving Prohibition. For good or ill, it was a lesson they did not forget.

CHAPTER 18

Strange Bedfellows

MANY SHARPLY CONTRASTING TYPES of women were involved in the feminine protest of the early twentieth century; so wide are some differences that the movement often appears to be the only thing the participants had in common. It has been remarked, too, that the geographical extent of the new ideas was nationwide; that Jane Addams' schoolfellows in Illinois were nearly all suffragists, and that even Mormon women in Utah wanted to vote. It must have been a powerful movement, too, that could include two women as widely dissimilar in background and education as Ellen Maury Slayden, Virginia-born wife of a Texas congressman in the House of Representatives, and Margaret Sanger from New York State, who devoted her life to the furtherance of contraception and coined the phrase "birth control." Ellen was a lady in the old sense of the word, whereas Margaret never stopped to wonder if she was one or not. Ellen was interested in political rights for women, Margaret in biological rights. Yet, as far apart as they were in many ways, both women aimed for the same thing—improvement in the lot of their sex.

Ellen Maury is probably best remembered for the journal she kept during her years in Washington, D.C. She was born in 1860 and grew up in Charlottesville; she could remember some of the effects of the Civil War and often cited examples of them in support of arguments for pacifism—she was passionately opposed to war. Like many other ladies of the South she had no formal education, but she was very well read, a good linguist, and an intelligent, original thinker. And she had an excellent vantage point from which to observe the activities of the suffragists and the tumultuous campaign they conducted in the nation's capital to win the right to vote. She favored the cause, while deprecating some of the methods of those who fought for it.

All her life Ellen Slayden favored women's rights, but strongly objected to the behavior of the militant suffragists. Her journal, *Washington Wife, 1897–1919,* has been edited by Dr. Walter Prescott Webb, who married the widow of one of her nephews and speaks with pride of her background: "The Maurys were related to the Lewises of Lewis and Clark fame. The Langhorne sisters, the Gibson girls, were cousins, and that includes Lady Astor."

Her photographs indicate her characteristic attitude toward life: the expression is pertly bland. One exception is a picture taken when she was nineteen, possibly for her coming-out party; she is wearing a broad-sashed white dress and looks adorably shy. Just under five feet tall, Mrs. Slayden was resignedly accustomed to hearing herself spoken of as "cute." Since her husband "J.," James Luther Slayden, was unusually tall, they were a striking couple. He too was a Southerner, born in Kentucky. As a young man he moved to San Antonio, acquired a ranch, and became a successful cotton broker until 1895, when the bottom dropped out of the market. Ellen probably met him when she was visiting her sister, the wife of a Texan named Albert Maverick of Maverick fame: their son became representative Maury Maverick.

The Slaydens married in 1883. There were no children. Having extricated himself from cotton, Slayden went into politics and was elected representative in 1896. His wife was a faithful taker of notes, and her journal is full of sidelights on Washington life.

Restricted finances prevented them from keeping a carriage, but it was the new fashion to ride bicycles, and this helped. "J. and I have beautiful wheels, and I hope I shall learn to enjoy it, but the divided skirt, for all its modesty, is so hideous and uncomfortable I feel as if I were in a bag," wrote the diarist in 1898.

Many parties she had to attend were made up exclusively of women. At one luncheon the table was beautiful and expensive, "but too much beribboned for my taste—ribbon and gravy are so incompatible." Broad pink-satin strips ran diagonally across the board, ending at each corner in a big bow like a little girl's sash. There were pink-shaded candles, a center piece of lace over pink silk, four wineglasses at each place, and ten courses "all wonderful to behold, especially the ice cream—pink roses falling out of a pink sugar umbrella into spun-candy snow."

The Slaydens themselves were having a dinner party on the day the news of the sinking of the *Maine* broke on the capital. Every morning for days afterward Ellen waited for the Capitol doors to open, then spent hours in the visitors' gallery listening to the workings of the government and chatting with the other women. "We talk of war and taffeta ruffles (very fashionable now) during the long wait," she wrote. "Most of the women are for war—'to the knife, and the knife to the hilt.' It is so safely glorious when only men are killed." When war was declared, she commented, "It does seem rather like a bully to fight such a poverty-stricken small country as Spain." Everyone wore little American flags, and people sang as much as they could remember, though it was not much, of "The Star Spangled Banner."

"Maps are searched to find the Philippines—few people ever heard of them before," she noted. "I am sure I never did. There is a general impression that they are the subject of one of St. Paul's epistles."

That summer had been a nightmare, she wrote in October; every day she apologized to J. for her lack of conviction that the war was necessary. She was haunted by the memory of troop trains they had seen on their way to Texas, those heading South filled with gay, shouting, often drunken boys, while those heading North carried more boys, sallow, dispirited, ill, or wounded. A few had been to Cuba and got what glory there was—"the little left by Colonel Roosevelt"—but more had simply been clearing land in Florida, where many died of typhoid.

In winter, evening receptions at the White House were rugged affairs: being a representative's wife had its drawbacks. No way had been devised to keep a blast of north wind from coming in with every guest, and one did not warm up for some time after reaching the drawing room. On a January night in 1899 the Slaydens found themselves among a more than usually distinguished company, with a great many foreigners and "an unblushing chase after them by the young girls—and their mothers who joined them in the view halloo." The cause of all this activity, Ellen said cattily, was that Mrs. Colgate, the scented-soap heiress, had just married the Earl of Strafford, and the young American women at the White House were stimulated by her example. If Mrs. Colgate and Jennie Jerome could win a title, why shouldn't they? They were in full cry after anything in foreign uniform no matter how insignificant. "A tiny Chinaman was surrounded by pretty girls hanging on to his words, and Turks, Hawaiians, and even the dark-brown Minister from Haiti had more attention than his charms called for."

Another manifestation of the social round that elicited Mrs. Slayden's scorn was the lavish use of calling cards during the visiting season. Every afternoon, from three to seven, the streets were thronged with carriages that usually carried two women, one holding a list, the other doing up cards in little packs held together with rubber bands—one for every adult female in the family receiving the call from every adult female in the family *making* the call, which added up to an appalling quantity. Sometimes Mrs. Slayden received packets of a dozen or more, all identical. One alone, she said, would make it perfectly clear who had called, and save her the trouble of burning the others.

Some other conventions seemed equally ridiculous. In every house, no matter how large or small it was, on visiting day a number of ladies in semi-evening dress had to stand about, passing the caller from one to another with a handshake as each remarked, "So good of you to come." One lady gave the visitor an ice with a rum cake, another a cup of sizzling tea; the visitor agreed with all of them on the state of the weather and the prevalence of grippe, and then left to a chorus of cheery "good-mornings" to go out into the black night. The ladies said "good morning" because it was morning, officially, until one had dinner, and it was considered smart to dine as late as possible.

The Slaydens heard of McKinley's assassination (1901) while they were in Mexico, and Ellen was sorry not only for his sake but because it meant that Roosevelt would now be President. Since his foray into Cuba she had not cared much for T.R. "What will it mean to the country to have him roughriding over it preaching war and the strenuous life?" she wondered. Two years later, however, she admitted that he had at least done one thing that entitled him to the country's gratitude: he had transformed the White House from a gilded barn into a comfortable residence, and one now entered on the ground floor through a warm, spacious corridor.

In her observations on the ladies of the White House, Mrs. Slayden has given us an unusually intimate picture of life as it was for young girls in her social set. She liked Mrs. Roosevelt, but the Roosevelts' daughter Alice did not enjoy a share of this approval. In several little comments Ellen showed that she considered Miss Alice far too free and easy. Writing to Jane Maverick in February 1904, she said: "Alice Roosevelt is getting to be almost pretty, but she has not quite arrived and still has awkward, bumptious manners."

Unwisely, Mrs. Maverick handed this letter to a friend who was a society reporter, expecting her to select passages from it. Instead, the reporter printed the whole letter in her column, and many Texas papers copied it. T.R. saw it, and though he did not exactly lose his temper, at a party of his wife's he taxed Mrs. Slayden with having used the word "bumptious" about his daughter. She *had* said it and there was no retreat, so she replied seriously: "Yes, Mr. Roosevelt, but I have had a great deal to do with young girls and feel sure it is just a stage in her evolution. Perhaps she will get over it."

The Slaydens kept in constant touch with peace organizations. In 1904 they helped to entertain a meeting of the Interparliamentary Union for the Promotion of Peace by Arbitration—"What a name!" as the diarist rightly said—and this entailed much moving around, first to St. Louis, where everyone visited the Exposition, then on a Western tour, and finally to Washington.

Again, Ellen scathingly commented on the feverish anxiety of some Americans to meet the titled men and women who had come to the meeting. "Some young girls in Colorado Springs spoke loudly of their joy at meeting a 'real live marquis' and gladly ran several hundred yards to catch up with and be introduced to a prince and a count." It gave her gooseflesh, she said, to think of how those foreigners must be laughing at such so-called republicans. But she also noted the republican lack of ceremony these same guests encountered at the White House. A Hungarian countess, for instance, was amazed to find that she need not remove her veil in the presence of Mrs. Roosevelt, and when Ellen invited an Englishwoman who wasn't feeling well to sit down by one of the windows, the lady asked in astonishment: "May we sit while the President is in the room?" A good question. Actually, people stood about for quite a while during the speeches, while T. R. "promised to hasten the millennium."

Many of the duties of a congressman's wife must have been onerous. Every February, for example, Ellen gave a reception for Texas schoolgirls, and every February there were more of them. In 1907 she thought that she would soon have to hire a hall for these occasions. "It was a dreadfully difficult party to entertain. They had a tendency to 'bunch' around the few young men I had corralled to help me, and they stayed bunched, charmed I never so wisely."

When the round began again in 1908, Ellen's entries in the journal sounded a little fatigued, as if the fun and excitement of being a representative's wife was not always worth the trouble. Without realizing it, she must have resented having to play a part in this pageant which her intelligence showed her was often absurd. But a congressman's wife should not have such subversive ideas. It was her husband's job to represent his state, and her job to represent him. For this she was honored, prettily dressed, and trotted out to parties: what more could a lady want? Nevertheless, the journalist does seem a bit tired. Once more, wrote Ellen, the streets were thronged with women earnestly doing their duty, paying calls not for the fun of it, but because they thought they had to. When a congressman's wife first arrived in town she was given a list—by the hotel clerk, or a milliner or dressmaker—of persons she must call on, which she doggedly worked her way through.

One day Mrs. Slayden was receiving with the assistance of a friend, Mrs. Gregg. The latter tried to hand a cup of coffee to a newly arrived wife, but that lady was busy studying a paper in her hand. At last she looked up and said: "Are you Representative Gregg's wife? Have I called on you?" Before Mrs. Gregg could answer, she went on: "No, but I'm going to. You live on Corcoran Street. Are you at home?"

"Always," said Mrs. Gregg. "Have you made many calls?"

The lady referred to her list again. "Yes, two hundred and fifty-seven," she said. "I have forty-six to make, though I've been calling quite assiduously. Soon I'll have a day at home. Ought to have a good crowd, don't you think?"

There was a Church Congress in 1910, and Ellen went to listen to a discussion of woman suffrage and its possible influence on education and religion. Dr. Henry Sylvester Nash of the Episcopal Theological School in Cambridge was in favor of votes for women. Women already had higher education, he said; to educate them like men and then tell them to stay at home and confine themselves to housekeeping was like manufacturing dynamite and then sitting on it. A man named Cyrus Townsend Brady, speaking in rebuttal, took what Mrs. Slayden bitterly called the highly intelligent position that women were slaves to their hats, their dresses, their shoes.

"I inferred that he thought when we abandoned them for trousers and derbies we would be qualified to vote," she said.

In the fall of 1912 Woodrow Wilson was elected, and Ellen Slayden, who had known him when he was at the University of Virginia when he was twenty-three, was not overjoyed. It was true, she said, that he had been admired even then for his intellect, but, she recalled, "We girls thought him too stuck on himself." Besides, she doubted if he was receptive to the cause of women's rights and especially female suffrage, which was naturally always much in the air at election time; she thought it should be paramount in any President's mind.

She was probably right to doubt that Wilson was pro women's suffrage, judging by a disgruntled comment he made in his notes during the time he was teaching at Bryn Mawr. Dated October 20, 1887, it read: "Lecturing to young women of the present generation on the history and principles of politics is about as appropriate and profitable as would be lecturing to stone-masons on the evolution of fashion in dress. There is a painful *absenteeism* of mind on the part of the audience. Passing through a vacuum, your speech generates no heat." And then, in charitable afterthought, he went on: "Perhaps it is some of it due to undergraduatism, not to femininity." Still, such an attitude betokened small help to the feminists.

On March 2, 1913, Ellen wrote that the inauguration was two days off and that the topic most discussed—no doubt, she meant most discussed by her female friends—was woman suffrage: "The inaugural procession follows the suffrage parade in public interest as in fact."

This sudden surge in interest was due chiefly to Alice Paul, a young Quaker who had done her apprenticeship in the school of militant suffrage work in England and developed a genius for public relations. There she had been put into prison and, when she went on a hunger strike, was forcibly fed. After three years in England—she went over in 1907—Alice came back to America in 1910 and began working for the National Suffrage Association. With Lucy Burns, another American experienced in the English struggle, she came to Washington in January 1913 to organize demonstrations at the inauguration. They gathered around them a few more women and organized a parade. Suffragist workers occupied a basement shop as headquarters, reported Ellen, a stifling place, but the busiest in town. There, crowds of men and tense-looking women sat at desks, handing out literature and pennants—unbecoming work, she thought, which would undoubtedly give the antisuffragists support for their argument that women, if they voted, would no longer be dainty. One "anti" actually wrote to the Washington *Post* to say that women were not made to vote but to be loved. Mrs. Slayden knew that letter was funny, but she criticized a squad of enthusiastic suffragists—the Pilgrims, they called themselves—who had hiked all the way from New York and looked far from alluring in their dingy brown cloaks and heavy shoes: "I admire their pluck, but can't see what use there was in hiking," said Ellen.

One way or another, walking or by train or auto, the women came. *The New York Times* described preparations on March 2: arriving trains were full of women; the delegates from New Orleans, Alabama, and other Southern points carried little yellow and white flags;

three special cars from New York were full of women wearing yellow gardenias. From New Jersey too, and Connecticut, Maine, Rhode Island, California, and Massachusetts they came, all in time for a full-dress rehearsal of a pageant that was planned, the high point of which was to be a tableau on the steps of the Treasury. Rehearsal day, March 2, was very cold and north winds blew across the city, but the practice went ahead. Two of the women, dancers, came barefoot.

Wilson was alleged to have said, when asked why he had not come out for or against women's suffrage, that it had never been brought to his attention. Very well, said Miss Paul, they would soon make up for that oversight. Of course, she had obtained a police permit for the parade and pageant—always a necessity for such demonstrations—and had announced in advance that it would take place on the day before the inauguration on March 4, because, she reasoned, the town would be full to bursting on that date. Woodrow Wilson arrived on the same day and was startled to find no crowds waiting to welcome him. He asked where everyone was, and was told they had all gone over to Pennsylvania Avenue to watch the suffragists' parade.

Next day the Baltimore *American* told what happened: how five thousand women had fought their way, foot by foot, up Pennsylvania Avenue through "a surging throng that completely defied Washington police, swamped the marchers, and broke their procession into little companies." They were able to finish their march only after cavalry troops were rushed in from Fort Myers to take charge. No inauguration had ever produced such scenes, said the newspaper writer, which in many instances amounted to riots.

The Baltimore *Sun* on the same date went into more detail and mentioned insults and jibes hurled at the women from the sidelines, so that many of them were in tears. It took more than an hour for them to go the first ten blocks, and at Fourth Street progress became impossible. When a Massachusetts National Guard regiment was told to help clear the way, some of the men laughed and refused. Finally the Thirteenth Regiment, Pennsylvania National Guard, agreed to go on police duty, as did students of the Maryland Agricultural College, who helped to protect the marching women. Where Sixth Street crosses Pennsylvania, police protection gave way entirely, and the two solid masses of spectators on either side came so close together that three women could not march abreast. At this point some of the Maryland boys formed in single file on each side of the marchers to keep them unmolested, while in front other students locked arms and broke through the crowd. Several newspaper correspondents had to use their fists fighting people back. Yet in spite of all, said the *Sun*, the parade was a great success because most of the marchers kept their tempers. "They suffered insult, and closed their ears to jibes and jeers. Few faltered, though some of the older women were forced to drop out from time to time."

On March 5 *The New York Times* reported that there were many protests, and the Senate was aroused into questioning why Pennsylvania Avenue had not been kept clear for the suffragists. No women were badly hurt, the *Times* reporter said, but some men had broken bones as a result of the crowd's unruly behavior, and there were bitter complaints. There were headlines such as the following:

POLICE IDLY WATCH ABUSE OF WOMEN
SHOCKING INSULTS, SEIZED AND SPAT UPON

The suffragists filed a complaint against the police, and at last the district commissioners investigated. In the end the Washington chief of police lost his job over the affair, but the publicity was invaluable for the women. Quick to follow it up, many of them went out on pilgrimages all over the country, collecting signatures for new petitions. Then their representatives came to Washington in an automobile procession on July 31 bringing the suffrage petitions signed with 200,000 names, and turned the papers over to a group of senators. Other delegations visited the President, and he at last, one assumes, began to pay attention to the subject of woman suffrage.

That summer the Slaydens visited London on their way to the Universal Peace Conference at The Hague, and Ellen discovered to her surprise that the English militant suffragists made more noise far away than they did at close quarters. In Washington, people had been saying that the English, to avoid suffrage demonstrations, were excluding women from public places like St. Paul's and Westminster Abbey, but it was not true. The Slaydens visited St. Paul's themselves and saw as many women as men in the cathedral. Later, at a peace ceremony in the Abbey, they joined a crowd that stood for an hour around a cart from which Mrs. Pethick Lawrence made a speech demanding votes for women. The lady was handsome, and so well dressed that no one could complain of her lack of womanliness. There was no actual disorder in the crowd, but the heckling, thought

Ellen Slayden, was brutal; in America such rude talk addressed to a woman would certainly precipitate a free fight. According to hearsay, a crowd at the Pavilion was not as gentle as that at the Abbey, for there was a genuine row at that place and several women were knocked down, though their leader, Mrs. Emmeline Pankhurst, escaped unhurt.

Woman suffrage was still very much in the public eye when the Slaydens returned to Washington. "A wearing week!" wrote Ellen in December. "The National Suffrage Association was meeting here and I had to go when there were so many pleasanter things to do." She went because she was the national committeewoman from Texas. She believed in suffrage for women, she said, in spite of the suffragists en masse, who bored her to death. If she had to deal only with Jane Addams, Florence Kelley, and others like them, she would ask no better company. "But the coy, coquettish suffragist who never lets you forget that she is a woman and therefore to be wooed, or the strident dead-in-earnest *female*, or those . . . who have ulterior motives, social or financial, shake my faith and paralyze my efforts."

As a committee woman, she was supposed to demand a constitutional amendment giving countrywide suffrage all at once instead of the commonsense method—as she considered it—of leaving the question to be settled state by state. The delay involved in this program did not dismay her, for, she argued, not one woman in ten in Texas wanted the vote, and if it was thrust upon them they would misuse or neglect it. Better to let them waken to the need for suffrage at their own pace; then they would use it wisely. But her "strenuous sisters" in the movement did not agree, and she had to bow to their judgment.

Then the war in Europe thrust such matters from her mind. All her pacifistic sympathies were aroused. Though like other women she busied herself with Red Cross activities, she was a leading spirit in the newly formed Women's Constructive Peace Movement. At a meeting of this body on January 11, 1915, Jane Addams presided.

". . . we may do some good if we are not swept off our feet by slushy sentiment or tangled up with women suffrage politics," Ellen reflected. If only they could get women to take as much interest in saving their sons from war as they did in preventing everyone from taking an occasional drink, their influence might be tremendous, but few women could see beyond the corner saloon. And at the Capitol, the legislators were sitting for a session of unprecedented length—nineteen months. Such anxious times were bringing about a change in American women, she declared, a kind of social ferment. Women had taken to making public speeches. Instead of the old tea, bridge, and dinner parties, they attended luncheons and made speeches afterward. She herself had become as incorrigibly loquacious as W. J. Bryan himself. Round-table luncheons at women's clubs, young girls' luncheons, a luncheon for "Free Discussion Among Advanced Women," the College Women's Club—at all these the ladies talked, and were beginning to talk surprisingly well. What did it all mean? Possibly it was a result of the suffrage question, but Ellen thought it more likely that women were stirred up by the fact that the European conflict was drawing nearer and nearer.

On the second of April 1917, President Wilson announced that a state of war existed between the United States and Germany. At the Capitol, Ellen sat in a group that included Mrs. Carrie Chapman Catt, president of the Woman Suffrage Party, whom she studied balefully, for Mrs. Catt had recently been guilty of high-handed action in offering the entire party for military service in case of war. "She has been called down sharply for it," wrote the diarist, "and will probably be dropped from the list of honorary chairmen of the Women's Peace Party at our next executive session." Mrs. Catt was handsome and well dressed, but if one judged by her expression, she was not in the same class spiritually with Jane Addams, Julia Lathrop, and other women considered by Mrs. Slayden to be the first ladies of the land, "and all of them lovable, the kind of women you can joke with."

One single vote had been cast against going into the war, by the government's first-ever woman representative—Mrs. Jeanette Rankin of Montana, who formally took her seat that same day. Approvingly, Mrs. Slayden watched her as she crossed the floor. "Not more than a year ago men would say when arguing against woman suffrage, 'Next thing you'll be wanting women in Congress,' " she reflected, "as if that was the *reductio ad absurdum,* and here she was . . . and the men were clapping, cheering in the friendliest way."

Mrs. Slayden was not in town at the time of a later incident in Washington. It happened on August 28, after the congressmen had left the city. Ten militant ladies picketed the White House and were arrested. Four drew prison sentences of six months.

On November 6 the suffrage movement got a shot in the arm when New York State adopted its own constitutional amendment granting the franchise to women. No doubt it was this triumph, of immense potential value to suffragists all over the country, that motivated the militants to picket the White House again a few days later, on November 10. This time forty-one women were arrested. Their leaders were duly sent to prison for sentences ranging from six days to six months.

Ellen Slayden failed to mention these earlier protests, but on January 2, 1918, she wrote: "Our militant sisters, whose methods I heartily disapprove, are bringing a lot of trouble to the suffragists. Last night on the street in front of the White House they brought on a riot by burning copies of the President's speeches, denouncing him as a 'false prophet' and doing a lot of spectacular things that do nothing that I can see but alienate dignified people from our cause."

Five of the women were arrested and taken to detective headquarters, but all were later released. Unrepentant, they announced that they intended to keep watchfires burning until the Senate passed the suffrage amendment, but Ellen Slayden's mind was occupied otherwise during those months. Her pacifism grew as the war fever mounted.

"September 7. Yesterday Congress voted eleven billions to carry on the war, to kill the bravest and best young men of the race, while scientists say that one billion wisely expended would eradicate tuberculosis from the earth." On December 15 she wrote that Jane Addams was in the capital rallying women of like mind. Miss Addams and Mrs. Slayden had spent three days together at Philadelphia, at a meeting of the Women's Peace Party—"a restful spiritual experience," even though the meeting was being shadowed and extra police guards were detailed to save the ladies from possible mob action. The executive committee met in Jane Addams' bedroom, "just like a lot of elderly schoolgirls sitting on the bed and the trunk, and she with her feet wrapped up in a sweater to keep off the draft," wrote Ellen. ". . . we didn't seem the dangerous traitors the Military Intelligence Office accuse us of being." There were excellent talks—"by Jane A., of course, Mrs. Post, that stormy petrel Crystal Eastman, and several of the Quaker women." Ellen spoke too.

There was exciting news of January 23, 1918, of the President's flying leap (or double back handspring) into woman suffrage by federal amendment, which he now supported. Ellen Slayden was amused and triumphant because she had foreseen this action and had won a bet with another lady, who had said that he wouldn't dare backtrack, that he couldn't. Hadn't he even refused to see the suffrage committee?

"But she doesn't know how many spurs there are for his single-track mind to run out on for political gain," said Mrs. Slayden wisely. "It is fun to see his thick-and-thin followers, who a few weeks ago opposed the suffrage even by permission of the states, trying to adjust their positions." She loved to stir them up by casually remarking that the pickets clearly knew what they were about; they had brought the President to terms.

"For months past women have stood like wooden Indians, one on either side of the White House gates," she now wrote, summing the matter up. "They never spoke unless spoken to, their appearance was irreproachable—except in the bitterest weather when poor Billy Kent said his wife had dressed them in his fur coats until he had nothing to wear." Mrs. Kent also sent her servants out at regular intervals with a barrowful of hot bricks, with which they built new platforms for the pickets to stand on. "We used to drive down to see it done, the servants, the pickets, and their friends perfectly silent, only rank outsiders making ribald remarks."

The public never complained, she continued, but the women got on the President's nerves until he ordered their arrest for obstructing traffic, and five or six of them were hustled off to the workhouse at Occoquan. They were all refined, intelligent women, so Mrs. Slayden and her friends were horrified to hear how they were being treated—denied the simplest toilet articles of their own, dressed in filthy prison clothes, given beds that were unspeakable, and seated at the table with the lowest drunkards and prostitutes, who had been arrested on the streets of Washington. It was planned by their companions to make a grand demonstration and parade the day they were let out, but the President took alarm and ordered their release a day sooner.

"I was at headquarters when our culprits came in and could hardly believe my eyes," wrote Mrs. Slayden. "They looked ten years older, unkempt, dirty and ill for want of the commonest conveniences and decencies of life." And now the President had flip-flopped completely! But the cause had not yet been won, and Mrs. Slayden found herself increasingly irritated by the suffragists' stepped-up propaganda.

On September 19, 1918, she wrote, "Sometimes I think I believe in suffrage for women in spite of the woman suffragists. Their ethics are so peculiar." Many of them had lost their sense of proportion and dignity and were becoming pests, like pretty little Mrs. Jessie MacKaye, who rushed up to Ellen one night on the street, her face lined with nervous strain, to say with delight that she had been arrested three times during the past week. They would go out from HQ every night to make speeches and wave banners until they got themselves arrested, then they marched off to jail, handbags packed in advance with toothbrush and nightie, to revel in martyrdom.

"The next day there is a spectacular trial at the police court, conspiracies of silence, threats of hunger strikes, and irritated husbands pleading 'Mother, come home.' They say they are doing it 'to influence the Senate.' . . . I can't believe it will succumb to such childish methods."

James Slayden was not reelected in 1918, because Wilson withdrew his support, motivated by what Ellen Slayden indignantly declared were trumped-up charges of disloyalty. The Slaydens left Washington for good at the end of the term, in 1919, so she was not there to witness the end of the suffragist struggle, when the Nineteenth Amendment went into force in 1920. But that was a formality. She had seen the opposition's back broken.

Margaret Higgins, later Mrs. Sanger, was born the year Ellen Maury married, in 1883, in circumstances very different from those of the Virginia lady. Until lately there have been only two public attitudes toward her, strongly against and adulatory, but the historian David M. Kennedy, in his book *Birth Control in America: The Career of Margaret Sanger,* has placed her in a more realistic light, as neither villainess nor heroine.

Margaret was predisposed by her origins to be a radical. She was born in Corning, a New York factory town, in a predominantly Catholic working-class neighborhood, the sixth in a family of twelve children. Her mother died at forty-eight of tuberculosis, the disease aggravated by so much childbearing—at least, so Margaret thought. Margaret's Irish-born father Michael, a stonecutter, was a lapsed Catholic who not only embraced but advocated atheism. This shocked his fellows and estranged the family from their neighbors. Margaret grew up an angry young woman, resenting her surroundings and especially her father, yet strongly affected by his philosophy. She tells us in her autobiography that she wanted to serve humanity and so became a nurse. She had nearly finished her training in New York when, in 1903, she met and married William Sanger, architect and painter. Because she soon fell ill with tuberculosis, the Sangers lived in the suburbs until she had recovered. Then they went back to New York City, where Sanger, a member of the Socialist Party, introduced his wife to Greenwich Village and its radicals.

This was in 1912. Havelock Ellis' *Studies in the Psychology of Sex* had just been published; Edward Carpenter's *Love's Coming of Age,* which extolled the pleasures of sex, had appeared the previous year, and the Sangers' friends were busy reading and discussing both books. Margaret read them too, along with the works of Ellen Key, the Swedish feminist. Freud too had just dawned on the American world and was part of her new education. With Emma Goldman, the Communist, Emma's lover Alexander Berkman, and Big Bill Haywood, the radical labor leader, she talked these ideas over; the importance of sex in society was a popular topic because they could discuss it openly for the first time. Margaret declared bravely that sex was central to social reconstruction and that emotion should be the cornerstone of the new morality, replacing the "old desiccated" rationalism, as she called this generally accepted philosophy of her day.

As a member of the Socialist Party she became a women's organizer, caught up in the new radical feminist thinking that urged an improvement of woman's place in industry. Bill Haywood brought both Sangers into the activity of the International Workers of the World during the textile workers' strike at Lawrence, Massachusetts, and the later one at the mills of Paterson, New Jersey. The eldest of the Sangers' three children attended the radical Ferrer School.

In her memoirs Mabel Dodge Luhan described Mrs. Sanger as "the Madonna type of woman," because she was gently, sweetly beautiful, with auburn hair parted in the middle, and her voice was soft and low. Mrs. Luhan said that Mrs. Sanger was the first person she ever knew who was openly a propagandist for the joys of the flesh, a topic of conversation that must have startled people after their first impression of the Madonna. At that time, in 1912, she was working as a nurse in the slums of Manhattan's Lower East Side, where socialistic emotions had full play and indignation could be untrammeled. There immigrants were packed tight in noisome tenements, and the people were horrifyingly ignorant about venereal disease—though if it came to that, even in more privileged circles VD was taboo in conversation or print. Mrs. Sanger quickly found this out, for soon after starting work she wrote a series of articles about it for the *Call,* a Socialist daily paper published in New York, and the *Call* was immediately banned from the mails.

Even social diseases, Margaret Sanger decided, were not the worst of slum life. Time after time, she wrote, poor mothers of large families would implore her to tell them how to keep from having more children, but she was forbidden by law to do this. At this point one must make up one's mind whether or not to believe her wholeheartedly. The experience of other social workers indicated that comparatively few women in underprivileged circles were much interested in birth control, and in any case, in 1912, before studying the subject intensively, Mrs. Sanger did not know very much. Nevertheless, according to her story, she was constantly besieged by women begging for information, medicine, or anything else that would prevent their bearing more children, and her heart went out to them. Some of them reminded her of her mother because they were threatened with death through overbreeding; others were simply frantic with worry over how to keep their families fed. On top of everything, there was the question of social disease; afflicted people kept producing unfit children, though they should not have been permitted, she thought, to breed at all. Yet the law decreed that she could do nothing. Even doctors were helpless in the matter.

According to her own account, however, she did not see contraception as an only or even an overriding cause. She was involved in too many other things, including her private life and increasing disagreements with William. In 1913 the Sanger family visited Paris, where Margaret and William made friends with French socialists and anarchists. At that time, for reasons she did not explain, she decided to leave William; perhaps she felt that she could express herself better without him. At any rate, at the end of 1913 she came back to New York with the children, while he decided to stay on for a while in Paris. Margaret had in mind a new project, the publication of a newspaper to give voice to IWW ideas. In the meantime, she resumed her work as a nurse and became interested once again in the plight of mothers who wanted no more children.

What brought her to a moment of decision, she wrote, was the tragedy of Mrs. Sadie Sachs, a poor immigrant with many children, who had been told by her doctor that she must avoid another pregnancy because her life was in danger. She asked him how to keep from getting pregnant, and he heartlessly suggested that Mr. Sachs sleep on the roof. Naturally, Mr. Sachs did not sleep on the roof, and in due course Mrs. Sachs found herself pregnant again. In desperation she attempted to abort herself, and died as a result. Mrs. Sanger, being a nurse, was present at the death, and in her autobiography she tells us that she was so overcome by the affair that she walked until late in the night through the city streets, thinking. Home at last, she looked down on the "dimly lighted city" and had a vision of "women writhing in travail to bring forth little babies; the babies themselves naked and hungry, wrapped in newspapers . . . children with pinched, pale, wrinkled faces . . . pushed into gray and fetid cellars, crouching on stone floors . . . making lamp shades, artificial flowers . . . white coffins, black coffins, coffins interminably passing in never-ending succession."

At that moment, she said, she decided to promote the dissemination of knowledge about contraception, or, as she began to call it in 1914, birth control.

Of course, the idea of contraception was not new. It was already popular among radicals and had even become a sort of football in Europe, where anarchists were advocating it to confound the capitalists by cutting down on the working classes so that there would be less fodder for factory and cannon, whereas the Marxists maintained that the more poor people the better, in order to revolt successfully. The argument had raged, in fact, since 1798, the year an English economist, the Reverend Thomas Malthus, warned the world that humanity reproduces itself a lot faster than it produces food and that we might well starve ourselves out of existence if we didn't take care. And for less world-wide reasons, women had long sought methods of contraception. French prostitutes tried to avoid pregnancy by inserting a vinegar-soaked sponge in the vagina before intercourse. Some men used sheaths made of sheepgut, a device invented by an English doctor named Condum. In the course of time, various people wrote books about the sponge and the sheath, for which they were heartily condemned by other people who had puritanical ideas.

Robert Dale Owen, son of Robert Owen and companion editor with Frances Wright in New Harmony, wrote such a book and was vigorously attacked for it. Naturally, Owen's attitude toward contraception was closely connected with his espousal of women's rights. In 1832 a Massachusetts doctor named Knowles issued another book and added to the list a new method: syringing, or douching, after copulation, with a chemical to kill the sperm. For this book the author was fined and imprisoned, and nothing more was published on the subject until 1849, when an English professor, Oldham, announced that he had found a "safe" period during which a woman was unlikely to conceive. She should avoid the time halfway between menstrual periods, he said.

By the middle of the nineteenth century a number of women knew something about the subject and managed to regulate the size of their families, but they were middle-class females with money and education. Those of the proverbially conservative working class did not avail themselves of such knowledge either because they had no access to it or because they thought it wrong to go against nature. Still, the idea was spreading however slowly, and in the 1870s two doctors, a father and son named Foote, published a magazine that openly advocated contraception on the grounds that parents should be carefully selected and "unfit" persons restrained from having children. The Footes in their magazine offered various contraceptive devices for sale, including something new, the "womb veil," a pessary or diaphragm. In 1876 Anthony Comstock pounced on the Footes. The elder Foote had written a pamphlet, *Words in Pearl for the Married,* which Comstock in his customary fashion sent for under a false name and got through the mail. Foote was heavily fined for his offense.

That was the situation when Margaret Sanger came onto the scene: contraception of a sort was available, but only to those who could afford it. The Sadie Sachses could not. As it happened, Mrs. Sanger's indignation was not calculated to worry people too much at that time. Malthus had proved a false prophet, and some people were growing alarmed, not at the shrinking food supply but at the fall in the American birth rate. According to a prediction made by Benjamin Franklin in 1755, the American people would double their numbers every twenty years, at which rate there should have been nearly 130 million inhabitants of the United States by 1900. In fact, however, there were not quite 76 million. One explanation for this fall in numbers is that in Franklin's day families commonly had eight or ten children, but by 1900 the average number was nearer three.

> There was an old woman who lived in a shoe:
> She didn't have many children, for she knew what to do.

Theodore Roosevelt, for one, viewed this tendency with alarm, and coined the phrase "race suicide." In 1905, in a message to Congress from the Presidential chair, he warned the nation that America would need larger families to withstand the attack of other, better-manned nations in warfare, Germany in particular. An even more frightening aspect of race suicide, he felt, was that the "right people" were not breeding as fast as the immigrants, who, if something were not done, would rapidly squeeze out the old guard. Thus, at just the same time that Margaret Sanger was proposing birth control for the masses, from a diametrically opposite direction pundits of the Ivy League were pointing with alarm at the fact that Harvard and Yale graduates had few children in comparison with their less privileged compatriots, and the very cream of the crop, college women, either failed to marry at all (only half the average Wellesley class did so) or, if they married, insisted upon having very small families. If the new eugenicists had their way, birth control would be taken away from the privileged but pressed upon the masses. In fact, time was to prove that the masses did not need urging, since the longer a family remained in America the more likely were its women to adopt birth control methods. After all, Sadie Sachs herself, if she was a real woman and not merely a symbol, sought a way to limit her family, and as Mrs. Sanger saw it, her duty was to provide this information.

In March 1914 the first issue of Margaret's magazine, the *Woman Rebel,* appeared. In its columns she discussed many matters, only two of which involved birth control. One was an excerpt from a lecture of Emma Goldman's concerning "free motherhood," and the other article advocated contraception, though no technical advice was included. In it, she asserted that contraception was a good way of confounding the capitalists. Nevertheless, she was promptly notified by the Post Office that the *Woman Rebel* could not be mailed because it contravened a section of the Comstock law in that it contained "obscene, lewd and (or) lascivious material."

The same fate overtook nearly all successive numbers of the *Rebel,* though in none of them did Margaret Sanger or anyone else speak directly of birth control methods. What she had done, though the authorities did not know it, was write a pamphlet, *Family Limitation,* full of such information, which was printed but had not yet been distributed.

The guardians of the nation's virtue were so watchful that without realizing it they silenced Mrs. Sanger in advance. However, after being called to trial for having violated the Comstock law on nine counts with her *Rebel,* she ran away to England—this was late in 1914—and sent back word that *Family Limitation* was to be distributed by William, who was back in New York. The couple had not resumed living together, but they remained friendly.

Though troubled by uncertainty and loneliness for her children, in England she had the chance to become better acquainted with Havelock Ellis and others interested in her work. Ellis told her what books to read and persuaded her to concentrate on birth control and leave other radical interests alone. On his advice she visited the Continent and spent some time in Holland, where a specialist corrected some of the information she had given in her first pamphlet. She wrote three more pamphlets on birth control, and was preparing to edit them for publication in Paris when she heard disturbing news from New York. One of Comstock's agents had fooled William Sanger and persuaded him to hand over a copy of *Family Limitation,* after which Comstock got him arrested.

The case attracted much attention. A large number of people were on Sanger's side against Comstock, and committees were organized to raise money for his defense. He was tried in September 1915 before a judge who was obviously prejudiced against the whole idea of birth control and equal rights for women. If, he said, some of the women going around advocating equal suffrage would advocate women having more children, they would do a greater service. The outcome of the trial was predictable, and Sanger chose thirty days in jail rather than pay a $150 fine.

The case, and the fact that Comstock died during September, impressed the public and made them more conscious of the birth control controversy, but Margaret Sanger resented her husband's sudden prominence. After all, it was *her* cause, not his. She had to get used to sharing the stage, however, since others too were moving in. Emma Goldman and Ben Reitman, who was now her companion, had already been arrested in Oregon for distributing literature about contraception, and while Margaret was away in Europe the National Birth Control League had been formed. It was not really her style, this league. Kennedy observes that the officers—Mary Ware Dennett, Jessie Ashley, Clara Gruening Stillman, Bolton Hall, and Lincoln Steffens—were liberals, not radicals; that many members were of the upper middle class; and that they deliberately excluded extreme radicals like Emma Goldman from their ranks. Instead of striking dramatic attitudes they worked within the framework of the law, attempting to change it so that birth control would not be categorized as "obscene."

Soon after Margaret Sanger's return she was overtaken by personal tragedy: her only daughter, Peggy, died of pneumonia. She fell ill through grief and was for a time unable to attend to her affairs. Then she found that she was still to be tried on the old indictment. Friends in the legal profession advised her to plead guilty, since she was bound to get off with a light sentence, but she stubbornly refused to do so, until they had almost lost patience with what they considered her muddleheaded attitude. Just before the trial, in February 1916, the court withdrew the indictment. "We were determined that Mrs. Sanger shouldn't be a martyr if we could help it," said the Assistant U.S. Attorney.

Probably she was disappointed in a way, but it meant one worry the less, and she now embarked on a coast-to-coast lecture tour. She impressed her audiences; they had expected somebody big and raucous, instead of which they found on the platform a small, pretty, soft-voiced woman who spoke in a reasonable manner. In each lecture she told her story of Sadie Sachs, pleaded for new moral standards that would allow free discussion of sexual knowledge, and decried the dangers of abortion. She presented an attractive picture: she was charming, idealistic, and fervent as well as knowledgeable, and she convinced many of her audience. Naturally there was some resistance too, but incidents of protest were grist to her mill: she welcomed the publicity. In Portland, Oregon, she was arrested—though soon released—for handing out literature on birth control, and in St. Louis the theater where she was to speak was locked against her, almost certainly through the action of a Catholic group. She could have asked for nothing better, because it all got into the papers—excellent preparation for her next action, the opening of a birth control clinic in Brooklyn. For the purpose she chose 46 Amboy Street in Brownsville, then inhabited by poor Jewish and Italian immigrants. With her sister Mrs. Ethel Byrne, a trained nurse like herself, and a friend from Chicago named Fania Mindell, she moved into the two rooms she had rented and made them ready. Then the three women walked around the neighborhood and slipped leaflets under all the doors. These were printed in English, Yiddish, and Italian, and read:

> MOTHERS!
>
> Can you afford to have a large family?
> Do you want any more children?
> If not, why do you have them?
> Do not kill, do not take life, but prevent . . ."

The clinic's address was added.

Margaret opened the clinic's doors on October 16, 1916, to find a long line of women already waiting for the information that had been promised. In the back room Margaret and Ethel gave lectures and distributed contraceptive devices, while in the front room Fania kept the records. One hundred and forty women passed through the clinic that day, and more were waiting on the seventeenth. Things continued like this, busily, until a policewoman disguised as a patient came on October 25 and collected evidence.

The next day the law arrived in force. They confiscated much of the material, and in due course Margaret, her sister Ethel, and Fania

Mindell were arrested and charged with violating Section 1142 of the New York State Penal Code, which forbade anyone to sell, lend, or give away, or to advertise or distribute any recipe, drug, or medicine for the prevention of conception.

One of Mrs. Sanger's supporters, Mrs. Amos Pinchot, had organized the so-called Committee of 100, consisting of wealthy women who all attended the trial, which took place January 4, 1917, before the Court of Special Sessions. Ethel Byrne was first to stand in the dock. Mrs. Byrne's counsel argued that Section 1142 was unconstitutional because it denied a woman the absolute right of enjoyment of sexual intercourse unless the act was so conducted that pregnancy would be the result. Furthermore, he said, it worked to the detriment of public health; in large families one often found a high mortality rate among infants and mothers, and enforced celibacy could lead to insanity, nervousness, sex perversion, and homosexuality. He did not convince the court, who found Mrs. Byrne guilty and sentenced her to thirty days on Blackwell's Island. It all made the front pages of the newspapers, especially when Mrs. Byrne went on a hunger strike and had to be force-fed. Public indignation heightened rapidly. Mrs. Pinchot went to the governor to plead for mercy, and he agreed to release Mrs. Byrne if she promised to refrain thereafter from the activities that had brought on her punishment. Ethel Byrne duly agreed and was permitted to go home, but so much anti-court feeling had been engendered that the authorities approached Mrs. Sanger's trial on January 29 more warily.

To Jonah J. Goldstein, her counsel as he had been Ethel's, the court offered to let his client go if she would promise not to repeat her offense. Margaret said she could not respect the law as it stood, so she was declared guilty, with the option of paying a fine or going to jail for thirty days. She chose jail. Unlike her sister, she enjoyed the experience, perhaps because she did not go on a hunger strike but proselytized her fellow prisoners and became a heroine in their eyes. When she came out she immediately appealed the conviction, first to the New York Supreme Court, which denied the appeal, and then to the state Court of Appeals, which also denied it. Yet the triumph was hers, for before a year had elapsed after her trial the judge of the Court of Appeals considered a loophole in the law in Section 1145, which stated that doctors *could* supply contraceptive material and information "for the cure and prevention of disease." Obviously this was intended to mean venereal disease only, and men rather than women had been in the minds of the legislators who framed the law.

But Margaret Sanger argued that it could equally well apply to women, who should be protected from ills connected with too much childbearing, and the judge agreed to accept her interpretation of the word "disease." From then on, doctors were permitted by law to give advice on contraception to married women in order to protect their health. The definition was a milestone in the history of birth control.

The rest of Mrs. Sanger's story, a long one, is much involved with her struggles to retain control of the movement. As children would put it, if she couldn't be boss she wouldn't play. She couldn't be boss of the National Birth Control League, formed in 1915 and the first of its kind, so she left it to set up the New York Birth Control League. Ultimately displeased with that organization for similar reasons, she formed the American Birth Control League, of which for a time she was president.

On November 13, 1921, a mass meeting was supposed to be held at Town Hall in New York to discuss the question "Birth Control, Is It Moral?" The featured speaker, Harold Cox, editor of the *Edinburgh Review*, came over to America expressly for the meeting. But Mr. Cox, Mrs. Sanger, and a large number of others discovered when they got to Town Hall that they were barred from entry by a guard of a hundred policemen, who had locked the doors to prevent the meeting. The lawmen arrested Margaret Sanger and took her to the West Forty-seventh Street police station. She was speedily freed, but like everyone else in the group she was still mystified. Who on earth had instigated the affair? It took about twelve hours to get the answer, and even then it was never proved absolutely. There is no real doubt, however, that Monsignor Joseph P. Dineen, secretary to the Roman Catholic archbishop Patrick J. Hayes, had telephoned Captain Donahue of the West Forty-seventh Street station to put a stop to the meeting at Town Hall. Captain Donahue, like a good Catholic, had simply done it, that was all.

In the midst of a lot of angry indignation, Margaret Sanger rearranged the meeting, and it was held five days later at a New York theater, this time with police protection rather than interference.

In 1922 Mrs. Sanger, who had been divorced from William in 1920, married J. Noah Slee. He was a rich, elderly widower, president of the Three-In-One Oil Company. He had been superintendent of his church's Sunday school for twenty-five years, he said grace before meals, he frequently read the Bible to his children, and—

along with all this—he was an ardent supporter of birth control! The marriage was something out of the ordinary. Margaret Sanger stipulated before agreeing to it that she should retain the name Sanger, and Mr. Slee agreed that they would maintain separate suites of rooms wherever they lived. It soon became clear to Mrs. Sanger's friends that the new husband was a great help to the cause. For one thing, he was exceedingly generous, practically underwriting the new American Birth Control League, founded in 1921, at times when its finances were particularly rocky, and for another, he put his wife's office on a businesslike basis. He persuaded her, for example, to install file cases for the league's correspondence.

One cannot declare roundly, with proof, that marriage to a rich man was responsible for Mrs. Sanger's change in philosophy, but the change was there. At the beginning, she had often declared that birth control was necessary first and foremost to help the working class. Now she turned on that same working class, and represented birth control as a weapon with which to control their numbers. The "unfit" must not be allowed to outnumber the "fit," among whom, of course, she included herself. It is true that a wide disparity between the fecundity of the classes stubbornly remained, but she always hoped to improve matters, and the nation's attitude toward contraception was actually swinging toward hers. According to the President's Committee on Social Trends, by 1931 66 percent of the opinions expressed in the press on birth control were favorable, and the trend continued. An article in *Fortune* in 1936 stated that 63 percent of Americans believed in the teaching and practice of birth control—and this figure included 42 percent of Roman Catholics. Henry Pringle in the *Ladies' Home Journal,* in 1939, said it was 79 percent. In 1943 this figure rose to nearly 85.

Mrs. Sanger's reputation had risen with these numbers. She had become a cultural heroine, and so she remained until her death in 1966, at the age of eighty-seven. Her name is preserved in birth control clinics all over the country and beyond: it is well known, for example, in Japan, to people who have never heard of the ladylike Ellen Maury Slayden.

CHAPTER 19

The Bacchanalian Maidens

IT WAS 1920 WHEN A TRAVELER just returned from other, wetter climes gazed around the dusky interior of a New York basement. It was his first speakeasy. "My God," he said in hushed tones. "We'll never get the women out of the saloon now."

Though it had taken the Eighteenth Amendment to ease them in without benefit of law, the deed was done and no one could undo it. Before Prohibition, only special types of females, cleaning women and the like, had entered bars for any reason save to buy a pailful of beer to go. A few old beldames, low on the social scale, frequented saloons, but they knew their place and tucked themselves away in back rooms where they did not disturb the gentlemen. More ladylike females did their imbibing, if any, in private, taking an occasional glass of wine at dinner parties. And, of course, there were the pretty ladies of the chorus or the streets who sipped champagne at racy restaurants; they were comparatively few. Some middle-class women ingested quite a lot of alcohol in patent medicines, but it was done in all innocence. Social drinking was an occupation for men only, until the "Noble Experiment" got under way, after which the rule, like so many others, was broken beyond repair.

It is unfair that women should be blamed as they are for the introduction of the Eighteenth Amendment into our Constitution, because in spite of Carry Nation and other zealots of her sex, it simply couldn't have been done that way. They didn't have the vote, and womanly persuasion could not have accounted for the number of men who brought it in. Furthermore, women were actively discouraged from temperance work, as we have seen in the accounts of Amelia Bloomer and Susan B. Anthony. Both these ladies, and no doubt many more, were forced to occupy second-class positions in temperance societies because it was believed that women hadn't the stamina to be of much use to the cause. As if to disprove this idea, Mrs. Nation and her sisters in the West played a showy part in the campaign to close down saloons; even those who did not quite behave like Carry Nation went forth in numbers to kneel down before saloon doors, as she had done, sometimes venturing in and plumping down on their knees in the filthy sawdust to pray until the proprietor and his customers departed. But they had no formal part in the introduction of Prohibition. Men did that.

It was a man, Herbert Hoover, who gave Prohibition the name "Noble Experiment," at a time when he should have known better, in 1928, when for eight disastrous years the country had been officially dry but was actually sopping wet. Hoover should have seen the situation clearly by then—almost everyone else did—but he was a politician, and he didn't want to look at it squarely.

It is often confusing to amateur historians that the Eighteenth and Nineteenth Amendments so nearly coincided in time, the Eighteenth, or Prohibition, Amendment being ratified on January 16, 1920, and the Nineteenth, or Woman Suffrage, Amendment on August 26 of the same year. Some have said that it was the Nineteenth Amendment, not the Eighteenth, that brought about so startling a change in the behavior of American women, but this theory seems unlikely. Much to the disappointment of feminism's old campaigners, young girls who now had the right to vote—thanks to those same old campaigners—did not seem to appreciate it, but took it for granted. Unless a girl was deeply involved in politics it would scarcely seem to matter more than once every two or four years that she had a voice in electing government officials. Much closer to home was her social life and the behavior expected of her on a date. It was thanks to the Eighteenth that girls became accustomed to a life style any knowledge of which would have sent their mothers into hysterics only a few years earlier, and this style, in turn, changed their idea of themselves. No girl used to sitting in speakeasies or sharing the contents of a hip flask in the rear seat of a parked car was likely to see herself as something rare and fragile, a hothouse plant. Nor could she accept the idea, if she was logical, that her only proper place was the nursery or kitchen.

Everyone today knows that the Noble Experiment did not work, but at the time this was not quite so apparent, at least not to the "drys" who were responsible for it. Curiously, it was the American woman who seemed to realize first that the act was, if anything, counterproductive, encouraging more people to drink more. Prominent among the protesting groups was the Women's Committee for Modification of the Volstead Act—the act prohibiting the sale of intoxicating liquor. Then in 1927 this committee declared, in sum, that modification was not the answer. Never mind haggling about wine and beer, they said; they wanted a clean sweep of the whole business, and as an earnest of their intentions they changed the name of their society to the Women's Committee for Repeal of the Eighteenth Amendment. Their stand attracted other organizations.

By 1929 the labor unions too were urging the government to scrap the amendment, and soon they were joined by bar associations throughout the country, who argued that the Eighteenth violated the Bill of Rights. In 1929 too, a banker's wife, Mrs. Charles H. Sabin of New York, who was the first woman to be a member of the Republican National Committee, resigned that post to found the Women's Organization for National Prohibition Reform. At the original meeting only seventeen people attended, but by 1932 the membership numbered 1,326,862. Obviously, a lot of middle-class American women were tired of drinking and watching their husbands and children get drunk. The drys naturally were concerned by these developments. Dr. Mary Armour, president of the Georgia WCTU, spoke bitterly of Mrs. Sabin and her "cocktail-drinking followers," and Dr. D. Leigh Colvin, a moving spirit of the Prohibition Party, referred to them as "Bacchanalian maidens, parching for wine."

Unrepentant, the bacchantes worked hard during Prohibition's last days, organizing and getting the vote out when President Franklin D. Roosevelt made up his mind at last to take action. In 1933 the Eighteenth Amendment passed into history, but it was a long time before people got used to drinking openly, in rooms where the doors were not locked. And, as the traveler had prophesied, women were never to be the same again. Having found their way out of the home into the saloon, they were not ready to pop back into domesticity. For better or worse, they lived in what had been a man's world—except for sex morality and the double standard.

Standards, whether single or double, had taken a bad shaking during the Prohibition days, and divorce was not the shameful thing it had been, but lip service was still paid to the sanctity of the home, the overriding responsibilities of motherhood, and the desirability of virginity in young girls. In the midst of change, Americans clung to the old beliefs, the virtues that made them feel safe. They read nostalgic stories like Edith Wharton's *Age of Innocence* or John Galsworthy's *The Forsyte Saga,* but in 1920 a new kind of novel appeared, F. Scott Fitzgerald's *This Side of Paradise,* and in spite of themselves they read it too. Similar books now came out depicting the new moral standards, and though they were decried by critics and railed at from pulpit and lecture podium they were eagerly, if secretly, read by many people.

Permissiveness had crept in. Among books that were in demand during that decade, James Hart, author of *The Popular Book,* listed Robert Keable's *Simon Called Peter,* James Branch Cabell's *Jurgen,* D. H. Lawrence's *Women in Love,* James Joyce's *Ulysses,* and Gertrude Atherton's *Black Oxen.* Percy Marks's *The Plastic Age* (1924) purported to be the true, unvarnished picture of the American undergraduate male, and possibly it was, for it showed the hero and his friends losing their faith in Christianity, drinking, and indulging in sex, a program that naturally resulted in VD. Marks faithfully discussed this version of sin's wages, but even worse followed: inevitably, women too were discussed in novels as having their share of the sexual urge. *The Green Hat* (1924), because it was about an Englishwoman, not an American girl, who was sexually promiscuous, and also perhaps because it was written by a foreigner, Michael Arlen, who was an Anglicized Armenian, was comparatively acceptable, but many of the stories that followed were not thoughtful of national sensibilities. Nevertheless, they were read.

There were also psychology and the new vogue for analysis, contained in what someone has called "the current profundities"—big, heavy books that people bought and sometimes read in an earnest desire to keep up with things. There were H. G. Wells' *Outline of History* and Will Durant's *Story of Philosophy* and *The Mansions of Philosophy,* most readers of which were women. As Hart said, "At the Mah Jong tables women spoke as glibly of complexes as of calories." Everything considered, they were more than ready for Freud, and delighted when his translated works were published. The Lynds in their study *Middletown* told of women eagerly thronging to lectures on "How We Reach Our Subconscious Minds," and of a number of them paying twenty-five dollars for a course of psychological instruction on gaining and maintaining bodily fitness and mental poise, and building personality. The Depression put an end to all that.

Eleanor Roosevelt's life spanned an important period of American transition, during which she herself underwent one of the most remarkable metamorphoses ever seen outside a terrarium. This is clear in Joseph P. Lash's two-volume biography, *Eleanor and Franklin* and *Eleanor: The Years Alone*.

The Roosevelts, from Holland originally, have lived in America since the seventeenth century, and most of them have prospered. When Eleanor was born in 1884 they were among the leaders of United States aristocracy, though she was a member of a comparatively poor section of the family. Her father Elliott, brother of Theodore, wasted his substance in drink and estranged his wife, and plain little Eleanor after her mother's death was brought up by her maternal grandmother, who sent her to finishing school in England. The eighteen-year-old girl returned to New York in 1902. The women's rights movement was gathering impetus, but feminism did not meet with her approval. *Womanly* women, she thought, ought not to make a noise about their rights but should engage in good works. Accordingly, Eleanor joined the new Junior League and went to work among the poor at the Rivington Street Settlement House. On Sundays she listened approvingly to a fashionable preacher who attacked women's suffrage. Eleanor disapproved of gambling, drinking, and women who smoked.

"Somehow I can't bear to see women act as men do!" she wrote to her cousin Franklin Delano Roosevelt, who was at Harvard Law School. She and Franklin were in love, and though his possessive mother opposed the match they were married as soon as FDR had his degree. Eleanor, like most of her class and generation among women, thought the sexual side of marriage distasteful, but she loved her husband dearly. They had six children in rapid succession, of whom five survived.

The erstwhile ugly duckling of a girl was gravely happy in her marriage and began to feel sure of herself, but she was suspicious of the lighter side of life and was often disappointed with the behavior of her pleasure-loving husband. Even more than other young wives in her circle she left her partner to his own devices, yachting and staying late at parties and flirting with pretty girls. She was pleased when he showed signs of settling down and going into politics, like other Roosevelts. In 1910 he was elected state senator in New York on the Democratic ticket. Until then Eleanor had merely managed her own small household—three children at that time, a nurse for each, and the usual domestics—but now she learned quickly to play hostess to the big crowds at the Albany mansion. FDR changed his attitude toward women's rights at this time and began speaking in public on behalf of the distaff side of humanity, but Eleanor, the homebody, did not agree. She felt that woman's sphere was something else; a man's world was not for her.

In 1913 Franklin became Assistant Secretary of the Navy. The family now lived in Washington, with time out for New York City, Franklin's mother's home at Hyde Park, and the Roosevelts' summer house on the island of Campobello. Often these journeys were undertaken by Eleanor and the children without FDR, who remained in the capital. However, the First World War enlarged Eleanor's horizons, especially after the armistice. Wounded men were shipped back to the States, and she visited wards in the Naval Hospital, aided men in the insane ward and tried to help their families, obtained rest rooms for the women workers in the Navy Department, and so on—the model of an official's wife.

Just then, at the end of the war, Franklin came back from a European trip with double pneumonia, and Eleanor took care of his mail. Reading through his letters, she discovered that he was having an affair with her pretty secretary, Lucy Mercer. It was a severe shock, a complete surprise. Such a thing was not at all in her picture of what a woman's life should be, and she was bitterly hurt. The more she thought of it, the deeper the wound became. Franklin had certainly been making love to Lucy while she herself carried their youngest child, Elliott, who was born in 1916. Their marriage, like his affectionate letters, was a lie.

It was here that Eleanor Roosevelt's true quality proved itself. Most women in similar circumstances would have walked out, but she waited and controlled herself. She asked FDR if he wanted her to divorce him; she would, she said, if that was what he wanted. Painful conferences followed. It became clear that Franklin did not want a divorce, possibly because, as his political mentor and campaign manager, Louis Howe, anxiously reminded him, his career was at stake. In those days no man could be divorced and yet stay in politics. Finally Eleanor said that she would not divorce her husband if he promised not to see Lucy again, and his mother Sara Roosevelt added that if he did not give his word, she would cut off his money. Then too, Lucy Mercer was a Catholic: she couldn't marry a divorced man. FDR came to heel, and he and his wife were reconciled—or, at least, there was no public split. Eleanor continued to maintain the appearance and behavior of an affectionate wife. But, she wrote in her diary, "All my self-confidence is gone."

Somehow, she believed, she had failed Franklin or this would never have happened. But changes were taking place in her philosophy. However painfully, her consciousness was enlarged. She stopped being a prig, shedding prejudices and smugness. Her new tolerance manifested itself in many ways. The rights of women did not now seem such a stupid thing to fight for. She had not seen the merits of the case when she considered herself happily married, a protected mother and housewife, but she had discovered that the world was full of pitfalls, and matters now bore a different appearance. Unhappily married women should have some means of protecting and supporting themselves. The beginning of power, thought the politician's wife, was in the vote, and though women had won the franchise in New York in 1917, they still could not vote in national elections. No, said Eleanor when a number of friends asked her to join the National Association of Anti-Suffragists; she had thought things over, and would not join.

The Democrats lost the election of 1920 in which FDR campaigned for the Vice-Presidency. By that time Eleanor was working actively for the League of Women Voters, a new name for our old friend the National Woman Suffrage Association, and soon she became a member of its board: she attended its state convention in Albany as a Dutchess County delegate. The league was still struggling for women's rights, since getting the vote had not, after all, finished off all the difficulties facing females—for example, New York's Republican governor now came out in opposition to them for showing interest in social welfare, which he thought was none of their business. The league's Republican chairwoman, Mrs. Frank Vanderlip, retorted sharply that her sex had a perfect right to work for political measures, and the governor, belatedly remembering that ladies too had the vote, took back what he had said. Eleanor enjoyed this tussle, and thereafter she engaged in many similar battles. Franklin, now with a New York law firm, often counseled her in these matters. But she never approved of the actions of that day's equivalent of the Women's Lib militants. ". . . the harsh stridency of some feminists irritated her," wrote Lash in *Eleanor and Franklin*.

In the late summer of 1921 FDR fell victim to polio. It looked for a time as if his political career was over, and Eleanor realized that he might as well have died if this were true. However, it became evident that he would be able in due course to return to the arena, though he was partially paralyzed. Louis Howe urged Eleanor to go into politics herself while her husband was recovering, so that people would not forget him. She agreed, and what followed is history. Thanks in part to her band of women friends, Mrs. Roosevelt was so active and effective that FDR sometimes felt a twinge of jealousy. She understood this well enough to write to him, early in 1924, "I'm only being *active* till you can be again."

With her band, she directed her main efforts toward organizing New York State's women in order to get out their vote for the Democrats in the next election; by spring in 1924 all but five counties seemed safely for the party. Mrs. Roosevelt saw, during her travels around the state, that though women had the vote they didn't yet know what to do with it. She believed they wouldn't learn, either, as long as men remained hostile toward the idea of women in politics. The men, she said, took this attitude: "You are wonderful. I love and honor you . . . Lead your own life, attend to your charities, cultivate yourself, travel when you wish, bring up the children, run your house. I'll give you all the freedom you wish and all the money I can but—leave me my business and politics."

She said that women must get into the game and stay in it. If they didn't learn the machinery of politics, they wouldn't get anywhere. In April, Eleanor and her friends put this philosophy into action and openly rebelled at the Democratic state convention against the male monopolization of power. As she pointed out, women had had the vote for four years, but many suffragists felt, possibly rightly, that instead of gaining in power they had lost. To begin with, women should claim the right to name some of the delegates at the convention, she said at a women's meeting in New York. The Tammany boss, Charles Murphy, stood firm against the women's demand, so Eleanor led a committee that called on Governor Alfred E. Smith and put their proposal to him. He agreed readily that women should have the right they claimed, and Murphy had to back down. A delegation of women then attended the convention meetings, and when Smith was nominated again for governor, Eleanor was requested to introduce the Smith resolution. She accepted the task readily, and did her job most impressively: *The New York Times* referred to her next day as "a highly intelligent and capable politician." Afterward she toured the state speaking in behalf of Al Smith. She even attacked her uncle Teddy Roosevelt, leader of the opposing party, when he came out in support of Calvin Coolidge as Republican Presidential candidate. Coolidge won the Presidency—but Al Smith was reelected for a second two-year term as governor of New York.

Eleanor and her associates unleashed considerable power which until then had been deflected and diffused. Women in America were great joiners; their appetite for organizations was the marvel of foreign visitors. Not only the WCTU engaged their earnest, busy aid; before and after that society's prime there were myriad smaller clubs for women. Peace organizations alone accounted for many members. Page Smith in *Daughters of the Promised Land* had listed eighteen peace societies of which Fanny Fern was a member—and she also belonged to twenty-nine other groups. One wonders how she found time to attend meetings and yet earn her living by writing. Two years before woman suffrage was won, Beatrice Forbes-Robertson Hale spoke of the possibilities: "An enormous reservoir of power almost untapped, a vast potential force for good." If, in the first hint of their strength after the 1924 election, Mrs. Roosevelt and others overrated what might be done by women if they would organize, it is not surprising.

The busy years passed and the Roosevelts worked out a way of life that suited them both. Franklin had discovered that swimming eased him and improved the use of his muscles, so he spent much time at a Southern resort called Warm Springs; ultimately he bought and developed the property. Eleanor had long wanted to get away from her mother-in-law's Big House at Hyde Park. Knowing she must not go too far away, she built a cottage in the near vicinity. Here, at Val-Kill, she lived with two friends who designed luxury furniture which was built at a nearby factory and sold on the market. In spite of so much occupation she found life empty at that stage. Her daughter Anna was married; the boys were away at school. It was the sort of pause in life that has brought many women to nervous breakdowns, but Eleanor was resourceful and found a way out. One of her friends was vice-principal at Todhunter, a girls' private school in New York, which was in financial difficulties. Eleanor bought a part interest in the school and taught classes there.

In 1928 it was decided that FDR was well enough to enter politics once more, and he ran for governor of New York and was elected. This meant, of course, that the Roosevelts had to move back to Albany, where Eleanor started a campaign to further women in public life. Her husband was sometimes touchy about advice, and she went carefully. Once and once only she suggested that he make Frances Perkins labor commissioner because she would do well. Mrs. Perkins, removal from the post she already held, the chairmanship of the Industrial Commission, would leave a place that could be filled by one of the men, said Eleanor, and his place, in turn, might be occupied by another woman, Nell Schwartz. Having done this, Eleanor waited until she could send a good friend of hers since 1924, Molly Dewson (Mary W. Dewson, civic secretary of the Women's City Council), whom she knew FDR liked, to see him. While there, Molly made the suggestion again as if it were her own idea, and Franklin accepted it without argument.

In 1930 he was reelected, and it was a natural step from that position to the nomination as Democratic candidate for the Presidency in 1932. Eleanor's hard work campaigning for her husband did not keep her from disagreeing with him, sometimes sharply, on certain issues, mainly Prohibition and the League of Nations. She was inflexibly dry; though she realized that the Eighteenth Amendment was not working, she was shocked when he suggested repealing it. She was even more shocked that he stopped supporting the League of Nations.

"I simply had a fit of rebellion against the male attitude," she wrote to Molly Dewson about this, but she and her army did effective campaigning for FDR nevertheless. They knew their business.

Throughout the Presidency of her husband, Eleanor Roosevelt continued to battle to improve woman's status in government and to forward the interests of peace. Many of her actions, especially entertaining blacks at the White House, brought down floods of criticism on her head, but she went her own way and did what she thought right. With Molly Dewson she kept a careful eye on all appointments of women, because she felt that the rights of women to jobs on the basis of merit were still on shaky ground. For this reason she protested when Secretary of State Cordell Hull proposed sending a woman to succeed Ruth Bryan Owen in Denmark. That particular job had been established, she felt. Why shouldn't he send a man to Denmark now, she suggested, and put a woman in some other place? Such an action would open another door for women, and avoid the danger of cut-and-dried arrangements on the basis of sex. And she tried to help Frances Perkins, who as Secretary of Labor was often attacked. Nevertheless, she concealed as well as she could any sign of holding influence over the President, from him as much as anyone.

Before FDR decided to run for an unprecedented third term in 1940, Louis Howe thought seriously of trying to elect her as his successor, but she said that one politician in the family was enough. Besides, she considered the possibility of any woman becoming Chief Executive remote. Some day it might happen, she said, but not in the near future. In 1933 she published a book, *It's Up to the Women,* expressing this idea among others.

FDR did run again for a third term, of course, and a fourth, and was elected both times; he was becoming a habit with the American public, and when he died on April 12, 1945, many of them realized painfully that the habit was deeply ingrained. They were dismayed. But Harry Truman took hold, and so, after a very short time—and, admittedly, under a lesser burden—did Eleanor Roosevelt. The list of her activities in the following years is staggering, especially when one remembers her early sentiments about women and how they should behave. To quote only in part from Lash's index from the second volume of his biography: "long-hoped-for trip to Soviet Union: looking for job to do: concern for world peace: backs international control of atomic weapons . . ." *Atomic weapons?* What kind of subject was that to interest a woman who had written in her youth that she couldn't bear to see women doing what men do?

People do change over the years, of course, but Eleanor's changes were dazzling, and they terrified a lot of people. She must have stepped on any number of painful hidden corns to elicit the attacks in the press that followed many of her statements. Westbrook Pegler, the most extreme of her critics, exploded on the subject like a volcano full of poisonous gas and red-hot lava, but he wasn't the only one. She represented to many appalled men what they felt was happening all over the country to American women, *especially their own.* Would they ever again get the girls under control? Many a man wondered, and doubted it.

At the same time, she attracted much admiration. Women naturally thought her wonderful, but so did a lot of men, and they were right. She had outgrown a series of chrysalid skins at a breathtaking rate. All her talents, and they were many, might have remained hidden if they had not been stripped by unhappy experience. It makes one wonder how many other women there might be who are as capable as Eleanor Roosevelt but who have never had the painful motivation to prove it. Not that she is the only one; all of us know women who have come out into the world and proved themselves strong and able, simply because they had to. But she is foremost, not only because she was the President's wife but because she was a natural worker, strong in character, educated for the task, and willing to shoulder it.

Her physical strength alone was extraordinary. Look again at Lash's index: ". . . at seventy-five, famous, successful, active . . . television work . . . journalistic and literary work . . . knocked down by car, Anna urges she slow down . . ."

Of course she did not slow down, but hers was a long life anyway, and she left women's position in her country as much altered as she herself was. It was not only that they had the vote, something that many of them, including Eleanor, had not wished for at the beginning. The change was to be seen in their attitude toward their duties and their participation in running things. When Eleanor Roosevelt was a girl, preachers were still shouting in their pulpits against the pernicious custom just coming in of sending young ladies to college. Some young ladies went to college just the same, but Eleanor was not of their number. By 1962, when she died, any American girl of the middle classes who didn't go to college felt that she must explain why. Poor girls, too, often obtained a college education. In Eleanor's youth it was hard for middle-class women to find a way to earn their livings, except by teaching or looking after the old, though a few daring souls were learning to be nurses or stenographers. By the time she died, the career woman, successful in business or designing or a dozen other fields, was no longer enough of a novelty to rate a feature story in the press. Women were becoming doctors and even, like Frances Perkins, successful administrators.

In her young days Eleanor Roosevelt had been forced to conceal her feelings about her husband's infidelity. Rather than ruin his political career and cast a shadow over her children's lives, she refrained from divorce. But by the time she died those same children had been divorced, some more than once. One of her dearest friends, Adlai Stevenson, though divorced, was twice nominated for President by a major party.

Such loosening of the tight moral code naturally had an effect on all American women. In Eleanor's girlhood her associates lived according to the so-called double standard, which was really triple: it was founded on the assumption that there are good women, bad women, and men. Eleanor's parents may have read a shocking book, *The Awakening,* by Mrs. Kate Chopin, who spent the Civil War years in her husband's native Louisiana and later earned a living for herself and her children by the pen. *The Awakening,* people felt, really went too far. It was the story of a young married woman who felt the stirrings of libido toward a young man to whom she was not married: as a result of this awakening of the flesh she left her husband and children and engaged in a liaison with a New Orleans rake. Afterward, overwhelmed with hopelessness and the consciousness of sin, she drowned herself, but this expiation was not enough for many readers, who wrote outraged letters to the publishers and libraries. As a result,

Mrs. Chopin was punished. She was never able to publish again, and lived the rest of her life in straitened circumstances. If the heroine had paid the usual literary fine for her wrongdoing and borne a child as the fruit of her sin, the public might have been assuaged. Unfortunately, she was too original for that.

Yet, as the decades passed, this sort of situation became increasingly outworn. I remember that in 1923 or thereabouts my friends and I were fascinated by a serial story running in the newspapers, about a young stenographer who went out in a canoe with her date, a romantic young man with brown eyes, and was seduced by him. (We agreed that it must have been an untippable model. We knew a lot about canoes in Wisconsin.) The stenographer got pregnant, or course, and her young man disappeared, of course, and she had to give up her job and move to another town, where she had her baby and assumed the identity of a widow. Then she met Mr. Right, who proposed marriage. What was she to do? Take a chance, or confess? After several chapters of agonizing hesitation she took the only right way out: she confessed everything. Mr. Right forgave her, and they were married and lived happily ever after. I recall wondering, however, how happy a woman would be in those circumstances, depending as she must on her husband's charity and forgiveness. That story was published just in time: a year or two later fewer readers would have taken it seriously, because of Margaret Sanger.

Even so, birth control for a long time was not for everybody. Most workers at birth control clinics prudently refused to hand out information or contraceptive material to unmarried women. Of course, there were ways of getting around that rule, but if even then the stuff failed, women whether married or single had recourse to the illegal method of abortion. There was a Russian doctor in New York, a pretty young woman who came to America in the early thirties because, it was rumored, the USSR had changed its policy and no longer permitted legal abortions. Dr. Olga set up shop in a private apartment on Riverside Drive, and word soon got around that she was sanitary in her methods and not expensive as these things went. Of course, she didn't anesthetize her patients—few abortionists did that because it was risky. But for what she did, Dr. Olga was all right. Once I went to her place as assistant to a friend who needed the operation. I was impressed by the setup. In a long, oval room that must once have served as a salon, the white-coated doctor had put up screens all around the walls, behind each of which was a cot. At 11 A.M. some of these were already occupied—the doctor started work early. My friend lay down on an operating table in the middle of the room, and Dr. Olga did the job while the patient gripped my hand and screamed. An old woman, probably Dr. Olga's mother, shuffled around the room unmoved all through the proceedings, carrying glasses of tea with lemon to various patients behind the screens. Finally my friend was permitted to get up and totter to an empty cot, where she lay recovering and crying softly.

Sitting by her side, waiting to help her when she felt well enough to leave, I listened to conversations going on between Dr. Olga and other patients. One woman, who said she worked in a department store, had come in, she explained, because though she knew she couldn't be pregnant—she had been having the curse right along—she was getting embarrassingly fat and people were wondering. After a short silence I heard Dr. Olga say, "Yes, you are six months pregnant."

There was a gasp of horror and some murmuring.

"No," said Dr. Olga, "you must have your baby. It is too far along."

"But what am I going to do?" the woman cried sharply. "What about my job? What—"

Dr. Olga told her to get a good corset and hold out as long as possible. When the time came, she herself would make arrangements for the lying-in. The door closed. It had been a harrowing few minutes, and I was more harrowed when I heard it open again. I was getting used to the atmosphere of the salon, the smell of antiseptic and blood, and on every side the soft sniffling of patients recovering, but I was not prepared for this sound—a *man* talking. In fact it was the doctor's husband, home for lunch, but I understood my supine friend's reaction when she opened her eyes and said with venom, *"There's one of 'em."*

That's the way things used to be. Doctors far worse than Olga were operating, and a lot of women died of their efforts. Now that abortion laws have been liberalized, the operation is not so dangerous as it was, but in the long run even legalized abortion will probably turn out to be less of a solution than the Pill to the problem of unwanted children. The Pill was first tested in 1956, some years before the death of Eleanor Roosevelt. One form of it, Enovid, was the first of many varieties to appear commercially on the market: this was in 1960. Unlike the methods advocated at Mrs. Sanger's clinics, the Pill does not depend on the mechanical prevention of a meeting between the human ovum, or egg, and the inseminating agent, or semen. The idea of using such a pill started, oddly enough, when researchers, looking for a way to cure infertility, found that they could do so in certain cases by administering hormones, progesterone and estrogen, that would cause pseudopregnancy and inhibit ovulation. After being inhibited in this manner for several months, some women had a better chance of becoming pregnant when the treatment was discontinued. From this discovery it was a comparatively short step to developing a similar method to prevent ovulation altogether. This was the Pill, an oral contraceptive.

Suddenly women had something they have been wanting all through human history—a control over their own bodies, a protection against unwanted pregnancy. Only a woman knows how large a part of life is played by this matter of pregnancy. It affects, or used to affect, everything, not only in herself but the way she was treated by the world. She has always been enslaved by circumstances. Those who battled in the early days for women's rights knew this unalterable fact but would not acknowledge it. They thought that there must be a way out; the world could be educated to make allowances for women's handicap, so why harp on it? Some women, especially Charlotte Perkins Gilman, blithely declared that the sex could free themselves by ignoring their sexual and maternal urges. Others, like Elizabeth Cady Stanton, thought that the vote would be enough to make up for physical drawbacks. Mrs. Gilman's solution was impractical, and Mrs. Stanton hoped for too much. Margaret Sanger, though she came nearer to the right answer, didn't have the tools for the job. Despite all that can be said against it, the Pill has set free the women of America to make their own decisions as to children: whether or not to have any, and, for those who do want them, how many to have.

With their new freedom from the preoccupations of maternity, women have the time at last to think about other things, and some of the results of this thought have been startling.

The new feminism was announced in a book published in 1963, *The Feminine Mystique* by Betty Friedan. Ms. Friedan held a degree in psychology and had worked at it academically, but it was as an angry journalist that she wrote her book about what she described as a new, creeping form of slavery of women that became evident after the Second World War. An insidious ideal of femininity had been propagated, she said, in response to which American women were staying away in droves from the freedom that feminists had laboriously won for them. The American woman was retreating into her house and slamming the door. Significantly, the proportion of women attending college, in comparison with that of men, had slumped sharply between 1950 and 1960. Even those girls who did go to college wanted only to find husbands, have children, and run dream houses for their families in the suburbs.

Who persuaded them into this course of conduct? In part Ms. Friedan blamed the makers and advertisers of domestic appliances, but behind commercial interest she saw the sinister shape of something larger, a conspiracy, a campaign to make women more aware of their femininity and take them out of competition with men. And women fell for it. In alarming numbers they stayed at home, abdicating from higher education and public life. In the female mind sex became predominant. Women went to ridiculous extremes to attract mates, dieting fiercely, dying their hair blond, and spending much of the family budget on clothes and kitchens and sewing machines. They never went out except to shop, chauffeur their children, or accompany their husbands. Their daughters grew up in the same pattern, never getting jobs, so that there were labor shortages in teaching, nursing, and social work.

So much domestic preoccupation, said Ms. Friedan, caused a large number of women to feel "a strange stirring, a sense of dissatisfaction, a yearning." Now and then some housewife put it into words: "I want something more than my husband and my children and my home." Was this a new complaint? Ms. Friedan thought so. She ransacked women's magazines of an earlier day, in which most of the stories were of girls who left home and sought careers, for whom love was of course important but not the whole aim of existence. And she noted that after 1949 things were different, the same magazines giving more space to articles with such titles as "Femininity Begins at Home" and "Have Babies When You're Young." When Ms. Friedan asked editors the reason for this turnabout, they said it was what their readers wanted. But, she wondered, would readers have wanted it if they hadn't been conditioned to want it? What was going on? She decided that at least half the blame should be attributed to Sigmund Freud.

Freud reanimated old prejudices that have existed from the beginning of civilization, though for several generations they had been covered up. In their hearts, though not openly, people still believed that women are animals, subhuman, unable to think like men, born to breed and serve men—and then along came Freud and told them that they were absolutely right. Because he was a genius, his followers accepted everything he said, including his theories on penis envy, anatomy as destiny, femininity, the lot. Freudian psychology became more than a science of human behavior; it was America's new religion. That's how it all began, said Ms. Friedan, and American womanhood had been trapped. The question was how women were to get out of the trap, and there were no easy answers. Each woman would have to find her own, but Ms. Friedan had a few suggestions. To begin with, everyone would have to say no to the housewife image and look at housework not as a career, but something to be done as quickly as possible. Every woman must see marriage as it really is, brushing aside all near-glorification, and should try to get a job.

Considering the developments of the following decade, it is hard to realize that this book was published so recently. But remember, the Pill first went on sale in 1960, just about when Ms. Friedan was formulating her thesis: it made possible the enthusiastic acceptance of her ideas. Without the Pill, women wouldn't have had the leisure, let alone the freedom from anxiety, to act upon her suggestions. As it was, in a remarkably short time a number of females became active and vocal in public, urging that their sex make demands for an equality undreamed of even in the heyday of the former women's rights movement. The early feminists had had to count sex out of their programs: Susan B. Anthony wouldn't touch it, and even Mrs. Stanton had to wait for the menopause to free her from childbearing so that she could work her hardest for the cause. Now any woman, regardless of age or sex habits, could feel free.

Of course equal pay was one of the first rights they demanded, but they wanted other things too—equal opportunity in jobs and an end to discriminatory practices that people had always taken for granted such as men-only bars, men-only institutions of learning, and male chauvinism in children's early reading. Everywhere they found fuel for their fires of indignation. America was suddenly full of angry, protesting women. One particular element in their protests was played up most of all—the rejection of woman's role as a sex object. The new feminists resented beauty competitions and inveighed against all forms of allurement. Some of their gestures seemed puzzling—I myself never grasped the significance of bra burning, for example. Whoever claimed that bras are alluring? But the protests attracted attention and forced people to think things out instead of accepting inherited viewpoints. They broke down barriers in the brain. A number of women challenged the fundamental law of merchandising—sex appeal. They refused to look pretty, stopped brushing their hair, and adopted ragged unisex clothing. And still, somehow, they attracted admiration, because the new fashion became a fad (and scared advertisers to death until they learned to swing into line with garments that looked worn out but cost a lot). Sex still goes on, though the elder generation cannot understand what the youngsters see in each other.

Women's consciousness-raising groups made their appearance all over the place. At some meetings the prostitute became a symbol of downtrodden womanhood; puzzled tarts were suddenly taken up by middle-class female champions and praised to the skies. Fiery girls declared that man is an obsolete life force: Who needs him? There was a lot of talk about female spiders and Amazons. The public became alarmed. What did the girls want, anyway? The American woman enjoyed the respect of her men: the country was well known for the consideration shown to her by males. She had the vote, didn't she? Of course, she didn't use it very effectively, but everyone knows what women are. Here were these crazy girls saying all sorts of indelicate things, some even claiming to be lesbians. They invented new terms like "sexism," and made scenes when men wolf-whistled at them in the street. They learned karate and gave advice on how to cope with rape. Was nothing sacred any more? Even worse, women were declaring that men should do a fair share of housework. In the end, those who asked what women want were left in no doubt of the answer.

In 1966 Betty Friedan founded the National Organization of Women, or NOW. Soon kooky elements splintered off to form such groups as WITCH, Women's International Conspiracy from Hell; POWER, Professionals Organized for Women's Equal Rights; and SCUM, Society for Cutting Up Men. SCUM's founding mother, Valerie Solanas, actually shot her employer, Andy Warhol, with a revolver instead of cutting him up, but the motivation was no doubt the same. There were also many books about the feminine protest, some of which reached the best-seller lists and carried Ms. Friedan's ideas further along the road to what solid citizens considered lunacy and ruin. The fact that Betty Friedan inevitably came to verbal blows with some of her one-time followers need not detract from the effectiveness of her new women's rights movement. These protests, this noise, did lead to a large number of changes in American life and the status of American women. For example, after forty-nine years of unavailing effort the backers of the Equal Rights Amendment have succeeded in getting it accepted in some states, and have reasonable hopes of seeing it nationwide before many more years have elapsed.

Until 1973 there remained on the reformers' agenda one outstanding object that long seemed hopeless of attainment—the right to legal abortion. Women's rights advocates argue that termination of pregnancy should be a wholly personal matter between a woman and her doctor. For a long time the law did not agree, but in 1967 there was a breakthrough in several states, in 1970 more states followed their example, and in 1973 the Supreme Court declared many restrictive laws on abortion unconstitutional.

So there, at the start of 1974, we stand, down on the floor with the boys. Women now have a chance to arrange their lives both economically and biologically. There are still many awkwardnesses, of course. A retiring male professor told me the other day, with a touch of asperity in his voice, that his place is being taken by a woman—and this in a university that has never been noted for its welcome of women, especially as full professors. "Fortunately I like her work," he added, "but even if I didn't, she'd have been given the post." The implication was plain: you can't fight women.

His is a jaundiced view, but things are definitely looking up. We've had the vote for a long time, and in law we also have equal rights, though as to that there are still some ragged edges to be trimmed, a lot of discrimination to expose. If present-day progress is maintained, there will come a time when men can forget the old days when women were stuck up there on their pedestals, out of the way, and women can take those chips off their shoulders and learn to walk around like anybody else. We have a long time to wait, of course, before everything is all right—I find it impossible, myself, to keep out of my approach to life anger against men—but utopia is on the way, given luck and vigilance.

Vigilance . . .

BIBLIOGRAPHY

ADDAMS, JANE. *Twenty Years at Hull-House*. New York: Macmillan, 1966.

ALSOP, E. B., ed. *The Greatness of Woodrow Wilson*. New York: Kennikat, 1971.

ANTHONY, KATHARINE SUSAN. *Louisa May Alcott*. New York: Knopf, 1938.

———. *Susan B. Anthony*. New York: Doubleday, 1954.

ANTHONY, SUSAN B. AND OTHERS. *The History of Woman Suffrage*. 2 vols. New York: National American Woman Suffrage Association, 1881–1900.

ARMSTRONG, MARGARET N. *Fanny Kemble: A Passionate Victorian*. New York: Macmillan, 1938.

ASBURY, HERBERT. *The Great Illusion: An Informal History of Prohibition*. New York, Doubleday, 1950.

"ASTELL, MARY." *An Essay in Defence of the Female Sex*. London, 1696. Chicago: Library of the Women's Movement reprint, 1971.

BELL, MARGARET. *Margaret Fuller: A Biography*. New York: Charles Boni, 1930.

BROCKETT, LINUS PIERPONT with VAUGHAN, MARY C. *Woman's Work in the Civil War*. Philadelphia: Ziegler, McCurdy & Co., 1867.

CURTI, MERLE. *Learning for Ladies, 1508–1895*. San Marino, Calif.: Henry E. Huntington Library and Art Gallery, 1936.

DE FOREST, JOHN W. *Miss Ravenel's Conversion from Secession to Loyalty*. Gordon S. Haight, ed. New York: Rinehard Editions, 1955. Original edition, 1867.

FLEXNER, ELEANOR. *Century of Struggle: The Woman's Rights Movement in the United States*. Cambridge, Mass.: Harvard University Press, 1959.

FRANKLIN, BENJAMIN, and MECOM, JANE. *Letters,* Carl Van Doren, ed. Princeton: Princeton University Press, 1950.

FRIEDAN, BETTY. *The Feminine Mystique*. New York: Norton, 1963.

FULLER, MARGARET. *Woman in the Nineteenth Century & Kindred Papers Relating to the Sphere, Condition & Duties of Woman,* New York: 1845. Chicago: Library of the Women's Movement reprint, 1970.

GREER, GERMAINE. *The Female Eunuch*. New York: McGraw-Hill, 1971.

HAIGHT, GORDON S. "Male Chastity in the Nineteenth Century." *Contemporary Review,* November 1971.

———. *Mrs. Sigourney, the Sweet Singer of Hartford*. New Haven, Conn.: Yale University Press, 1930.

HALL, BASIL. *Travels in North America in the Years 1827 and 1828*. Philadelphia: Carey, Lea & Carey, 1829.

HART, JAMES D. *The Popular Book: A History of America's Literary Taste*. Berkeley: University of California Press, 1950.

JEBB, CAMILLA. *Mary Wollstonecraft*. Chicago: F. G. Browne & Co., 1930.

JEFFERSON. THOMAS. *Correspondence*, Vol. IV. H. A. Washington, ed.

JOHNSTON, JOHANNA. *Mrs. Satan: The Incredible Saga of Victoria C. Woodhull*. New York: Putnam's, 1967.

KEMBLE, FRANCES ANNE. *A Journal of a Residence on a Georgian Plantation in 1838–1839*. Northbrook, Ill.: Metro Books, 1969, reprint of 1864 edition.

KENNEDY, DAVID M. *Birth Control in America: The Career of Margaret Sanger*. New Haven, Conn.: Yale University Press, 1970.

LASH, JOSEPH P. *Eleanor and Franklin: The Story of Their Relationship Based on Eleanor Roosevelt's Private Papers*. New York: Norton, 1971.

———. *Eleanor: The Years Alone*. New York: Norton, 1972.

LERNER, GERDA. *The Grimké Sisters from South Carolina: Rebels Against Slavery*. Boston: Houghton Mifflin, 1964.

LUTZ, ALMA. *Emma Willard, Daughter of Democracy*. Boston: Houghton Mifflin, 1929.

MARBERRY, M. MARION. *Vicky: A Biography of Victoria C. Woodhull*. New York: Funk & Wagnalls. 1967.

MARRYAT, FREDERICK. *Diary in America*. Jules Zanger, ed. Bloomington: Indiana University Press, 1960.

MARSHALL, HELEN E. *Dorothea Dix, Forgotten Samaritan*. Chapel Hill: University of North Carolina Press, 1937.

MARTIN, RALPH G. *Jennie: The Life of Lady Randolph Churchill*. Englewood Cliffs, N.J.: Prentice-Hall, 1969.

MARTINEAU, HARRIET. *Society in America*, 3 vols. New York: AMS Press, reprint of 1837 edition.

MEYER, ADOLPH E. *An Educational History of the Americans*. New York: New York University Press, 1957.

MILLETT, KATE. *Sexual Politics*. New York: Doubleday, 1970.

MORGAN, EDMUND S. *Puritan Love and Marriage*. Boston: "More Books," 1956.

NOYES, JOHN H. BEREAN. *The History of American Socialisms*. New York: Hillary, 1961.

O'NEILL, WILLIAM L. *Everyone Was Brave: The Rise and Fall of Feminism in America*. New York: Quadrangle, 1969.

———. *The Woman Movement: Feminism in the United States and England*. New York: Barnes & Noble, 1969.

SEYERSTAD, PER. *Kate Chopin: A Critical Biography*. Baton Rouge, La.: State University Press, 1969.

SHAPLEN, ROBERT. *Free Love and Heavenly Sinners: The Story of the Great Henry Ward Beecher Scandal*. New York: Knopf, 1954.

SHEPARD, ODELL. *Pedlar's Progress: The Life of Bronson Alcott*. Westport, Conn.: Greenwood, 1968.

SINCLAIR, ANDREW. *The Emancipation of the American Woman*. New York: Harper & Row. 1970.

SLAYDEN, ELLEN MAURY. *Washington Wife, 1897–1919.* New York: Harper & Row, 1963.

SMALL, EDWIN W. and MIRIAM R. "Prudence Crandall: Champion of Negro Education." *New England Quarterly,* Vol. XVII, No. 4 (December 1944).

SMITH, PAGE. *Daughters of the Promised Land: Women in American History.* Boston: Little, Brown, 1970.

STOWE, LYMAN BEECHER. *Saints, Sinners and Beechers.* Indianapolis: Essay Index Reprints, Series 1934.

SWISSHELM, JANE GREY. *Letters, 1858–1863.* Arthur J. Larsen, ed. St. Paul: Minnesota Historical Association, 1934.

———. *Half A Century.* Chicago: Library of the Women's Movement, 1970, reprint of 1880 edition.

TOCQUEVILLE, ALEXIS DE. *Democracy in America.* New York: Vintage, 1945.

TROLLOPE, FRANCES. *Domestic Manners of the Americans.* New York: Dodd, Mead, 1901.

TROLLOPE, THOMAS ADOLPHUS. *What I Remember.* New York: AMS Press, 1970, reprint of 1888 edition.

WATERMAN. WILLIAM RANDALL. *Frances Wright.* New York: Columbia University Press, 1924.

WINTHROP, JOHN. *A History of New England from 1630 to 1649.* James Savage, ed. Research Library of Colonial Americana reprint of 1825 edition. New York: Arno, 1959.

WOLLSTONECRAFT, MARY. *A Vindication of the Rights of Woman.* Charles W. Hagelman, Jr., ed. New York: Norton, 1970. Chicago: Library of the Women's Movement reprint, 1970. Original edition: London, 1791.

INDEX